ARAB SOCIETY
IN REVOLT

ARAB SOCIETY IN REVOLT

The West's Mediterranean Challenge

CESARE MERLINI

OLIVIER ROY

editors

BROOKINGS INSTITUTION PRESS
Washington, D.C.

Copyright © 2012
THE BROOKINGS INSTITUTION
1775 Massachusetts Avenue, N.W.
Washington, D. C. 20036
www.brookings.edu

Library of Congress Cataloging-in-Publication data
Arab society in revolt : the West's Mediterranean challenge / Cesare Merlini and Olivier Roy, editors.
    p.   cm.
 Includes bibliographical references and index.
 ISBN 978-0-8157-2396-7 (pbk. : alk. paper)
1. Social change—Mediterranean Region. 2. Mediterranean Region—Social condi-tions. 3. Mediterranean Region—Economic conditions. 4. Islam and politics—Mediterranean Region. 5. United States—Foreign relations—Mediterranean Region. 6. Mediterranean Region—Foreign relations—United States. 7. European Union countries—Foreign relations—Mediterranean Region. 8. Mediterranean Region—Foreign relations—European Union countries. I. Merlini, Cesare. II. Roy, Olivier, 1949–
 HN650.7.A8A73 2012
 303.409323—dc23   2012021021

9 8 7 6 5 4 3 2 1

Printed on acid-free paper

Typeset in Minion

Composition by R. Lynn Rivenbark
Macon, Georgia

Contents

Foreword

On December 17, 2010, a twenty-six-year-old street vendor named Mohamed Bouazizi doused himself with gasoline, lit a match, and set himself on fire outside the municipal headquarters of a provincial Tunisian town. His desperate act followed persistent harassment from local officials that interfered with his livelihood and culminated in the confiscation of his grocery cart. This tragedy was the spark that ignited a regional conflagration and the biggest geopolitical transformation since the fall of the Berlin Wall. Over subsequent weeks and months, protests swept across the Arab world and led to the fall of four dictators whose collective tenure in power totaled almost 120 years.

Scholars, officials, journalists, and people around the world reacted in the manner typical of all human beings who are confronted with the unexpected—they strived to understand what was happening. Grasping for the right words to describe the stunning chain of events unfolding before their eyes, broadcast on their television screens and conveyed through their social media accounts, the most common term deployed was the "Arab Spring," which evoked earlier bursts of peaceful revolts against totalitarian regimes in Europe, especially the Prague Spring of 1968. Others preferred to talk about an "Arab Awakening," in homage to George Antonius's 1938 book about the rise of Arab nationalism: whatever the season and however events turned out, whole populations and societies were rising from what often seemed to be decades if not centuries of somnolent acceptance of rule from on high.

Of course, every attempt to characterize the complexity of what unfolded in 2011 in a simple phrase, by necessity, failed to capture certain important issues or left plenty of pertinent questions unanswered. "Arab Spring" implied a parallel with earlier events in a vastly different region. It also said nothing about what the summer, or indeed winter, following the spring would yield. Likewise, "Arab Awakening" offered no view of what is likely to happen once those societies stirred to political life.

For every pithy conceptualization of complex events, there are additional lenses through which to examine them. One of the several virtues of this book is precisely that it brings different perspectives to bear on the complexity, diversity, and uncertainty of recent and current events in the Arab world. The thirteen authors concentrate on the critical social forces shaping the region—demography, religion, gender, telecommunication connectivity, and economic structures—and they are painstakingly analyzed and evaluated. Cesare Merlini, nonresident senior fellow in Brookings's Center on the United States and Europe, and his coeditor, Olivier Roy, point out in their introduction that months before Mohamed Bouazizi's self-immolation, the contributing authors were already thinking deeply about the societal trends across the Mediterranean's southern shore and the subterranean pressures that were building. Of course, the resulting earthquake gave added impetus to the project, while also generating a wealth of new observable trends to be analyzed.

One theme running through a number of chapters is the increasing importance of the individual—including the individualization of religious faith; the lighter family burden being borne by individuals due to falling fertility rates; an ever-increasing yearning among women for a more active role in society; individuals connecting with one another in cyberspace; and the individual's desire for economic opportunity. Societies are ultimately comprised of millions of people, and this book points to the profound importance of individual empowerment in societal change across the region.

Another recurring topic is the need to resist the temptation of applying inappropriate historical analogies to contemporary events. History must inform the way we grapple with what is unfolding before us. But, we must refrain from merely transplanting ideas and assumptions drawn from other eras, contexts, and geographical locations to a different one. There is no substitute for a nuanced, detailed understanding of the vortex of forces at work in the region, and this book contributes much to that body of knowledge.

In the best tradition of policy-oriented scholarship, it also offers recommendations for policymakers in the United States, Europe, and around the world. It presents new analytic frameworks for thinking about the region, building on the comprehensive analysis of social forces, rather than relying on old paradigms.

Arab societies are in revolt—a process that will not be completed for years, if not decades. The basic human desire to understand is often followed by another one, the urge to assist. The chapters that follow help to meet both desires—they help us to comprehend what is going on, but they also inform how external actors might assist the process of societal change in North Africa and the Middle East to ensure that change is ultimately positive and that the demands for individual empowerment and good governance are realized.

As my Brookings colleague Salman Shaikh, director of our Doha Center, wrote in the midst of the upheaval, "In today's Middle East, people matter. Many are now engaged in what could be a lifelong struggle to fight long-standing grievances and take greater control of their lives." The ideas and prescriptions in this book are an important part of the arsenal for waging that lifelong struggle.

STROBE TALBOTT
President, Brookings Institution

June 2012

Acknowledgments

The draft texts of the chapters of this book were first discussed in a seminar hosted by the Robert Schumann Center of Advanced Studies at European University Institute in Florence in February 2011. A second version was the object of a conference held in the Paris premises of the World Bank in November 2011. The entire exercise profited highly from the qualified contributions to the debate that came from the following participants in either or both events: Samir Aita, editor in chief, *Le Monde Diplomatique*, Arabic edition; Margot Badran, Center for Muslim-Christian Understanding, Georgetown University; Assia Bensalah Alaoui, ambassador-at-large, Kingdom of Morocco; Jon Anderson, Catholic University of America; Jonathan A. C. Brown, professor of Islam and Muslim-Christian Understanding, Georgetown University; Nathan J. Brown, Carnegie Endowment for International Peace; Anna Carrabetta, Promos, Milan; Silvia Colombo, Istituto Affari Internazionali, Rome; Alain Dieckhoff, Centre d'Etudes et de Recherches Internationales—Sciences Po (Institut d'Études Politiques de Paris); Francis Ghilès, Centro de Estudios y Documentación Internacionales de Barcelona; Giorgio Gomel, Bank of Italy; Mohammed Hachemaoui, Université Paris 8 and University of Algiers; Thibaut Jaulin, European University Institute; Mustapha Kamel Al-Sayyid, Cairo University; Mats Karlsson, director, Center for Mediterranean Integration, Marseille; Bichara Khader, Catholic University of Louvain; Eberhard Kienle, Centre National de la Recherche Scientifique, Paris; Francois Lafond, then with the German Marshall Fund of the United States; Ian Lesser, head of the German Marshall Fund European office in Brussels; Nadia Marzouki, European University Institute; Karim Mezran, then with the Centro Studi Americani, Rome;

Boris Najman, Université de Paris-Est; Massimiliano Paolucci, World Bank, Rome; Raed Safadi, Organization for Economic Cooperation and Development, Paris; Luigi Sampaolo, Eni, Rome; Giuseppe Scognamiglio, Unicredit, Rome; and Mohammad Selim, Cairo University.

This project could not have been completed without the support of these sponsoring institutions: the Italian Institute of International Affairs, Rome; the Robert Schuman Center of Advanced Studies, Florence; the Center for the United States and Europe, Brookings Institution, Washington; and the Paris office of the World Bank.

Generous grants from the Bank of Italy, Eni, Finmeccanica, and Unicredit are also acknowledged here with gratitude.

CESARE MERLINI *and* OLIVIER ROY

Introduction

In our time civil society has growing relevance in the global polity and in international relations. At the same time, it is undergoing profound and rapid change in almost every corner of the planet. People today increasingly communicate, interrelate, and enter into conflicts outside the representation and intermediation of their respective national governments. Nonstate actors such as ethnic and religious groups, corporations and smaller businesses, nongovernmental organizations and impromptu street demonstrators, and radical or terrorist networks have become more prominent in a time of relatively little warfare, high economic interdependence among nations, partial attempts at global governance, and an unprecedented degree of interpersonal communication.

Outbursts of interstate conflict and wars of independence have become increasingly rare. Even civil or interethnic conflicts, though still frequent (witness Syria or South Sudan), appear to be trending downward both in number and lethality, particularly since the end of the cold war. Yet the world continues to be seen as a dangerous place. Words such as instability, anxiety, threat— even apocalypse—enjoy widespread use. One explanation is that today's conflicts are watched worldwide, in detail and in real time, wherever they occur. Houses in flames and corpses on the pavement—not to speak of the collapsing Twin Towers—are brought by the media into people's living or dining rooms almost daily. The changing typology of violence, reflected in increased impersonal and cowardly killings of many innocent civilians by politically or religiously inspired fanatics, may also bolster this perception.

1

Regarding the world economy, per capita income has shown unprecedented growth over the long run, despite the constant increase in global population. In particular, the outlook for what used to be called the third world a few decades ago has changed drastically, especially in recent years. From 2005 to 2010, half a million individuals escaped absolute poverty (defined as an income of $1.25 a day or less). Three quarters of these people are from China or India, but the poverty rate of sub-Saharan Africa has also fallen below 50 percent. The main engines of development have been trade expansion in both goods and services and investment liberalization, with the consequence of dramatically enhancing interdependence among nations. Yet the prevailing perception is either of economic uncertainty, particularly after the 2008 financial crisis and economic downturn, or of an unacceptably unfair distribution of wealth, or both. Again the mass media bear some responsibility for this unbalanced perspective in that they apparently prefer to spread bad news while, at the same time, broadcasting fictions that are mostly about the more affluent.

Governance both within and between countries is undergoing transition. The totalitarian states that made the twentieth century so tragic have almost disappeared from the face of the earth. Conversely, the number of democracies has increased since the late 1980s at the expense of authoritarian regimes, with a significant grey area remaining in between. Although international institutions are often viewed as being of little significance, they actually make their presence felt more than ever before. The number of peacekeeping operations undertaken by the international community—both UN- and non-UN–sponsored—surged steeply after 1989. The 2011 Security Council resolution that contemplated a military intervention in Libya was based on the principle of the "responsibility to protect" civilians—a first application of that international framework. The International Criminal Court, the first such treaty-based body established in the framework of the UN, entered into force in 2002 after ratification by 60 countries, and as of this writing, 120 states are committed to it (excluding China, Russia, and, interestingly, the United States, originally a sponsor of the concept). Moreover, a notable indication of a more widespread respect for human life is the decreasing implementation of capital punishment: the number of countries that are "abolitionist for all crimes" has exactly doubled from 48 in 1991 to 96 in 2010. Yet again, as with conflict resolution and economic interdependence, powerful opposition to international governance exists on the grounds of absolute state sovereignty and the Westphalian principle of noninterference.

Both the ongoing changes and the corresponding resistance by the powerful are subject to the influence of rapidly expanding global communication technology. Individuals and households, often including those earning incomes below average or living in small cities or villages, are increasingly endowed with the capability of spreading as well as receiving informative messages and images. The explosion of interaction with fellow countrymen and -women—and even across borders—although often temporary or ephemeral, has the potential to generate mass mobilization and thus oblige authorities to be more accountable.

Changing societies, greater economic interdependence, the spread of democracy, and attempts at global governance are the result of the long predominant Western influence. Civil societies are stronger in the Old World and in North America than in almost any other areas of the planet. Yet Europe lost its dominant role more than half a century ago, and even the United States now appears increasingly unable to steer world matters in keeping with its status as the only global superpower. Not only are new powers emerging, but the societal and cultural model largely shared by the two sides of the Atlantic is also increasingly being challenged. In order to face the new realities and compensate for the decline in influence, the West has to develop new paradigms for foreign policy options, choices, and instruments to enhance the efficacy of its actions toward what has been called "the rest," possibly with outdated condescension. The project that led to this book concentrated on that portion of the rest that is the Muslim Arab world, whose societal change is widely perceived in the West as susceptible of generating outcomes incompatible with the established (Western) order, whether secular or religious.

The area of interest is further limited to the southern Mediterranean shores, from the Atlantic Ocean to the Sinai Peninsula. At the beginning of the project, back in 2010, the authors chose to so restrict their focus because transformations in this part of the Middle East are less likely to be affected by the geostrategic issues associated with the southeastern Mediterranean and the Persian Gulf. However, a few months after this choice was made, a Tunisian fruit vendor set himself on fire to protest the hardships imposed by the police state, catalyzing what soon looked like a revolution throughout North Africa. This turn of events was unexpected by many, including the contributors here, but it was not unpredictable. Occasionally political science resembles seismology, which cannot pinpoint when an earthquake will take place nor its exact intensity on the Richter scale but which can predict that a certain geographical area is likely to experience a serious seismic event sooner or later.

The uprisings in the Arab squares were not isolated phenomena. In a world that is less bellicose and more interdependent than in any time in history, the legitimacy and stability of states today may derive less from their ability to defend their citizens from external threats, as in the Westphalian system, than their ability to provide them basic services, internal security, an independent judiciary, and fairer income distribution, and to accept public scrutiny, beyond the façade of more or less formal democracy. Thus heterogeneous and variously motivated protests have arisen in different parts of the world, from the *indignados* ("angry ones") spreading from Madrid and the Occupy-Wall-Street movement propagating from New York, to the Russian "Awakening" (a label borrowed from the Arab precedent)—all of which, by the way, have been urban in nature and dimension.

In a way, the currently uncertain outcome of the transformations occurring in a number of Arab countries may also be another element in common with these other instances of widespread and sudden protest movements—besides, of course, the practice of pitching tents in the squares. The heterogeneity of the participants, the organizational improvisation, and, above all, the lack of sound alternative projects have generated limited or even unintended political consequences, at least in the short term. The disgruntled Spanish youth may ultimately have contributed to the decline of the Socialist Party, to the benefit of the conservative and Catholic Popular Alliance in the subsequent parliamentary elections. The New Yorkers camping in Zuccotti Park apparently included socialist sympathizers as well as supporters of Ron Paul, a libertarian Republican presidential candidate, who later fell out of the race. Vladimir Putin's return to the presidency was not jeopardized by demonstrators defying Arctic temperatures along the Moskva River's banks in December 2011.

Yet the Arab Spring, whether or not it may have turned—temporarily?—into a winter in some cases, has its own specificities in terms of both origin and context. One such specificity is that only here do the countries concerned have a colonial past that marks their recent history and thus their culture, their institutions, and even their borders. As a consequence, they are still going through a process of finding an identity, developing a sense of belonging, and building a state—a process in which they are at different, often unstable, yet probably irreversible stages of advancement. The colonial heritage can hardly be erased, and this may make it, along with the factors of proximity and interdependence, an inescapable challenge for Europe and the United States to address.

A Revolution without Revolutionaries

As the dust painfully settles on the stage of the uprisings, a few observations can be made. First, few, if any, members of the new generation that assembled in the North African squares well over a year ago are now in power. The young people and mostly secular intellectuals who were at the forefront of the uprisings had no clear political agenda and were not capable of building strong political parties and promoting an alternative platform for government. Many did not even plan to go into politics. In sum, they did not act like real revolutionaries. The countries are still in the hands of the previous generation, that is, the old political elites, including the Islamists who have been on the scene for decades, though kept on the margins by the regimes. These are people of the past—conservative, even traditionalist people—whatever their background in the establishment, the military, or the religious sphere. They are not revolutionaries, either.

Nonetheless, the widespread impression that a revolution has taken place is not entirely misplaced because the uprisings were the symptom of the profound social, cultural, and religious change that societies in North Africa, and in the Arab Muslim world at large, have undergone—and to a greater degree than in other places where there have been popular protests, which is another major specificity. Thus not only has discontent overthrown the symbols of the past regimes, but expectations, occasionally unrealistic, have been raised that are bound to have political consequences sooner or later. The current leaders, although people of the past, and the newly elected members of parliament—most of whom were, for various reasons, initially extraneous to or reluctant participants in the movement—have had to adapt to the new scene that came out of the movement itself. They must deliver on the economy as well as on governance and stability in order to show that they are trying to meet at least some of the expectations.

The Islamists are now part of the game, and this leads to a second observation: they, too, will have to adapt to this new political landscape. This implies that they will have to make compromises and build coalitions with partners who vary from country to country. The doctrine itself has to be recast in a new context, with no denomination being in a position to claim a monopoly on Islam. This is a way of becoming democratic without being liberal. Actually, the Islamists are very conservative, but they too have to respond in one way or another to the people who voted for them and want results, progress. To be under the scrutiny of the electorate is a new situation for them.

A third observation is about the predominantly domestic nature of the protest movement. Despite the contagion moving rapidly from country to country, first through North Africa and then extending to almost the entire Middle East (thanks to today's highly pervasive telecommunications), both the perspective of the uprisings and the aforementioned expectations they generated have essentially remained within the boundaries of each country. With more or less explicit surprise, Western media noted the fact that no American flags, or for that matter Israeli ones, were initially burned in the squares of Tunis, Cairo, or Alexandria. Throughout 2011 neither the nationalists nor the Islamists substantially raised the issue of the treaty with the Zionist state, not even in a country as sensitive to the issue as Egypt is. Instead, patriotic rhetoric has been widespread and rarely, if ever, associated with militant advocacy to spread the movement abroad, despite the common perception of being watched by the world.

The suggestion here that there was a revolution without revolutionaries, with all the implications just discussed, is reinforced by the striking differences from the Islamic upheaval in Iran back in 1979. There the rebels took over power, did not care about building coalitions, and ended up in charge of the country. Then they tried to export the revolution into the Middle East and to confront the superpowers of the time. Those were revolutionaries.

An Irreversible Transformation

Though the protest movement that shook most of the North African countries stopped short of effecting the replacement of the political class, the transformation that led to the "Arab Spring" is irreversible because it affects the very fabric of society. Three aspects of the process are of the most evident significance. The first one is generational. The demographics of the region have changed, particularly during the last twenty years, because of the drop in fertility rates. Today Tunisia has a lower fertility rate than France, for instance. The current young generation, however, is the last from a period of wild population growth, while also being the first to reach adulthood in a new sociological context. To start with, there is more gender equality than ever before—equality in terms of education and age of marriage. People marry later—in their twenties or thirties—and have fewer children, if they have children at all. They also are more educated than their parents, and since they are more likely to understand and speak foreign—especially Western—languages, they are more connected globally and better informed. Consequently, this younger generation tends to be less defined by the roles of the family framework and the traditional patriarchal society at large. The undermining of the old social structures carries with it the seeds of a change in the way people see themselves.

As a consequence, the father figure embodied in the great charismatic leader no long resonates—which brings us to a second aspect of the change, one related to political culture. The fall of the great leader, under whom the people were supposed to be united, goes hand in hand with the diminishing appeal of the traditional ideologies, be they Arab, nationalist, or Islamic. People have become more individualistic. They tend to ask for good governance and citizenship rather than ideology. Even the call for dignity, a personal reference, instead of honor, a collective value, is significant in this respect. Thus people are less amenable to the standard propaganda, such as democracy being a foreign, indeed a Western, plot to destroy the unity of the Arab people. Instead, they believe in democracy, though possibly less as a deeply felt cultural conviction than as something that simply must be—a fact of life.

The third aspect of the transformation concerns religion. As stated above, the Islamists are now in the political forefront, which is, however, a pluralist scene in which they do not form a solid bloc. They too are confronted with the surge of individualism and the increased rejection of top-down authority; in addition, the decline of ideology can be extended to faith. The fast-growing access to communications and the Internet may help preach the word of God and spread *fatwas,* but it is a two-way street that puts the hierarchy under a new kind of scrutiny from the believers. Furthermore, half of these happen to be women, whose rapid empowerment in terms of personal choice about reproduction and also access to education affects the basic structure of the family and hence inevitably that of the religious community. In sum, while most observers focus on the issue of Islam taking over the polity and society in Arab countries, what is happening appears to suggest that it is the societal transformation that will affect the religious outlook of the Muslim world in the future.

There are precedents for similar kinds of development in other countries, including Western ones. One telling example can be found in the United States during the second half of the twentieth century. Throughout that period of their national history, Americans consolidated their specificity among Western countries in terms of the nearly unanimous importance given to religion and worship attendance, two features that declined only in part during the eighties and nineties. Most of the Christian denominations initially resisted but then accommodated successive societal transformations that directly affected church doctrine, such as divorce, premarital sex, contraception, and unmarried couples, all of which were ultimately accepted by a large part of the population—often to a greater degree than in secularist Europe. More recently, faith-based resistance to societal change has retrenched on the issues of abortion and homosexuality. Something not that different has been occurring, by the way, among Muslim societies.

This leads us to underline the fact that there have been religion-related misjudgments in the West about the movement in Northern Africa, at least in its early phase. The widespread view has been that a political upheaval, such as the advent of full democracy, or a social metamorphosis, such as the emancipation of women, among the Arab Muslims had to be preceded by a phase of secularization or some sort of theological reform. This perspective ignores the history of Christianity, which demonstrates that while the same theology has been there for twenty centuries, the reference to religion in the political sphere has taken very diverse and divergent forms. And those who advocate a religious reformation of Islam, on the model of Protestantism, tend to forget that though Martin Luther was a religious reformer, he espoused neither democracy nor liberalism.

The parliamentary elections, held in Tunisia and Egypt in late 2011 and at the beginning of 2012, confirmed both the feasibility of a sufficiently fair vote and the strength of religion among the population. However, their outcomes made plain that it is not the entire society that has been experiencing the transformations just discussed—be they political, religious, demographic, or gender related. The movement that became so visible at a time of crisis turned out to involve perhaps only a minority. The electoral geography revealed the important differences between urban and rural populations. The conservative backlash has come primarily from citizens located in rural areas. But even among urban people, there are those who are afraid of going too far, who are concerned about instability, losing tourists, and seeing the economy at risk of irreparable collapse. The subsequent presidential elections in Egypt have, in fact, illustrated this state of affairs. The standard bearers of conservatism prevailed on both the secularist and religious sides. At the same time, the highly heralded breakthrough of the Islamist vote in the parliamentary elections failed to find confirmation, and the candidate closer to the spirit of Tahrir Square did not end up as marginal as many had predicted. Above all, the first turn manifested a relatively normal "balance of power" among Egyptian political subjects, with none of the candidates getting more than one-fourth of the vote. Hence, we witness the apparent oxymoron of the conservative revolution happening in the area, at least in the short term. Over the longer term, however, it appears inevitable that the generation behind the Arab Spring, including the teenagers who breathed the air of the uprisings and are likely to grow up clicking incessantly on a personal computer or cell phone, will have growing influence on the way their societies evolve during the next decades. How this will affect national political and institutional frameworks the day after tomorrow—as well as international relations and crises within and beyond the region—is of course an open question.

The Geostrategic Context

For the first time in the history of the Middle East since decolonization, the upheavals within the area were not related to geostrategic issues, such as great power rivalries or security of oil supplies—or indeed a conflict with Israel—nor to supranational movements, such as pan-Arabism or pan-Islamism. Nonetheless, they have set in motion a profound change in the geostrategic picture of the region, either directly whenever the spread of the revolt takes a sectarian form, as in Bahrain and Syria, or indirectly as the rules of the game for policymaking—foreign policy included—come under increasing public scrutiny. Gone is the era of the dictators' club, within which disagreements could be settled by personal phone calls or private meetings, occasionally followed by a generous exchange of cash—the favorite tools of Saudi foreign policy.

The end of this era is confirmed by the actions of the surviving authoritarian regimes, which are attempting to overshadow the reform movements by shifting attention to issues that could fuel a broader regional crisis. Today the main divide in the Middle East is less and less related to the Israel-Palestine issue. The Palestinians have been unable to adopt the new tools of protest that developed out of the North African squares, so Israel can continue to have a substantially free hand in developing settlements in East Jerusalem and the West Bank. At the same time Israel has resented the changes brought about by the Arab Spring, above all with regard to its future relationship with Egypt, and has tried to minimize its impact by focusing attention on Iran and its uranium enrichment activities. Tehran, in turn, has threatened to retaliate against Western pressures and more or less open Israeli threats of attack by blocking the Persian Gulf, an act that would translate into a direct challenge to the Sunni Arab kingdoms and emirates of the Gulf. Thus the remaining Sunni authoritarian regimes of the region find themselves sharing with Israel both the dislike of Arab populaces taking to the streets and the Iranian leadership seeking regional dominance.

In fact, the emerging geostrategic divide of the Middle East appears to be between a Sunni camp, led by Saudi Arabia and comprising also the Muslim Brotherhood, and a Shiite camp, led by Iran and including the Assad regime in Syria as well as Hezbollah. To an extent, Turkey could be seen as part of the former, at least as long as Erdogan's Justice and Development Party (AKP) is in charge, and Iraq part of the latter, thanks mainly to the U.S. intervention of 2003. The protagonists of the Arab uprisings, particularly in Bahrain, would reject this new divide but have little choice other than being enlisted on either side of it and conforming to the new rules of the game. Hamas, for instance, despite its political proximity with Iran and Hezbollah, closed its offices in Syria and moved to Egypt.

The events in Syria have absorbed much of the international attention during the first half of 2012. This is not surprising because in contrast to what has been happening in North Africa, related developments in Syria are key to the geopolitical transformation in the Middle East and come as a confirmation of the new divides. The crisis of the Assad regime and the protracted and bloody civil conflict in that unfortunate country have the potential to strengthen the Sunni camp, diminish Iranian influence in the Arab Middle East, and isolate Hezbollah.

At the same time Turkey has gained soft influence throughout the upheavals as a paradigm of a relatively successful Muslim and democratic state. It is regarded as an emerging regional power because of its role in the sectarian and multiethnic conflict taking place across its southern borders—notwithstanding a potential recrudescence of the Kurdish issue to trouble the waters in Ankara.

The other game in the area that has attracted media coverage is the interplay of negotiations, sanctions, and possible military action to stem the Iranians' potential nuclear capability. The scenario of a major Israeli strike against a Muslim country has been held out as a way to mobilize the Arab streets against imperial Zionism and its American protector—and that scenario may, in fact, be developing, at least at a preliminary stage. But the assumption that this contingency would turn into a systematic rally in favor of Iran, thus offsetting the growing Sunni-Shiite divide, will likely prove groundless. Instead, the Tehran ayatollahs might ultimately find themselves as isolated as the Assad regime.

The Syrian crisis has further highlighted the decreased role of the great powers that was demonstrated throughout the Arab Spring. This applies to the United States in particular. The war in Iraq contributed to this state of affairs because it had unexpected and unwelcome consequences, such as the already mentioned strengthening of the Shia camp. Moreover, democratization is not making progress in that country—nor is that happening in Libya either, by the way—further demonstrating the failure of the policy of exporting democracy. European leverage has proved even weaker, both at the national and EU level, despite the recurrent clauses of conditionality (linked to human rights protection) in the scattered attempts at cooperation with the countries of the area. Democratization, when and where it takes root, is done through laborious national and domestic processes, and the resulting regimes, while not necessarily anti-Western, are not going to be indebted to the West should they achieve some political stability.

The United States and the European countries have a limited capacity to influence the unfolding of events in the Middle East, both in terms of soft economic power, because of the limited incentives they have to offer, particularly in the current adverse economic circumstances, and of hard military power, notwithstanding the successful intervention in Libya to which the Americans contributed reluctantly and in which the Europeans soon reached the ceiling of their modest war-waging capability. The hope of reproducing the convergence of favorable circumstances that brought about the fall of Qaddafi has proved illusory in other contexts, such as in Syria. Moreover, further options for initiative have largely been held hostage to the "poker game" with the Iranian regime. Thus, in the short run, the West appears to have little choice other than to assume a low profile in the region and follow a realistic approach based on a cool assessment of national interests.

In a time when there is much talk on both sides of the Atlantic about rising new powers (the BRICS: Brazil, Russia, India, China, and South Africa), it may be worth noting, however, that none of these emerging actors has taken advantage of the changes in the Middle East—either by choice or through lack of clout—to substantially increase its role in the region. Those having a seat in the UN Security Council, either permanently or by turn, gave a lukewarm green light to the action in Libya and then dragged their feet when resolutions concerning Syria were put on the table, while the protesters were being massacred by the regime. Regarding Iranian nuclear capabilities, neither Moscow nor Beijing—nor for that matter Delhi, Brasilia, or Pretoria—favors nuclear proliferation, but they also dislike the idea of international pressure being exerted, via sanctions or other methods, on sovereign states. In general, the more or less shared preference among the BRICS seems to have been to let the West burn its fingers with the hot potatoes while confronting a loss of leverage in the area rather than to seek for themselves new popularity and influence among the changing Arab polities and societies through active engagement in the region.

Thus, Americans and Europeans would be well advised not to limit themselves to the realistic and sober approach just suggested for the immediate future in view of the current constraints. They should give due consideration to the longer-term and deeper causes of change in North Africa and the Middle East. The innovative foreign policy paradigms presented in this volume are an attempt to adapt to an international system experiencing societal transformations. Leaders on both sides of the Atlantic may find that the implementation of policies based on these paradigms is most fruitful in those countries of the region that are undergoing the agonizing processes of renewal while being less subject to the distortions of broader geostrategic factors.

Presentation

The preceding introductory remarks were intended to help the reader understand the rationale and organization of this volume. The first part examines the transformations that have occurred in Arab societies. Although the primary focus is on the countries along the southern shores of the Mediterranean, this discussion also covers what is shared by the broader region in terms of geography, history, religion, and culture. Six areas of change have been chosen as particularly relevant and thus deserving of specific analysis.

Demographics and two-way migrations between North Africa and Europe constitute the first such area and are treated by Philippe Fargues, director of the Migration Policy Center at the European University Institute (EUI). The issue of compatibility between Islamic revival and democracy is discussed in the context of Egypt and Tunisia by Olivier Roy, head of the Mediterranean Progam at the Robert Schuman Center for Advanced Studies of EUI. How the fast-changing roles of women in Arab society interact with both demographics and religion is a topic covered by two Italian university professors, Maria Cristina Paciello and Renata Pepicelli. Another case of rapid transformation is the extraordinary penetration of telecommunications—particularly the Internet—into Arab societies so as to become a vehicle of Islamic expression, as Gary Bunt of the University of Wales, himself a blogger, claims in his piece. Modern small and medium-size commercial and social entrepreneurship is also an important factor of change, at least potentially, as two academics from Madrid, Gonzalo Escribano and Alejandro Lorca, explain in their chapter. Moving from the micro to the macro level, the subsequent contribution by

Caroline Freund and Carlos Primo Braga of the World Bank examines the economic framework and consequences of the current Arab transitions.

The second part of the book is about those cultural and religious as well as political and economic factors that have influenced the Western response, or lack of it, to the Arab Spring. It is also about the policy options that remain open. To begin with, Jonathan Laurence, of Boston College, deals with the policies the United States has pursued toward North Africa in recent years and the future choices to be made. American attitudes underlying foreign policy are frequently affected by stereotypes, and Middle East policy is no exception, as another academic from Boston, Alan Wolfe, discusses in his contribution. Turning to Europe, the unsatisfactory political response of the European Union to the ongoing societal change occurring on the other side of the Mediterranean is treated by Roberto Aliboni of the Italian Institute of International Affairs. The problem is not only political but cultural since the Islamist challenge has to be confronted by the Europeans, and Western culture at large, at a time of changing religious perspectives in the world, as discussed in the subsequent chapter by Olivier Roy. The final chapter by Cesare Merlini, of the Italian Institute for International Affairs and a nonresident senior fellow at the Brookings Institution, analyzes the reactions on both sides of the Atlantic to the unexpected events in North Africa and explores the policy options still open to a less influential West.

PART I

SOCIETAL CHANGE IN THE ARAB MUSLIM WORLD

PHILIPPE FARGUES

1

Demography, Migration, and Revolt in the Southern Mediterranean

For the people of the Mediterranean, the early 2010s will be remembered as a period of great change. In the south, Arab citizens' claims to fundamental freedoms and dignities have toppled—or at least seriously shaken—decades-old dictatorships, while in the north the market's failures have confronted governments with an unprecedented crisis concerning the equally old and unsustainable production and welfare systems. The two crises, political in the south and economic in the north, have no common origins except that they are both partly rooted in the progressive, inexorable transformations brought about by demographic change.

Historians will certainly highlight the crises' concomitance with a radical demographic turning point that is barely noticeable in real time, as shifts in population evolve slowly and therefore invisibly for those who focus on the short term. The period around 2010 will indeed be remembered as the time when the population of young adults peaked in the Arab world while an enduring population decline gained momentum in Europe. Demography offers a key to understanding changes that separately affect the southern and northern shores of the Mediterranean while, at the same time, linking them together through international migration.

This chapter will, first, briefly review how demographic trends challenge Europe's ambitious economic, social, and political goals and will ask to what extent immigration can help in addressing demographic challenges. The rest of the chapter focuses on Europe's closest neighborhood, the Arab Mediterranean region, from which large flows of recent immigrants have originated.[1] It describes the lack of economic prospects, political freedom, and individual agency that young adults—more numerous but more excluded than ever—suffer in the context of the powerful social changes that accompany such a demographic shift, such as women's empowerment, the spread of education, and, for the first time, the birth of the individual in societies that have been based, since time immemorial, on families and communities.

The chapter then offers an interpretation of emigration and revolt as two possible responses of the young, whose new aspirations are frustrated by the patriarchal order of both the family and the polity, which largely negates individuals' aspirations. After recalling that Arab countries have their own "south" and thus constitute a migrant receiving as well as a sending region, the chapter finally examines what happened when migration and revolt met in the course of 2011. By way of conclusion, it will speculate on the future of migration in relation to long-term demographic and short-term political changes in the Arab region, as well as on the future of European policies regarding Arab migration.

Generational Contracts at Risk

For the first time in history, Europe must prepare for a long-term decline in population that will not be the result of wars or epidemics, as in the past, but rather the outcome of individual choices freely made by its own people over the last half century regarding procreation. Demographic recession cannot be stopped unless the downward trend is offset by large-scale immigration. Moreover, below-replacement fertility rates will combine with continuous gains in life expectancy to produce unprecedented population aging. While this process is potentially universal, it will affect Europe first and more acutely than any other part of the world.

Europe's demographic recession will have three facets. The first will be a shrinking Europe. While the total population of Europe will decrease or stabilize, depending upon migration scenarios, the number of people in most other regions will continue to increase so that the relative weight of Europe in world population terms will dwindle. Europe's closest neighbors will continue to follow their own demographic paths. For example, if the members of the League of Arab States eventually accomplish the dream of its founders and build one Arab nation, this nation will have 633 million inhabitants in 2050 (versus 357 million in 2010), whereas the twenty-seven member states of the European Union (EU27) are projected to have only 448 million inhabitants in 2050 (versus 506 million in 2010) if no immigration takes place.[2]

The second facet will be a fast decline in Europe's workforce, endangering its wealth. If no immigration occurs between 2010 and 2050, the EU27 will lose 84 million working-age persons, a relative change of –27 percent (compared with an absolute gain of +1,349 million working age individuals, or +34 percent, at the world level).

The third facet will be an unprecedented rise in the elderly population, jeopardizing Europe's social contract. Booming numbers entitled to pensions combined with shrinking numbers subject to taxation will soon make the whole welfare state unsustainable. With no further immigration, the EU27 old-age dependency ratio (population aged sixty-five and over divided by population aged fifteen to sixty-four) will jump from 0.256 in 2010 to 0.468 in 2050.

Europe has recourse to a range of strategies to address the consequences of these population trends. Pursuing enlargement by including new countries in the European Union would increase the weight of the EU in world population but hardly mitigate distortions in its age pyramid, even if new member states have younger populations (for example, Turkey). Adopting pronatalist policies, raising the retirement age, increasing economic participation among women and immigrants of former migration waves, and elevating labor productivity would partly address the consequences of an aging population. Finally, redesigning pro-immigration policies—instead of suspending them in response to rising unemployment with the economic crisis, as most EU states are doing at the time of this writing—is a strategy that states must not dismiss, keeping in mind that the economic crisis will pass, but the demographic recession is here to stay.

Not far to the south, the Arab world presents a demographic pattern that contrasts strikingly with that of Europe (see figure 1-1). Until the 1980s Arab populations were viewed as the epitome of the demographic explosion. The "population problem" was felt as early as the 1930s in Egypt, when intellectuals and scientists pointed at overpopulation and rapid population growth as a major cause of underdevelopment, and a *fatwa* allowing contraception was pronounced by Egypt's grand mufti in 1937, decades before the issue became a matter of debate for the Vatican.[3]

From that time until the 1980s, the population problem centered on high birth rates, which caused the population to grow faster than the economy. A demographic measure—birth control—was seen as the solution, and family planning programs were initiated in the early 1960s in Egypt and Tunisia, then in the following decades across all the Arab world except the Gulf states

Figure 1-1. *Population of Young Adults in the Middle East and North Africa (MENA) versus the European Union*[a]

Millions

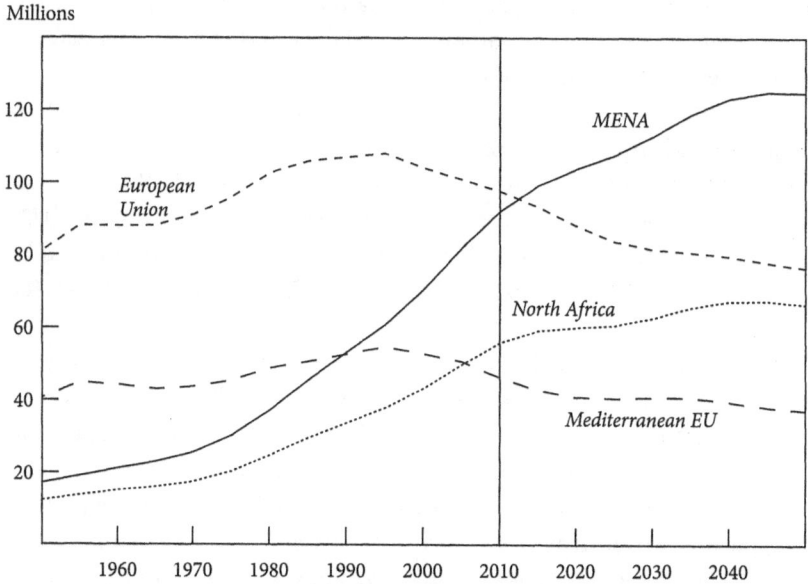

Sources: United Nations, Population Division, "World Population Prospects, the 2010 Revision" (http://esa.un.org/unpd/wpp/index.htm [May 2012]).

a. Young adults defined as those aged twenty to thirty-five. The Mediterranean EU states are Cyprus, France, Greece, Italy, Malta, Portugal, and Spain.

(where governments considered national populations too small in relation to the size of their oil-driven economies). Finally, the annual number of births began to grow more slowly and stabilized between the mid-1980s and the mid-1990s (dates varying slightly from country to country), the years during which the largest generations were born.

Twenty to thirty years later, in the early 2010s, these generations now constitute the twenty- to thirty-five-year-old age group, which stands at its historical peak, and the population problems associated with this cohort can no longer be addressed through demographic measures. Because the numbers of young adults have grown faster than resources available to them—from labor access to employment and income to enjoyment of freedom, and more particularly the freedom to act—the solution now must be both economic and political. Before examining the various options available to the young in the Arab world, it is useful to reflect on two key determinants of demographic change: the condition of women and the spread of education.

Figure 1-2. *Total Fertility Rate in the MENA, 1960–2010*

Average number of children per woman over her lifetime

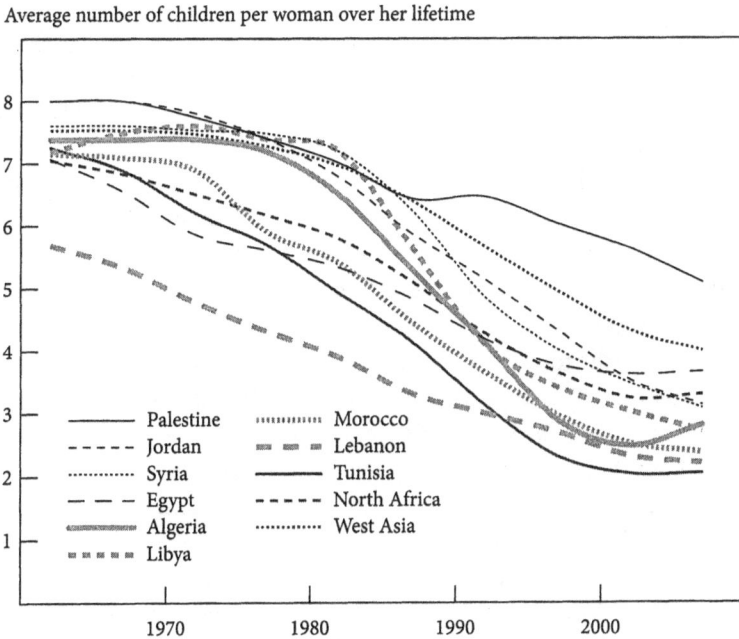

Sources: United Nations, Population Division, "World Population Prospects, the 2010 Revision" (http://esa.un.org/unpd/wpp/index.htm [May 2012]) for all countries, except between 2000 and 2010 for the following countries: Egypt—CAPMAS 2011 (same source as table 1-1); Algeria—Office National des Statistiques, "*Démographie Algérienne 2010, Etudes Statistiques no. 575*" (Algiers, 2011); and Tunisia—Institut National de la Statistique, "*Annuaire Statistique de la Tunisie 2005–2009*" (Tunis, 2011).

Women, Fertility, and Patriarchal Traditions

The average total fertility rate (TFR) in the Middle East and North Africa (MENA) was 3.3 children per woman in 2005–10. Although this is relatively high compared to the world average (2.5), it is low compared to the six to eight children per women that were the norm for the previous generation (figure 1-2). The global decline in birth rates began later in the Arab world than in Southeast Asia or Latin America, but once under way it progressed faster. There are still significant differences among MENA countries. Tunisia and Lebanon are now just at replacement level (between 2.0 and 2.1 children per woman), Morocco and Libya are slightly above (2.4 and 2.7, respectively), and Egypt, Jordan, and Syria fall in the middle range (3.0 to 3.5). The TFR is still high in the Gulf states and

Sudan (around 4) and in the Palestinian Territory (5.1), where the factors that would promote fertility decline have largely been countered by the economic and social ramifications of the Israeli occupation and the associated conflict.[4]

Fertility also varies across regions in the same country. As a general rule, cities and the richer regions have lower levels of fertility than villages and poorer regions. For example, in Morocco in 2004, urban women had a TFR of 2.1 (replacement level) compared with 3.1 for rural women.[5] In Tunisia in 2009, the district of Tunis had a TFR of 1.65 (with a minimum of 1.50 in Ariana)—a level comparable with the very low fertility observed in Mediterranean Europe—while the district of Centre-Ouest (Kasserine, Sidi Bouzid) had a TFR of 2.46.[6] In the Arab world, as elsewhere, factors that explain birth control include the roles of women and the place of children in the family and society, all of which change dramatically with urbanization, the shift to service economies, and the spread of school education.

Why have these universal causes for lower birth rates acted later in the Arab countries than in other parts of the world? The common view among Western social scientists is that Islam held back two key engines of demographic transition: women's autonomy and the emergence of civil society that fosters community self-empowerment.[7] If so, then how can one explain that Iran has experienced one of the fastest fertility declines in history—with a TFR literally collapsing from 6.54 in 1980–85 to a far-below-replacement level of 1.77 in 2005–10—precisely when the country was ruled by the most fundamentalist of clergies?[8] Likewise, how can one understand the fertility collapse in Algeria in the 1990s that coincided with the rise of Islamic radicalism?

Another explanation may be found in the political economy of the Arab countries. All these countries (except Morocco) share a heavy dependency on oil revenues. Dependence is direct in the case of major oil exporters (the Gulf states and Iraq in Western Asia, Libya and Algeria in North Africa) and mostly indirect for minor exporters and for nonexporters where Arab oil wealth arrives in the form of development assistance, foreign investment, and migrant workers' remittances.

The dramatic oil boom between 1973 and the early 1980s generated an income that enabled Arab governments to subsidize a wide range of household needs from food to school education and health, thereby cutting the cost of children for families—in other words, it made high fertility affordable. In an enduring patriarchal context valuing large families, the wealth from the oil boom extended the era of high levels of fertility. The redistribution of significant oil wealth effectively pitted the forces of conservatism and change against one another. A low level of economic participation among married women, whose maintenance in the home directly fostered high fertility, reflected social conservatism. Social change, meanwhile, was seen in the rising school attendance among the young, who later would act as catalysts for political change.

The oil crisis in the mid-1980s put an end to the oil-supported pattern of high fertility rates. Collapsing oil prices affected states' and households' revenues in all Arab countries, oil exporters as well as nonexporters indirectly depending upon oil revenues, and governments, except in the Gulf states, adopted International Monetary Fund economic reforms under which families lost out. Average age at marriage among Arab women rose—from under twenty years of age in the 1960s to between twenty-five and thirty years in the early 2000s—and couples started to drastically limit the number of children they had in order to be able to provide them with educational opportunities. The universal mechanism described by Gary Becker as a child quantity-for-quality trade-off was no longer deactivated by oil wealth.[9]

Will fertility continue to decline and reach replacement level in Arab countries (by around 2030 as is assumed in the population projection of the United Nations)? While there seems to be no question that demographic transition is an irreversible process here as elsewhere, it responds to changes that are themselves unidirectional, making its actual pace uncertain. Indeed, the declining trend in fertility was curbed or even slightly reversed in several Arab countries in the early 2000s. In Algeria the TFR has regularly increased from a historical minimum of 2.4 reached in 2001 to 2.5 in 2002, 2.6 in 2005, 2.8 in 2008, and 2.9 in 2010.[10] In Egypt it has never fallen below 3.5 children per woman, and its level in 2009 (3.9) was already reached in 1992 (table 1-1); in Tunisia, the Arab forerunner in demographic matters, it has imperceptibly risen from 2.04 in 2005 to 2.05 in 2009.[11] This list could be extended. One cannot rule out that the resilience of patriarchal views that a woman's role should be confined to being wife and mother is currently at play in the Arab region, whether or not it is fueled by Islamic fundamentalism.

Women have gained considerable visibility and an accompanying capacity to act for themselves over the last half century, but their empowerment is not complete. While schooling has allowed girls, previously confined to the family house, into the public space (see the following section), many workplaces are de facto closed off to women. In the 2000s, Arab countries had by far the world's lowest rates of female economic participation. In the mid-2000s (last available statistics), the rate of economic activity among women aged fifteen

Table 1-1. *Total Fertility Rate (TFR) in Egypt, 1990–2009*

Year	TFR	Year	TFR	Year	TFR	Year	TFR
1990	4.68	1995	3.82	2000	3.73	2005	3.49
1991	4.38	1996	3.87	2001	3.66	2006	3.52
1992	3.89	1997	3.74	2002	3.63	2007	3.63
1993	4.04	1998	3.76	2003	3.59	2008	3.74
1994	3.95	1999	3.69	2004	3.52	2009	3.95

Source: Calculated by the author, using data from Central Agency for Public Mobilization and Statistics (CAPMAS), "Egypt in Figures, March 2011, Vital Statistics, Number and Rates of Births, Deaths and Natural Increase (1990–2009)" (www.sis.gov.eg/VR/egyptinfigures/pages/note.htm [May 2012]).

and over was 24.7 percent in Morocco (2004), 24.2 percent in Tunisia (2004), 16 percent in Egypt (2006), 14.6 percent in Syria (2004), 15.7 percent in Palestine (2007), and 14.2 percent in Algeria (2008), compared with a world average of 55 percent.[12] While female employment exists in Arab countries, as elsewhere it is mostly held by never married, divorced, and widowed women, not by married women—a fact suggesting that society may allow women to work in the public space, but husbands do not.

Demographic change, however, is slowly undermining the patriarchal system that has governed the family since time immemorial. That system rests on two pillars: younger brothers' subordination to the eldest brother, and women's subordination to men. Fertility decline breaks the first pillar. Schematically, the current trend towards two-child families—on average, a boy and a girl—undermines a hierarchy among brothers, for lack of brothers. The second pillar can still be based on Islamic law, but the gap between law and practice is widening. Rising educational levels are shaking the hierarchy of genders. Young adult women have now received an education comparable to education for men of their age (which makes them much better educated than their fathers), and a new competition, between the genders, is appearing in the upper reaches of the labor market.

Expansion of Education and Its Effect on Inequality

Almost all of today's children in the MENA spend at least a short period of time at school. In their grandparents' (or, in a number of countries, their parents') generation, the same majority had never been to school and remained illiterate all their lives. Like mosques, schools have become familiar buildings in urban and rural neighborhoods, and the majority of the population is too young to recall that school education is a recent social achievement. School has introduced a modern kind of hierarchy based on educational level, one that differentiates between the most elementary groupings in society, those of gender and age.

Arab countries share three characteristics with most other developing countries with regard to education. First, despite the fact that school education is so well established that it is taken for granted as one of the fundamental rights of the individual, it only recently has become accessible to the greater public. Only a few decades have elapsed—at most a century—since the time when school did not feature in the lives of ordinary people. The second characteristic of school education is that it only provides for children and young people. Third, the level of childhood and adolescent education remains one of the few stable characteristics of an individual, in the same way as eye color or date of birth (a fact that adult literacy programs are too limited to alter).

From these three characteristics, it follows that a generation can be characterized by its level of education, from the time when that generation passes school age (twenty years) until its death. In times of change, when different generations coexisting at a given time have not had the same access to education in their youth, education introduces vertical differentiation in the population, between the generations and invariably to the advantage of the youngest ones.

Arab societies have a continuous scholarly tradition dating back to the establishment of Islam, when elementary schools (*kuttâb*) and higher-level establishments (*madrasa*) were instituted to teach the Koran and religious disciplines. However, public education, as a prerogative of the state, was not established until the twentieth century. Whatever the level of schooling being considered, from simply learning to read to graduating from the university with a diploma, education has not ceased to make up ground since then. This has resulted in a remarkable and continual rise in the average educational level of the population. In Egypt the average number of years of education goes from less than one year for the generations born before 1900 (0.9 years for boys and 0.1 for girls) to 8.4 and 7.2 years, respectively, for men and women in the generations born around 1980.

Initially, the pupils were mainly boys, but the great majority of boys, as well as girls, never became pupils at all: almost all children were excluded. Therefore schools did not introduce inequality to the mass population, but only to

Figure 1-3. *Gender Gap by Level of Education and Generation in Egypt, 1929–94*[a]

Percent

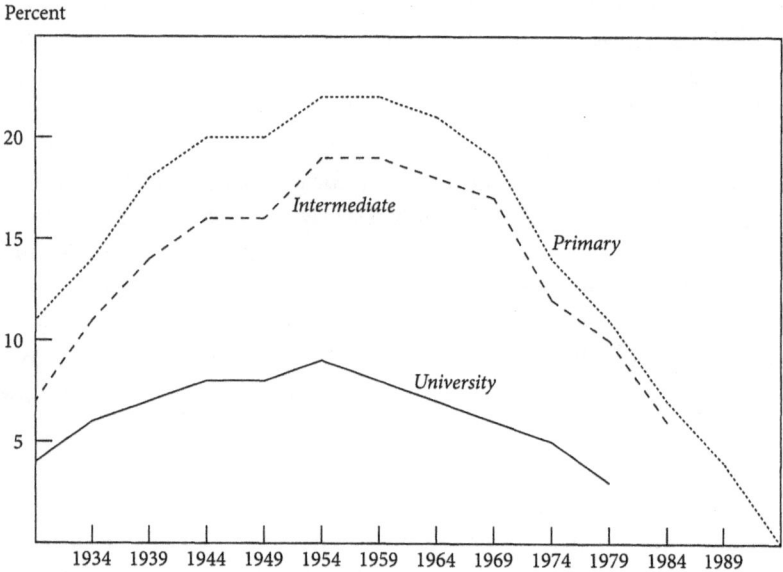

Source: Calculated by the author from the distribution of the Egyptian population by sex, age, and level of education, using data from CAPMAS, "Population and Housing Census of Egypt 2006" (www.sis.gov.eg/En/Story.aspx?sid=9 [May 2012]).

a. Gender gap = proportion of males − proportion of females with given level of education.

the privileged minorities who, in the early days of schools, only sent boys to them. Gender inequality in modern education was thus confined to the top of the social ladder. As schooling spread, it became commonplace for boys from diverse social classes before it expanded to take in girls as well. As a result, the institution of the modern school reinforced the traditional hierarchy between the sexes by following the traditional, male-dominant patriarchal model. In Egypt the generations with the highest gender inequalities in education were born in the 1950s (figure 1-3). In more recent times, a new gender equality emerged when access to school at all levels became the norm among girls as well as boys in Egypt—as was also the case, indeed, in most Arab countries.

This movement from an old equilibrium dominated by illiteracy to a new one dominated by (some) education inspires three remarks. First, the most elementary inequality between the sexes, regarding reading and writing, has declined across the social hierarchy, starting among the privileged classes and ending with the underprivileged groups (the only groups where some residual illiteracy among the young remains). Second, although women have gained access to education, men have had access longer, so gender equality in education has yet to be fully achieved. Third, educational inequality between the sexes peaked in the generations born in the 1940s, 1950s, and 1960s, and it is the men from these generations who occupy positions of power in society and politics at the beginning of the twenty-first century. These generations are the heirs of the patriarchal tradition, which paradoxically was reinforced by the hierarchies arising from the earlier gender inequalities in modern public education.

The continuing spread of education had another effect: it inverted the hierarchy between age groups. While the patriarchal model placed elders at the top, schooling has given preeminence to the young, who are better educated than their elders. The decrease in illiteracy exemplifies this reversal of the traditional order. Until the generations born around 1920, children were more or less on a par with their parents in terms of education: for the most part, none of them would have received any, and illiteracy was their common destiny. As the widespread diffusion of schools benefited only children, it created a distance between them and their parents, a generation gap that is constantly widening. In Egypt the biggest gap exists between parents from the generation born around 1945 and their children from the generation born around 1980. From this perspective, the young adults of today have reached a critical point where their knowledge exceeds their elders' to a greater extent than ever before. These elders, however, still hold the key positions of authority in the family and, indeed, in society.

Growing access to education has been accompanied by a profound change in the aspirations of individuals. However, the ever-expanding educational factory soon ceased to be matched by concomitant growth in the employment market. During the last quarter of the twentieth century, the young of the MENA have been confronted with the phenomenon, unknown before 1975, of unemployment among college and university graduates. The Egyptian case described here applies across all Arab countries.

The vast majority of those unemployed in Egypt are under thirty years of age and have never been employed before. Out of every ten young adults, four start their active life with a period of unemployment lasting on average 2.5 years. The numbers of unemployed women and men are equal, a fact that makes women's unemployment rate (number of unemployed per number of economically active) much higher than that of men (25 percent versus 9 percent, respectively, in 2008) simply because there are fewer women than men in the active population.[13]

A major change occurred in the 1980s and 1990s, namely, a steady rise in the education level of the unemployed. In the 1960s the unemployed were below average in terms of education, with almost 90 percent being illiterate or having only partially completed their primary schooling. A generation later, the situation was reversed: 2008–09 unemployment rates were 14.7 percent among young people with a secondary education and 25.6 percent among those with university or higher education.[14] The irruption of unemployment among university graduates challenged the myth that had once elevated the value of schooling to the point where it was seen as a guaranteed route to individual well-being and social progress.

The expansion of education in the countries of the MENA has generated powerful consequences. By giving the young an advantage over their elders and gradually erasing gender inequality, educational institutions establish a new order that openly contradicts the old order that still rules day-to-day relationships, both public and private, and gives precedence to older people and to men. School, which previously opened the doors of the civil service to the sons of a peasant or a local shopkeeper, has seen its value eroded in a labor market that is dominated by the *wasta,* the influential person who will intervene on your behalf and without whom your diploma is worthless. This situation sets the stage for widespread frustration among the young, which in turn may lead to resignation, rebellion, or emigration.

The Birth of the Individual

Declining birth rates are expected to relieve pressures on labor markets, but not for another twenty to twenty-five years. In the meantime, the number of new job seekers (age group twenty to twenty-five) continues to grow and will reach its maximum sometime between 2005 and 2030, depending on when fertility starts to decline. The growing number of youth seeking employment is only one aspect of the changes that Arab labor markets will experience during the next two decades. Indeed, the other trends associated with declining birth rates—fundamental change in women's roles and the dramatic spread of school education—will sharpen the competition for employment. The quantity of human capital entering the labor market is soaring.

Is this massive, demographically driven flow into the Arab labor markets an opportunity or a burden? One rather optimistic view considers demographic change a "gift" for it opens a window of opportunity to endogenous economic development.[15] As a consequence of recent, but sharp, declines in

Figure 1-4. *The Youth Bulge in North Africa, 1950–2050*

Age group 20-35 as percent of total population

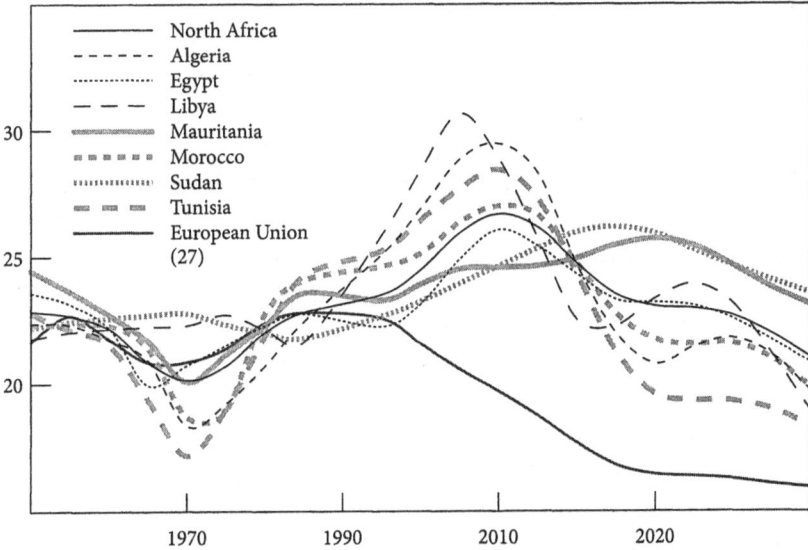

Source: United Nations, Population Division, "World Population Prospects, the 2010 Revision" (http://esa.un.org/unpd/wpp/index.htm [May 2012]).

the birth rates, the dependency ratio is minimal.[16] This is an opportunity that must be seized because declining birth rates will soon lead to an aging population, and the child dependency of the recent past will give way to the dependency of the elderly.

The current decade is a unique period, then, during which the proportion of potentially active to inactive individuals is exceptionally high (figure 1-4). For young people now beginning their working life, the future benefits of their work are no longer mortgaged to support numerous children (as was the case until recently) or the burden of the aged (as will soon be the case). This is a situation that favors savings and investment. Investment can now be economic rather than demographic: it may serve to improve the quality of life for future generations rather than meet the immediate demands of an exploding population.

The problem with this interpretation, however, is that for young people to be able to save, they need to work and to earn a sufficient income. In reality, young Arab adults are confronted with high unemployment, underemployment, low wages, and poor returns on education. On average, it takes a young educated person two to three years to find a first job, then again two to three years to accumulate enough savings to get married. Transition to adulthood occurs at the price of a long period of expectation and exclusion.[17]

In Algeria, a country where oil wealth could never translate into job opportunities for everyone, unemployment is the lot of 31 percent of young adults aged twenty to twenty-four and 26 percent of those aged twenty-five to twenty-nine.[18] In Morocco unemployment is highest among the young (in urban areas, 33 percent among those aged fifteen to twenty-four and 26 percent for those aged twenty-five to thirty-four) and the highly skilled (24 percent of people with a university diploma are unemployed versus 9 percent of those with no diploma). Between 1999 and 2004, unemployment declined for every category except those with a university degree, and the higher the degree, the higher the probability of being unemployed. Unemployment starts as soon as education ends, and the higher the education received, the longer the duration of subsequent unemployment; two out of three first job seekers with a university diploma are unemployed for more than one and up to three years.[19] Egypt, Tunisia, and Syria have patterns similar to those of Morocco.

Another perspective on the demographic transition focuses on the implication of low birth rates at the family and individual levels; familial constraints of earlier times will ease for new generations. Due to their own (expected) low fertility, they no longer bear the burden of numerous children. Due to their mothers' high fertility, they still have numerous siblings to share the burden of looking after the elderly. As a result, young adults today bear a lighter family burden. From a demographic point of view, the Arab world is now witnessing the birth of the individual. For the first time, there is personal freedom of movement. The transition sets the backdrop against which the young and often educated adults now arrive on Arab labor markets, for they are increasingly free from family charges. The resulting freedom of movement also enables younger individuals to assume a greater level of risk.

More human capital flooding into the labor market not only means more capabilities but also higher expectations. Human capital has a potential for progress but also for protest. If expectations are frustrated, then the response can be anything from voicing dissatisfaction to exiting. The former is dealt with elsewhere in this volume. Two decades before the revolution of 2011, a statistical analysis of political violence in Egypt in the early 1990s showed striking correlations between the rise of education, the rate of decline in births, urban growth, and the increase in violent political action.[20] But exit (emigration) has been the most salient response to frustrated expectations over the last decades.

Exiting Instead of Voicing

Emigration from the Maghreb to Western Europe—initially to France—had actually started long before the demographic mechanisms described above, in the interwar years. It gained momentum after World War II in response to the large-scale labor needs of postwar reconstruction and accelerated when Tunisia (1956), Morocco (1956), and Algeria (1962) became independent nations, confronted as they were with huge unemployment problems at home. Migration was then driven by economic forces—the search for a labor force in Europe meeting the search for employment in the Maghreb—and managed by guest worker programs defined under bilateral agreements between sending and receiving states. Migrants were all men moving back and forth between their homes in the Maghreb and their workplace in Europe, according to labor agendas.

This situation dramatically changed with the severe economic crisis, triggered by soaring oil prices, that hit the industrial economies in Western Europe starting in 1973 and that soon resulted in mounting unemployment in Europe. One after another, all the concerned governments responded by closing the borders to foreign workers in an attempt to end migration. However, this measure produced just the opposite outcome: migrants who were in Europe at that time did not return to their home countries for fear of not being allowed to reenter Europe, and since they stayed, their wives and children could join them, thanks to European laws supporting family reunification. In a few years, it became obvious that visa restrictions had transformed the two-way mobility of temporary male migrant workers into one-way permanent immigration of mostly inactive family dependents of former migrants. Immigration was no longer driven by the economic logic of labor markets but by the sociological stimulus of families and networks. Legislation on naturalization and *jus soli* consequently made populations originating in the Maghreb and their descendents a genuine part of national populations in Europe.

Two observations must be made here. First, European labor markets always remained more open than their respective governments were to migrant workers, for migrants accept jobs that are no longer attractive to natives and more generally allow a flexible adaptation of labor supply to demand. If there is no legal way to enter or reside in the country, then unauthorized entry or unauthorized stay offers a second best solution. And irregular migration grew in the late 1980s in response to visa restrictions as well as to employers' strategies of hiring underpaid, informal workers. Second, soon after Western Europe experienced the 1973 crisis, Southern Europe emerged as a new magnet for migrant workers. Starting again in the late 1980s, the steady growth of the Italian economy and, even more strikingly, the boom of the Greek, Spanish, and Portuguese economies with the fall of their dictators and their subsequent admission into the European Union transformed these countries with a long tradition of emigration into new destinations for southern and eastern Mediterranean migrants. From there, due to the implementation of the Schengen Treaty in 1990, they could reach the whole European space of free circulation. The term Fortress Europe may work to describe policies limiting labor migration, but it never reflected the reality on the ground as European borders were never sealed up.

Farther away from Western Europe, emigration from Egypt and the Mashreq (Iraq, Israel, Jordan, Kuwait, Lebanon, and Syria) followed a different route. In the Arab east, where the Ottoman Empire had once established a vast area of free circulation, the movement of people has remained the most significant form of regional exchange. Contrasting with the peaceful relocations of the past, however, modern migration has constantly been linked to wars and conflicts in the Mashreq. The wars of Palestine (1948–49 and 1967) as well as the low-intensity conflicts continuing since then have been instrumental in fostering emigration: directly, locally, they caused two Palestinian exoduses and a constant flow of emigration from the Palestinian occupied territory; indirectly, beyond Palestine, the protracted Arab-Israeli conflict bolstered military regimes claiming their solidarity with the Palestinians (and belligerence toward Israel), whose authoritarian rule also became a strong driver of Arab migration.

During the October 1973 war, with a battlefront along the Suez Canal, the supply of oil became a new weapon, and the price of crude oil quadrupled, creating vast wealth in the Arabian Peninsula and the Gulf. The commensurate need for labor from outside was decisive in orienting migrant flows from Egypt, Syria, Jordan, and Lebanon toward Arab oil states, which still remain the most popular destinations for migrants from these countries.

However, the 1990–91 Gulf War was an unprecedented trauma in that region. Virtually overnight some 3 million migrant workers were cast out simply because they were the wrong nationality: Egyptian peasants in Iraq, unskilled Yemeni construction workers in Saudi Arabia, and Palestinian white-collar workers in Kuwait.

In the 2000s, the largest wave of Arab refugees since 1948 was triggered by the sectarian violence in Iraq that erupted all over the country after its invasion and occupation by the United States, Great Britain, and several other countries. An estimated 2 million Iraqis fled their homeland from October 2005 through 2007. The previous waves that had fled Iraq under Saddam Hussein in the 1990s could find refuge in a number of countries, including several EU member states, but those fleeing Iraq under American occupation found shelter almost exclusively in nearby Arab countries. They arrived first in Jordan, at least until 2005, then in Syria and Lebanon, and finally in Egypt, four countries located in the Euro-Mediterranean area and linked to the EU by association agreements. Not only were Jordan, Syria, and Lebanon the main countries hosting Palestinian refugees, but now they also became the largest recipients of Iraqi refugees, with only tiny numbers of these refugees subsequently being allowed into nearby Europe. (A later section shows how history repeated itself in 2011, this time with refugees fleeing Libya.)

By around 2010 Arab Mediterranean countries were the source of a recorded 10.8 million emigrants (table 1-2)—12 million or more if unrecorded migrants are included.[21] Migrants represent 5.3 percent (or more likely 6 percent) of the population of their origin countries, which is twice the 3 percent world average and demonstrates the very high propensity for migration among young Arabs. Moreover, emigration was steadily rising until the 2008 economic crisis hit the principal destinations in Europe and the Gulf, and the 2011 war in Libya, which triggered a return migration from Libya to Egypt and Tunisia.

Figure 1-5 shows the considerable increase in the number of Moroccan migrants in the 1990s and 2000s. Their total population rose from 1.545 million in 1993 to 3.293 million in 2007, an average rate of 5.4 percent over that time period, which is more than four times higher than the rate of growth of the total population in Morocco (1.2 percent during the same period). It is worth stressing, first, that emigration from Morocco kept growing steadily precisely at a moment when demographic growth started to decline and when the youth bulge started, a bulge that correlates with migration; and second, that Moroccan migrants kept going to France, Italy, and particularly to Spain after the crisis, despite soaring unemployment there.

Surveys of the young in the Middle East reveal that the proportion of that population who wish or intend to emigrate ranges from a quarter to an enormously high three-quarters of that age group, depending on which country is under analysis. In the second half of the 1990s, a Eurostat-coordinated survey already found high proportions: 14 percent in Egypt, 27 percent in Turkey, and

Table 1-2. *Migrants from Arab Mediterranean Countries,*
by Region of Residence, 2011[a]

Country of origin	Region of residence					
	European Union	Gulf States	Libya	Other Arab countries	Other countries	Total
Algeria	1,475,662	19,595	4,593	21,850	56,310	1,578,010
Egypt	199,153	1,132,091	164,348	121,082	226,661	1,843,335
Libya	43,646	2,035	...	6,928	10,947	63,556
Morocco	2,390,174	46,544	19,839	26,279	92,522	2,575,358
Tunisia	516,440	15,985	14,124	11,311	20,308	578,168
Mauritania	26,518	1,012	...	3,174	2,648	33,352
Jordan	25,745	168,668	2,053	48,990	78,195	323,651
Lebanon	153,196	52,543	966	6,635	296,065	509,405
Palestine	8,401	136,573	28,596	2,699,280	34,530	2,907,380
Syria	109,913	120,524	17,017	91,477	82,482	421,413
Total	4,948,848	1,695,570	251,536	3,037,006	900,668	10,833,628

Source: Unpublished table obtained from national population census data of the countries of residence, compiled by A. di Bartolomeo for the Consortium for Applied Research on International Migration, European University Institute.

a. Migrants are defined as "foreign-born residents" (best option) or "foreign nationals" according to countries of residence.

20 percent in Morocco.[22] More recent surveys suggest even higher numbers. Tunisia, a country with a successful economy but a stalled democratization process, is a case in point (table 1-3): in 2005, 76 percent of fifteen- to twenty-nine-year-olds declared that they were contemplating emigration, compared to 45 percent in 2000 and 22 percent in 1996. Many of them, of course, may simply dream without making concrete plans, but their dreams relay much about the discomfort that characterizes the young of MENA countries.

Potential future migration from Arab Mediterranean countries depends not only on the proportion of their youth bulge, which is known, but also on a number of unknown economic and political factors. Whether and in what proportion migrants will choose Europe as their destination is also a matter of conjecture. What is less debatable, however, is that due to demographic change, future patterns of migration will not resemble those of the past and not even those of the present day. Family profiles of young Arab migrants are changing radically. Yesterday, they had a family left at home, and their emigration was motivated by the need to feed and educate their families. Remitting money to those at home was the main reason for leaving the country, and

Figure 1-5. *Moroccan Migrant Populations in France, Italy, and Spain, 1992–2010*

Number of migrants

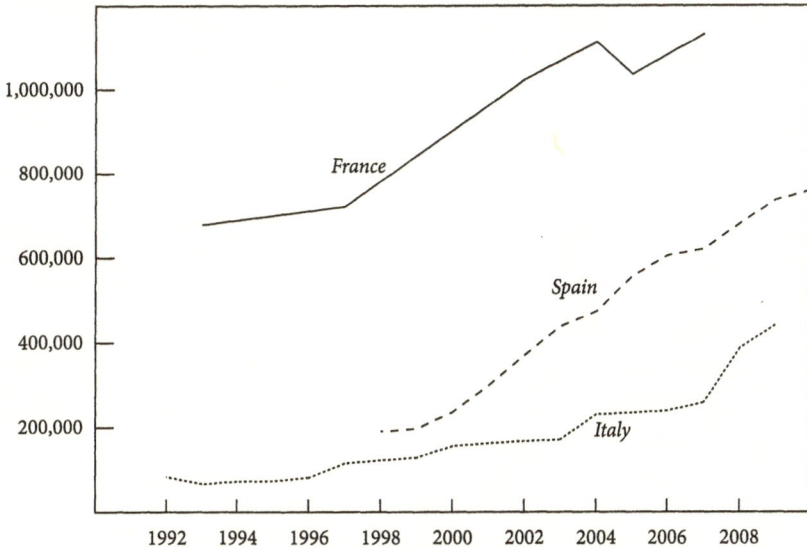

Sources: France, consular records; Spain, municipal registers, Instituto Nacional de Estadística; Italy, residence permits, Istituto Nazionale di Statistica.

in many cases return was part of the migration plan. Tomorrow's young emigrants will typically have no children or wives, and their goal will rather be self-accomplishment.[23]

The "South" of the South

Arab Mediterranean countries are not only sources but also recipients of international migration. In 2010 they had some 4.5 million immigrants (table 1-4). A majority are migrant, mostly low-skilled workers coming from less developed countries further to the south or east, migrants who take jobs that have become unattractive for natives. Refugees form a second category, whose numbers soared in the 2000s with conflicts in, for example, Iraq and Darfur as well as in several sub-Saharan countries. Most then find themselves stranded in countries of first asylum where they cannot obtain residency or even a proper refugee status, and there they either wait for resettlement in a third country or for return to their country of origin when the conditions allow. A third category of

Table 1-3. *Desire to Emigrate among Tunisian Youth, 1996–2005*[a]
Percent declaring a wish to emigrate

Characteristics	1996	2000	2005
Gender			
Male	29	54	84
Female	14	37	66
Age			
15–19	21	44	76
20–24	24	47	77
25–29	23	45	74
Education			
Illiterate	6	3	66
Primary	19	45	77
Secondary	26	49	77
University	24	46	73
Activity			
Employed	25	48	77
Unemployed	31	54	85
Student	26	48	75
Total	22	45	76

Source: Habib Fourati, "Consultations de la jeunesse et désir d'émigrer chez les jeunes en Tunisie 1996–2005," Analytic and Synthetic Notes 2008/47 (Florence: CARIM, 2008) (http://cadmus.eui.eu/handle/1814/10091 [May 2012]).
a. National representative samples: 20,000 in 1996; 10,000 in 2000; 10,000 in 2005.

migrants, by far the smallest group, are transit migrants stuck on their way to Europe, which they cannot enter for lack of a visa.

A salient characteristic of the early 2000s is the dramatic rise in irregular migration from south of the Mediterranean. While much attention is given to those who clandestinely attempt or succeed in crossing the Mediterranean to Europe, very little is said about the bulk of this migration, which is actually destined for or stranded in the countries of the southern Mediterranean. Some of these migrants had entered the MENA country where they now live irregularly, but many others had their passport regularly stamped at the border and assumed irregular status only after their permit to stay expired or was invalidated due to changes in laws regarding the conditions of work and residence for foreign nationals. For example, in Egypt the legal status of the Sudanese, who form the largest migrant population, has varied over time, from full freedom of movement and residence (1956–95) to visa requirement

Table 1-4. *Regular and Irregular Immigrants in Southern and Eastern Mediterranean Countries, circa 2005*
Number of persons, except as indicated

Country	Regular immigrants	Irregular immigrants			Minimum total	Total immigrants	Ratio irregular/ regular (minimum)
		Labor	De facto refugees	Transit			
Algeria	80,238	Tens of thousands	95,121	Tens of thousands	≥10,000	≥185,000	0.1
Egypt	115,589	Tens of thousands to hundreds of thousands	104,390	n.a.	≥100,000	≥215,000	0.9
Jordan	392,273	100,000 or more	519,477	n.a.	≥600,000	≥1,000,000	1.5
Lebanon	302,315	400–500,000	22,743	n.a.	≥400,000	≥700,000	1.3
Libya	449,065	1.0–1.2 million	4,754	Tens of thousands	≥1,000,000	≥1,450,000	2.2
Mauritania	48,000	Few thousands	861	Tens of thousands	≥10,000	≥60,000	0.2
Morocco	62,348	Thousands to tens of thousands	1,878	Tens of thousands	≥10,000	≥70,000	0.2
Syria	55,000	Thousands to tens of thousands	707,422	n.a.	≥700,000	≥750,000	12.7
Tunisia	35,192	Thousands to tens of thousands	161	n.a.	≥10,000	≥45,000	0.3
Total	1,540,020	2–3 million	1,456,807	50,000–150,000	≥2,840,000	≥4,475,000	1.8

Source: Philippe Fargues, "Work, Refuge, Transit: An Emerging Pattern of Irregular Immigration South and East of the Mediterranean," *International Migration Review*, 43, no. 3 (2009): 544–77.
n.a. = Not available.

(1995–2004) to again, at least theoretically, freedom of residence by virtue of a bilateral agreement signed in 2004 but never fully implemented. In Syria, a country open to nationals of all other Arab countries in the name of pan-Arabism, a visa obligation was suddenly imposed on Iraqis in 2007, transforming hundreds of thousands of refugees who had originally been admitted as "guests" into irregular migrants.

Libya before the fall of Qaddafi was a case in point. Persistently subordinating migration policy to changing foreign policy interests, its government successively opened the country's borders to Arabs in the name of pan-Arabism, then to Africans in the name of pan-Africanism, before imposing visas on both Arabs and Africans to please Europe at a time when Libya had become a major gateway for irregular migrants from Africa. Potentially all those who had entered Libya without a visa were made irregular by measures taken in 2007. Irregular migrants have recurrently been scapegoated by being presented as a threat to public security, and as such they were subject to mass deportations in 1995, 2003–05, and 2008.

Revolt and Its Impact on Migration

At the beginning of 2011, revolt flared across the entire Arab region in response to the long-standing frustrations of the population. Uprisings spread in predominantly migrant-sending countries (Tunisia, Egypt, Syria, Yemen) as well as in predominantly migrant-receiving countries (Libya, Bahrain). While the Arab Spring already has had a massive impact on immigrants in war-torn Libya, it will probably produce far-reaching consequences for migratory movements both originating in and destined for the region.

In Libya the exodus caused by the war strikingly resembles what happened in another oil-rich, labor-importing part of the Arab region twenty years earlier, when the Iraqi army invaded Kuwait, provoking the then unprecedented exodus of 3 million migrant workers. Between February and October 2011, more than 1 million people crossed the border out of Libya (table 1-5), 37 percent of them Libyans seeking refuge and the rest mostly temporary migrant workers returning to their homes. But in and among these two groups, there were also an unknown number of de facto refugees from other regions who were trying to find another shelter. Many of these were nationals of conflict-torn Sudan, Somalia, Eritrea, Chad, and a few other African countries, who needed protection but could not claim refugee status in Libya since the country does not recognize refugees.

Table 1-5. *Persons Fleeing Libya, by Nationality, 2011*

Number of persons

Libyans seeking refuge abroad[a]	422,912
Migrants[b]	706,073
Tunisians returning to Tunisia	96,913
Egyptians returning to Egypt	140,642
Third-country nationals reaching Tunisia or Egypt	292,772
Other migrants reaching an African country bordering Libya	148,281
Migrants and refugees of all nationalities fleeing from Libya to Italy or Malta	27,465
Total migrants and Libyans[c]	1,128,985

Source: International Organization for Migration, "Humanitarian Emergency Response to the Libyan Crisis," December 5, 2011 (http://publications.iom.int/bookstore/index.php?main_page= product_info&cPath=41_7&products_id=750 [May 2012]).

a. Arrivals of Libyans in Tunisia, Egypt, and Algeria as of June 8, 2011.

b. Movements of non-Libyans as of September 30, 2011.

c. As of September 30, 2011, for migrants and June 8, 2011, for Libyans.

Many Libyan nationals may have returned to their homes at the time of this writing. On the other hand, among those who were migrant workers in Libya, the vast majority (96.1 percent) have reached an African destination, either their own or a third country (see table 1-5). Only 3.9 percent of them, including all the European expatriates in Libya, went to Europe when the country erupted in riots (table 1-6). Not all migrants and de facto refugees were able to flee the conflict in Libya. Many were stuck there, where they often suffered widespread abuse and human rights violations from both ousted regime loy-

Table 1-6. *Migrants Fleeing Libya, by Country of Arrival*

Units as indicated

Country	*Number*	*Percent*
Tunisia	304,127	43.1
Egypt	226,200	32
Niger	80,329	11.4
Other African states	67,952	9.6
Italy	25,935	3.7
Malta	1,530	0.2
Total	706,073	100

Source: See table 1-5.

alists and forces of the National Transitional Council, who accused them of being mercenaries of Colonel Qaddafi.[24]

Contrary to fears expressed by some European governments, waves of migrants and refugees fleeing Libya did not flood into the European Union. As of September 30, 2011, 27,465 had arrived in Italy and Malta compared to 678,608 migrants (Libyan nationals excluded) who reached an African destination. The road to Europe was not only the less traveled, it also was by far the most dangerous. According to the Italian blog "Fortress Europe," 1,931 migrants died in the Mediterranean between January and July 2011, most in the Channel of Sicily (1,674).[25] When the number of migrants dying at sea is compared to the number who arrived safely in Italy and Malta, one finds the probability of dying while traveling from Libya to Europe to be a shockingly high 6.5 percent, certainly many times higher than the probability of dying while traveling across the desert to an African destination.

The EU took measures to contain flows toward its shores and also to alleviate the burden on Tunisia and Egypt, the two countries that actually took in the largest refugee waves at a time when they themselves were destabilized by revolutions. It must be noted, however, that the EU took no action to accommodate the refugees in Europe. The Libyan crisis suggests that European states need to critically reassess their asylum policies, not the least since their migration policies had led some of them to support, and thereby strengthen, the Qaddafi regime in order to contain irregular migration across the Mediterranean.

In Egypt and Tunisia popular revolts will certainly have repercussions for migration. What is unknown though is how, and this will depend, of course, on their political and economic outcomes. If the revolts succeed in establishing regimes that respond to the peoples' demands for freedom and dignity, and if they generate economic prosperity and social equity, the deep causes of emigration will fade, outflows of migrants will slacken, and return migration from the diaspora might even begin. However, if the revolts fail to achieve democracy, and if economies flounder, the opposite outcome is more likely, and emigration will soar and return migration will fall.

In Egypt the trends since January 2011 have generated mixed signals. On the one hand, political unrest has already cost its economy an estimated $9.8 billion, and tourism, a sector from which more than 10 percent of Egyptian households directly or indrectly earn their living, has at least temporarily disappeared.[26] In a survey of young Egyptians performed by the International Organization for

Migration (IOM) in the summer of 2011, 15–20 percent declared an intention to emigrate in the near future, a proportion strikingly close to those found in two previous surveys: one conducted in 2009 by the Population Council among 15,000 Egyptians aged ten to twenty-nine (18 percent intented to migrate) and the other carried out in 1998 by the Egyptian Central Agency for Public Mobilization and Statistics in the framework of a Eurostat survey (14 percent intended to migrate).[27] The Summer 2011 IOM survey among young people with an intention to migrate found that almost half of them (44 percent) had already decided to migrate before the uprising, and most of the rest (41 percent) were only slightly influenced by events; but still a significant proportion (15 percent) admitted that the uprising had made them want to migrate.[28]

On the other hand, the response from Egyptian expatriates has run contrary to expectations. It was believed that Egyptians abroad would wait before sending any more money home while they observed from a distance the economic evolution in their home country. Thus remittances for fiscal year 2010–11 were expected to fall below the ones for the previous year ($9.5 billion). Instead, remittances reached a historical high of $12.6 billion.[29] Was this the result of a campaign to incite migrants to remit through official channels, or a burst of trust in the Egyptian economy and an upsurge of patriotism among Egyptian expatriates? Or, instead, did soaring remittances simply reflect an unusually intense movement of Egyptian migrants returning from the Gulf?[30] At this writing, it is still too soon to assess what actually took place. Finally, it must be noted that the topic of irregular emigration, which was regularly making the headlines in the Egyptian press before the revolution, simply disappeared from the mainstream media in January 2011 as other matters closer to home took precedence.

A different situation unfolded in Tunisia, where the onset of popular uprisings was followed by a surge in irregular emigration to Italy: in the first quarter of 2011, some 20,000 Tunisian nationals were recorded as irregularly landing on the Italian island of Lampedusa. However, irregular migration rapidly lost momentum when many migrants were repatriated to Tunisia when the terms of the readmission agreement, passed in 2009 between their country and Italy, were applied; indeed, the number of Tunisian irregular migrants arriving in the second quarter of 2011 fell to 4,300.[31] The larger than usual emigration in the first months of 2011 has been explained not by a surge in the intention to migrate so much as by the opportunity provided by the fall of the dictatorship.[32]

Conclusion

The old, established demographic order of the Mediterranean is being over-turned. For the first time since the Roman Empire, the African shore is about to overtake the European shore. Egypt, which barely had 2.5 million inhabitants at the beginning of the nineteenth century, became in 1995 the largest Mediterranean nation, more populous than either France or Italy, and is expected to exceed the population of those two countries combined in just one generation, reaching a population of 120 million somewhere between 2040 and 2050. During the same time frame, the population of Algeria will be greater than that of Italy, and Morocco's population will exceed that of Spain. However, that migration from the south to the north will gain momentum, as these numbers might suggest at first glance, should not be taken for granted.

As of this writing, no one knows when the economic crisis will be over and full employment resume in the north, but one can assume that the European Union will sooner or later recover and remain a magnet for global migrants. Unless unprecedented demographic aging is accompanied by major resistance to accepting newcomers, a number of jobs in EU labor markets should again be open to immigrants. From where will they come? Migration is asymmetric in essence, and the receiving end—the state, the market, and to a certain extent networks of former migrants—is where the origin of new migrants is ultimately determined. With migration becoming global, geographic proximity is no longer the primary factor it once was, and states and employers are just as likely to favor immigrants from more distant regions, as happened in Spain when massive flows arrived from Latin America in the early 2000s.

In the Arab region, demographic trends are likely to remain favorable to emigration, but not for very long and not at the same level in each country. The youth bulge, which has been historically concomitant with emigration peaks in many parts of the world, is already receding in those Arab countries farthest along the demographic transition (Tunisia, Lebanon, and Morocco) but is likely to persist in others, such as Palestine, Syria, Jordan, Algeria, and also Egypt. [33] Egypt, once the Arab pioneer of family planning and birth control under President Nasser, is now following a different path, with birth rates halfway between pre- and post-transitional levels. This corresponds with the unachieved empowerment of women, who still are largely secluded from the workplace, even though girls have now gained parity with boys at school and university.

The resilience, or return, of traditional patterns of fertility and family building in Egypt may well reflect a broader change under way in the MENA, triggered by models and values borrowed from Saudi Arabia and spread by oil money and migrants returning from the Gulf. In Egypt, as in other Arab countries, future political developments will be instrumental in determining whether emigration will slacken or amplify and where it will go. The economic successes or failures of future regimes and, as important, their inclination to respect or disregard the dignity and freedom of their people will be key factors affecting the scale of emigration. Their options in international politics, their relations with Europe, and, perhaps more significant, their view of the West and the values they choose to promote will play a role in orienting would-be migrants toward Europe or elsewhere.

There are currently 5 million first-generation migrants from the Arab countries in the European Union, and that number increases if their sons and daughters born in Europe, the so-called second-generation migrants, are counted. Despite the fact that some of them are poorly integrated—as has always happened in the history of migration—many others fully interact with the natives of their host society, with whom they share increasingly equal opportunities. In the neighborhoods where they live, migrants often share social spaces with natives, with whom they work and trade and whom they sometimes marry. Migrants are continuously exposed to the mainstream values and practices of the society where they live, which they progressively make their own and transmit to their society of origin according to a mechanism described as "social remittances."[34] Thus migrants make an invaluable contribution to reducing cultural divides by bringing part of their culture of origin to the host society while transferring to their society of origin elements of the host society's culture. Migration has been the most critical form of exchange across the Mediterranean over the last half century, building cultural as well as economic bridges. Whether it continue or recedes will largely depend on political choices.

Notes

1. The countries that are the focus of this chapter—from west to east, Morocco, Algeria, Tunisia, Libya, Egypt, Palestine, Jordan, Lebanon, and Syria—are both Arab and Mediterranean (except Jordan). While they are viewed as one region by the European Union (EU's southern neighborhood, sometimes called MEDA in EU' jargon, designating the Mediterranean countries linked with the EU by an Association agreement), they do not form an entity that would be recognized as such by the concerned peoples, who rather identify with the wider Arabic-speaking world, which also includes (Northern) Sudan, Iraq, Yemen, and the Gulf states. In order to stay

close to common perceptions among Arabs, this chapter also uses the following terminology: Arab world, which encompasses all the above countries; Northern Africa (from Morocco to Egypt); Maghreb (from Morocco to Libya); and Mashreq (from Egypt to Syria).

2. Population numbers cited in this section are taken from Philippe Fargues, "International Migration and Europe's Demographic Challenge," Background Paper EU-US Immigration Systems 2011/09 (http://cadmus.eui.eu/bitstream/handle/1814/17839/EU-US%20Immigration%20Systems%202011_09.pdf?sequence=1 [May 2012]). Data used are computed from Eurostat for Europe and from the UN Online Population Database for the Arab countries.

3. See, respectively, Wendell Cleland, "Egypt's Population Problem," L'Égypte contemporaine 28 (1937): 67–87; Philippe Fargues, "Croissance et mutations démographiques au XXe siècle," in L'Égypte au présent—Inventaire d'une société avant révolution, edited by Vincent Battesti and François Ireton (Paris: Sindbad, 2011), pp. 41–74; A. R. Omran, Family Planning in the Legacy of Islam (London and New York: Routledge, 1992).

4. Philippe Fargues, "Protracted National Conflict and Fertility: Palestinians and Israelis in the Twentieth Century," Population and Development Review 26, no. 3 (2000): 441–82.

5. Royaume du Maroc, Haut Commissariat au Plan, "Recensement général de la population et de l'habitat 2004—Caractéristiques démographiques et socio-économiques de la population," National Report (Rabat: Centre National de Documentacion du Maroc, 2008).

6. République Tunisienne, Annuaire Statistique de la Tunisie, 2005–2009, no. 52 (Tunis: Institut National de la Statistique, December 2010).

7. Philip Morgan and others, "Muslim and Non-Muslim Differences in Female Autonomy and Fertility: Evidence from Four Asian Countries," Population and Development Review 28, no. 3 (2002): 437–515.

8. Marie Ladier-Fouladi, "Population et politique en Iran. De la monarchie à la République islamique," Les cahiers de l'INED, no. 150 (Paris: Institut National d'Études Démographiques, 2003).

9. Gary S. Becker, A Treatise on the Family (Harvard University Press, 1993).

10. République Algérienne, Démographie Algérienne 2010 (Algiers: Office National des Statistiques, 2011).

11. République Tunisienne, Annuaire Statistique de la Tunisie, 2005–2009.

12. These figures come from the following sources: Morocco 2004: Royaume du Maroc, Recensement général; Tunisia 2004: Republic of Tunisia, Ministry of Planning and International Cooperation, National Institute of Statistics, General Population and Housing Census for the Year 2004 (Tunis, 2005); Egypt 2006: Central Agency for Public Mobilization and Statistics (CAPMAS), 2006 Population Census (Cairo); Syria 2004: Syrian Arab Republic, "Population and Housing Census" (Damascus); Palestine 2007: Palestinian Central Bureau of Statistics, "Population, Housing and Establishment Census of 2007" (Ramallah); Algeria 2008: Office National de la Statistique, Résultats

du recensement général de la population et de l'habitat 2008—Ménages ordinaires et collectifs (Algiers); world average: International Labor Organization, "LABORSTA" (http://laborsta.ilo.org [May 2012]).

13. Heba Handoussa, *Egypt Human Development Report 2010: Youth in Egypt, Building our Future* (Cairo: United Nations Development Program–Institute of National Planning, 2010), p. 27.

14. *Ibid.*, p.82.

15. David E. Bloom, David Canning, and Jaypee Sevilla, *The Demographic Dividend: A New Perspective on the Economic Consequences of Population Change* (Santa Monica, Calif.: RAND, 2003) (www.rand.org/pubs/monograph_reports/2007/MR1274.pdf [March 2012]); World Bank, "Development and the Next Generation: Regional Highlights—Middle East and North Africa," *World Development Report 2007* (Washington, 2007) (http://siteresources.worldbank.org/INTWDR2007/Resources/1489782-1158076403546/WDR2007RegionalHighlights_MENA_Aug29_draft6.pdf [March 2012]); Ragui Assaad, "Labor Supply, Employment and Unemployment in the Egyptian Economy, 1988–2006," Working Paper 0701 (Cairo: Economic Research Forum, 2007).

16. Dependency ratio = population 0 to14 plus population 65 and over/population 15 to 64.

17. Navtej Dhillon, Paul Dyer, and Tarik Yousef, "Generation in Waiting: An Overview of School to Work and Family Formation Transitions," in *Generation in Waiting: The Unfulfilled Promise of Young People in the Middle East,* edited by Navtej Dhillon and Tarik Yousef (Brookings, 2009), pp. 11–35 (www.brookings.edu/~/media/Files/Press/Books/2009/agenerationinwaiting/agenerationinwaiting_chapter.pdf [March 2012]).

18. République Algérienne, *Enquête sur l'emploi de septembre 2004* (Algiers: Office National des Statistiques, 2007).

19. Centre d'Études et de Recherches Démographiques, *Formes d'activités économiques, emploi et chômage des jeunes* (Rabat, 2005).

20. Philippe Fargues, "Violence politique et démographie en Égypte," in *Le phénomène de la violence politique: Perspectives comparatistes et paradigme égyptien* (Cairo: Dossiers du Centre d'Études et de Documentation Économiques, Juridiques et Sociales, 1994), pp. 223–43.

21. The total number in table 1-2 underestimates real migrant populations in 2010 for three reasons: estimates for the Gulf states refer to year 2000 data, but subsequently emigration to the Gulf has been intense in the early 2000s; counts of Egyptians and Tunisians in Libya—where they do not need an entry visa—are obviously underestimated; and a number of other host countries are not included.

22. Eurostat, *Push and Pull Factors of International Migration; A Comparative Report* (Luxembourg : Office for Official Publications of the European Communities, 2000) (www.nidi.nl/Content/NIDI/output/2000/eurostat-2000-theme1-pushpull.pdf [March 2012]).

23. Philippe Fargues, "International Migration and the Demographic Transition: A Two-Way Interaction," *International Migration Review* 45, no. 3 (2011): 588–614.

24. Amnesty International, "Europe, Now It Is Your Turn to Act—Refugees Forced Out of Libya Urgently Need Resettlement," September 20, 2011 (www.amnesty.org/en/library/info/MDE03/002/2011/en).

25. Migrants at Sea, "Fortress Europe Calculates 1,931 Deaths in the Mediterranean during First 7 Months of 2011" (http://migrantsatsea.wordpress.com/2011/08/15/fortress-europe-calculates-1931-deaths-in-the-mediterranean-during-first-7-months-of-2011/ [March 2012]).

26. Peter Middlebrook and Claire Hajaj, "Re-Thinking the Arab Spring: A Roadmap for G20/UN Support?" October 2011 (www.geopolicity.com/upload/content/The-Cost-of-the-Arab-Spring.pdf [March 2012]).

27. See, respectively, Roberto Pitea and Reham Abdel Mohsen, *Egypt after January 25: Survey of Youth Migration Intention* (Cairo: International Organization for Migration, May 2011) (www.egypt.iom.int/Doc/IOM%20%282011%29%20Egypt%20after%20January%2025%20Survey%20of%20Youth%20Migration%20Intentions.pdf [March 2012]); Population Council, West Asia and North Africa Office, *Survey of Young People in Egypt—Final Report* (Cairo, January 2011) (www.popcouncil.org/pdfs/2010PGY_SYPEFinalReport.pdf [March 2012]); Eurostat, *Push and Pull Factors.*

28. Pitea and Mohsen, *Egypt after January 25.*

29. Dina Abdelfattah, "Impact of Arab Revolts on Migration; The Case of Egypt and Libya," Analytic and Synthetic Notes 2011/68 (Florence: Consortium for Applied Research on International Migration [CARIM], 2011).

30. *Ibid.*

31. Frontex (European Agency for the Management of Operational Cooperation at the External Borders of the Member States of the European Union), *FRAN Quarterly 2: April–June 2011* (Warsaw, September 2011).

32. Souhayma Ben Achour and Monia Ben Jemia, "Révolution tunisienne et migration clandestine vers Europe : Réactions européennes et tunisiennes," Analytic and Synthetic Notes 2011/65 (Florence: CARIM, 2011).

33. Timothy J. Hatton and Jeffrey G. Williamson, *Global Migration and the World Economy: Two Centuries of Policy and Performance* (MIT Press, 2006).

34. Peggy Levitt, *The Transnational Villagers* (University of California Press, 2001).

OLIVIER ROY

2

Islamic Revival and Democracy: The Case in Tunisia and Egypt

In this short analysis of the role of the religious factor in the societal change occurring on the southern shores of the Mediterranean, it may be appropriate to begin from a point already hinted at in the Introduction. An entrenched prejudice in Western public opinion is that there can be no process of democratization in the Muslim world if there is no prior process of secularization or reformation of Islam. This is one of the reasons why the West supported supposedly secularist dictatorships, as in Tunisia, in the hope that these regimes would have an impact similar to the Kemalist regime in Turkey: forced secularization from above. It also explains the frantic quest for "liberal" Muslim thinkers, reformist theologians, and "moderate" Muslims. Books, articles, and conferences repeatedly ask the same rhetorical question: is Islam compatible with democracy, human rights, women's rights, and Western values?[1] But the Arab Spring took place outside the debate on Islam: it was not a conflict between "liberal secularist" and "conservative Islamists"; neither Islamism nor secularism was on the demonstrators' agenda.

So the issue is not that religious reformation is a prerequisite to democratization, nor is it about theology. The issue here is *religiosity*—the way people experience their relationship to religion, the way they experience their faith. During the last two decades, a number of scholars, including this author, have observed a transformation in religiosity.[2] That does not necessarily mean that religious practices have become looser or more superficial; rather, there has been a process of individualization of faith and diversification of the religious field.

47

The stress is on individual belief, individual faith, not on collective belonging to the *ummah* or community of believers or on blindly following the *ulama* (Muslim scholars). This individualization of faith also means the possibility to choose, change, and adapt as well as potentially more acceptance of other choices. We are accustomed to hearing people proclaim they have been "born again" in religious terms in reference to neo-Protestant confessions, particularly in the United States. The born-again phenomenon also occurs in the Muslim world. And when we speak about born again, it is always about somebody who is breaking with tradition, somebody who does not consider religion something traditional, something inherited from his or her parents. He or she regards religion as something that has to be saved from tradition, culture, and social inertia.

These new religious activists have tried, for better or for worse, to rebuild faith communities outside the framework of traditional kinship and social bonds. Thus most of them seem to be "fundamentalists" because they stress the autonomy of religious norms from the dominant culture, but they could also follow more liberal lines—including a quest for spirituality. So what appears as a "return" to fundamentalism is, in fact, some sort of transformation and individualization of religiosity—an endeavour to rethink and recast religious norms in a modern society. The paradox is that some apparently rigorist forms of religiosity, like Salafism, are a way to recast the religious norms outside the bounds of culture and tradition. And paradoxically this kind of religious revivalism is based on the same principles that promote modern forms of citizenship as opposed to the more traditional conception of the social bond: individualization, choice, openness to diversity.

The consequence of the Islamic revivalism that has engulfed the Arab world during the last forty years is that the religious field has become far more diverse and autonomous. The implication is that traditional religious authorities everywhere have lost credibility, as has happened with Al-Azhar or with the different sorts of state-appointed clerics.[3] There has been a surge in individual religious entrepreneurs, TV preachers, and minor imams with a local following. Many young people are inventing their own kind of religiosity. The Salafist movement, which is seen as a very conservative and rightist movement—which is true—is also a product of this individualization of religion and deculturation of religion.

Fundamentalism is not a return to traditional religion. It is rather an endeavor to recast religion as a pure system of norms (*sharia*) disconnected from both the history of Muslim civilization and local anthropologic cultures. Thus it could be compatible with a transformation of religiosity on an individual basis. And it is this individualization that provides the common ground between religious transformation and a quest for democracy, even if, by definition, the political parties that represent a religious constituency may clash in parliamentary setting with more secular parties.

After the Arab Spring, the Islamists find themselves in a pluralist political scene and accept this pluralism. They accept elections. They accept the concept of a constitution drafted by an elected body instead of, say, chanting "the Koran is our constitution." But they cannot give up the idea that Islam should have some centrality. They cannot become secularist. If they become secular, they will disappear. So the issue for them is to recast the centrality of Islam into a more democratic, open, and realistic political space.

Moreover, the Islamists do not enjoy a religious monopoly over the public sphere. There are other movements, such as the Sufis and the Salafists. The paradox of the Arab Spring is that the Al-Azhar Mosque in Cairo, one of Egypt's most important religious institutions, is seeking to regain the legitimacy that was jeopardized by its close association with the Mubarak regime. The imam of Al-Azhar, Sheikh Ahmed el-Tayeb, has suddenly become an advocate of human rights, liberty, and, above all, the separation of religious and state institutions. This means that, in contrast to what has happened in Iran, the Muslim Brotherhood is unable to dictate what Islam says. The religious arena has become pluralistic and open to democratic pressure, even if, for the faithful, there are some things that remain nonnegotiable.

That said, there is no agreement over what is and is not negotiable beyond the centrality of Islam. Should there be a body that determines the Islamicness of laws? If so, who ought to be nominated to it and by whom? Should *hudud* or corporal punishment be applied in cases where religious laws have been violated? Is conversion to Christianity possible for a Muslim? Clearly the situation in Egypt, where the Salafists are outbidding the Muslim Brothers on Islam, is totally different from Tunisia, where the moderate Islamist al-Nahda Party has excluded both the implementation of sharia and the cancellation of the liberal laws on the status of women.

Beyond this opposition between the Muslim Brothers and the Salafists looms another rivalry, between Saudi Arabia, which supports the Salafists (who tend to align with the Wahhabi sheikhs of the Kingdom), and Qatar, which is helping either directly or indirectly (through the Al Jazeera TV channel) to promote the moderate Islamists. The entry of Egyptian Salafists into politics, in contradiction to one of the main points of their creed, would have been impossible without discreet encouragement from some Saudi quarters.

Religion, Identity and Universal Values

So what we see is an endeavor to recast the religious markers in the public sphere into more universal values. For instance, how would Islam work as a constitution? There is a consensus, even among many nonbelievers (at least in Egypt), that Islam is part and parcel of society, culture, and political life. But this centrality is expressed more in terms of identity than of sharia. This is clearly the case in Tunisia, where al-Nahda rejects the imposition of sharia but insists on the country's Islamic identity and culture. Rachid Ghannouchi, the Islamist leader in Tunisia, speaks most often about identity. The reference to identity is a way to mitigate and tame the born-again phenomenon, to reconnect it, not just with a faith community but with a national identity. In opposition to the Salafists, the Islamists want to reconnect Islam to a concrete society and to reconcile it with patriotism. Islam is the national identity in the same way that Catholicism was, until recently, the national identity in Italy. And precisely because it is a matter of identity, it remains quite vague and symbolic. It is a reference, not a legal system.

This idea is shared by the first elected president, Moncef Marzouki, who has never been an Islamist but insists on the fact that there is a Tunisian identity that has been systematically ignored, by both the colonial system and post-colonial Western intellectuals and media. Interestingly, the debate on identity versus an abstract definition of human rights and international law is also raging in Europe. What is the European identity? What is the role of religion in the European identity, and specifically in countries like Italy, Germany, and so on? There is a mirror effect here.

Besides identity, another way to give some centrality to Islam without creating an Islamic state is to recast the Islamic norms into more universal conservative values. And this is exactly what is going on now with respect to many issues of daily life, such as alcohol consumption. Should the new regime ban alcohol? This was the first question that French journalists asked Ghannouchi and other Islamist spokesmen, and the answers were interesting in that they did not refer to sharia. The reference for restricting the use of alcohol was public health, decency, and public order, not sharia. Such restrictions are more in line with local regulations in the United States, from Utah to New York, than with the ban in Saudi Arabia. Laws restricting the use of alcohol may be voted in, like banning the public drinking of alcohol, increasing the legal age for buy-ing alcohol, and increasing duties. The harsh criticism of single mothers by Souad Abderrahim, an al-Nahda member of the Constituent Assembly, was expressed in terms of morality and not in reference to religious law.[4]

Ghannouchi and his party say that they will not touch the status of the family in Tunisia. But they are supporting more gender separation in the pub-lic sphere by referring to decency; respect for equality; the right of women to work, study, and access the public sphere; and the need to fight sexual harass-ment. One can speak of a conservative modernization of public life, which is expressed not in sharia terms but in terms of universal moral values, as do many conservative Christians.

But by definition society is not managed through these kinds of moral norms and values alone. In terms of religion, the Islamists will have to deal with the de facto diversification of the religious field. As mentioned above, the dean of Al Azhar University, Sheikh el-Tayeb, said that Al Azhar should be sep-arated from the state. Of course, el-Tayeb is not a secularist, and what he wants is only the separation of religious institutions from the state. Yet this is precisely a step in the direction of the separation of the religious field from the political field, which is possible because there is a plurality of religious actors—the Sufis, the Salafists, the Muslim Brothers—that leads to a plural-ity of political actors.

Beyond all that, the real challenge for the Islamists is the economy. They have been elected not to impose sharia but to improve the way society works. Whether sincere or not, they cannot effect a coup d'état for a number of rea-sons: aside from not enjoying a monopoly on religion, they do not have the military power; they would need solid political alliances, which are yet to come; and their electorate is very conservative, not revolutionary. So they have to deal first with the economic situation. In the economic field, most of the Islamists are liberal. Their model is more Turkey than Iran or Saudi Ara-bia; in addition, these countries do not have the oil rent that allows many authoritarian regimes to ignore the issue of developing entrepreneurship, the private sector, and an autonomous middle class (that is, one not heavily dependent on the bureaucratic payroll). They are looking toward the AKP (Adalet ve Kalkınma Partisi, or Justice and Development Party) model in Turkey, which has succeeded in combining economic liberalism with a con-servative approach in terms of social values. To do that, they have to assure for-eign investors and the domestic business milieu that there will be no revolution. So it is in their interest to ensure a smooth transition to a more open political system and to institutionalize the democratization process. Thus the real issue is the institutionalization of democracy, not the secularization of the public space.

There will nevertheless be some other burning issues, such as that of the Christian minority in Egypt. For the Muslim Brothers, there is no problem with protecting a religious minority. They see the Christians as a sort of "closed" community, with its own rules and clergy—a view that is shared by the Coptic clergy. But the new generation—Christian, Muslim, or secular—does not consider religious liberty the collective right of a community but an individual human right, which entails the right not to believe or the right to convert, including from Islam to Christianity, a taboo for most Salafists and Islamists.

Another of the big issues facing Islamists in Egypt now and in the future will be the debate on apostasy and conversion. If ever a ban on apostasy is put in place, then it means that individual freedom will not reach the religious field. But if apostasy for Muslims ceases to be a crime, if freedom of religion is defined as an individual right and not a minority right, then there will be a correlation between religious and political freedom, the only way to reconcile citizenship and faith, democracy and religion.

Democratization is a process, not a sudden event. It supposes that the different aspects of social activity (such as demographic trends, politics, social structures, and religion) are undergoing changes that make a given political system obsolete. There is, of course, no direct correlation between these changes: a Salafist, for example, has no political program. But the changes in the religious sphere are making it more congruent with a process of democratization: in fact, it is religious revivalism, not secularization, that has reopened the old issue of the compatibility of Islam with democracy.

Notes

1. See, for instance, the quest for a "moderate" Islam in Cheryl Benard, *Civil Democratic Islam: Partners, Resources, and Strategies* (Washington: RAND Corporation, 2003). Moreover, dozens of books with "Islam and democracy" in their titles have been published since 9/11, by authors as different as John Esposito, Fethullah Gulen, Fatima Mernissi, Larry Diamond, Jocelyn Cesari, and Saeddin Ibrahim.

2. Olivier Roy, *Globalized Islam* (Columbia University Press, 2004).

3. Al-Azhar University in Cairo has been the world center for Islamic and Arabic learning.

4. In a live debate on Radio Monte Carlo, November 9, 2004.

MARIA CRISTINA PACIELLO *and* RENATA PEPICELLI

3

The Changing Role of Women in Society

In January–February 2011, Zine El Abidine Ben Ali in Tunisia and Hosni Mubarak in Egypt were overthrown by unprecedented mass mobilizations. Inspired by the Tunisian and the Egyptian revolutions, a wave of popular protest has spread to other Arab countries, although, apart from Libya, incumbent regimes are still in place. Contrary to the widespread view that Arab women are passive victims in their societies, they have played a prominent role in this large movement of protests, contributing as key actors of change. Women's massive participation in the so-called Arab Spring is emblematic of the direction and extent of gender role changes in the Arab region, in general, and in the North African (NA) region, in particular, over the last few decades.

Unsustainable socioeconomic conditions combined with a lack of political freedoms and repression lie at the root of the mass protests across the Arab world. As far as women are concerned, their political and economic exclusion, particularly among the young, has been even deeper than that of men. While women in NA societies have made considerable progress with regard to education and fertility rates, as this chapter shows, their integration into the economic sphere and formal political structures has been much slower. However, women's political agency in the public sphere is not a new phenomenon in this region. Over the decades, NA women, in growing numbers, have made their voices heard in various ways, from being active in women's organizations and in Islamist groups and political parties to participating in more spontaneous expressions of dissent and frustration such as sit-ins, strikes, and so on.

53

The Arab Spring did not arise from a void but rather built up through a long process of individual and collective awareness of men and women alike, suggesting that women have long been shaping change in the NA region. The revolutions in Egypt and Tunisia came at a time when civil society actors, such as women's associations, human rights groups, and political opposition forces—including Islamist groups—were increasingly incapable of effecting political and economic change, owing to growing repression as well as internal weaknesses. The absence of large, viable, organized opposition forces and formal channels of political expression, combined with the deteriorating socioeconomic conditions and political repression, explains the spontaneous and broad nature of the mobilizations.

Based on these observations, this chapter examines the NA region and assesses the direction and extent of gender changes in the economic and political fields as well as provides a broad overview of women's activism in its diverse forms, with a particular focus on the Arab Spring.[1]

North Africa Women: Between Progress and Resistance to Change

Over the past decades, women in NA societies have made considerable progress with regard to education and fertility rates. More girls than boys are now receiving secondary and higher education, and other aspects of demographic transition have proceeded rapidly since the early 1990s. Although there are variations across areas of residence and social classes, NA families have undergone important structural transformations: the age of first marriage has increased, family sizes have been reduced, the nuclear model has come to represent the majority of families, the percentage of unmarried women has increased, and a growing number of families are headed by women.[2]

These achievements, however, have not been accompanied by corresponding improvements in the participation of NA women in the economy. As shown in table 3-1, labor market indicators are comparatively more unfavorable for women in North Africa than in other regions. Yet, while participation of women in the labor force in the NA region has been rising since the 1960s, it remains among the lowest in the world, meaning that most women continue to be outside of the labor market. Together with the Middle East, the NA region also has the lowest employment-to-population ratio for women and the highest female unemployment rate in the world. Moreover, while unem-

Table 3-1. *Labor Market Indicators by Gender, Regional Averages, 2007*
Percent

Region	Labor force participation rates		Employment-to-population ratio		Unemployment rate	
	Females	Males	Females	Males	Females	Males
Developed economies and European Union	52.7	68.2	50.6	68.5	6.8	6.6
East Asia	67.1	81.4	69.7	83.1	2.9	3.9
Southeast Asia and the Pacific	59.1	82.8	58.9	87.8	5.8	5.3
South Asia	36.2	82.0	37.4	86.4	6.0	5.1
Latin America and the Caribbean	52.9	79.1	52.3	82.2	9.1	5.6
Middle East	33.3	78.3	24.3	81.9	13.4	8,7
North Africa	26.1	75.9	26.7	81.8	16.3	8.2
Sub-Saharan Africa	62.6	86.1	62.5	85.5	8.4	7.7

Source: International Labor Organization, *Global Employment Trends for Women 2008* (Geneva, 2008); International Labor Organization, *Global Employment Trends for Women 2009* (Geneva, 2009).

ployment is high for both men and women in the NA region, the gender gap is much wider here than in other regions.

The labor market situation in North Africa is even worse for young women (see table 3-2). In particular, in Algeria in 2010, unemployment among young female university graduates was 33.6 percent versus 11.1 percent for young men with corresponding levels of education.[3] Similarly, in Egypt in 2009, the unemployment rate among young women was about 32 percent compared to 12 percent among young men.[4] At the same time, wage discrimination against women and gender segmentation in the labor market continue to be marked in North Africa, with women being squeezed into a limited range of occupations that are mostly low paid, and concentrated in forms of temporary and precarious employment.[5]

The limited access of women to the labor market has been an important factor in perpetuating the Arab patriarchal contract and undermining gender role change in NA countries. The fact that NA women have problems in entering the labor market means that delayed marriage and declining fertility are not associated with greater empowerment of women and weakening of the patriarchal contract.[6] In Egypt, for example, young women and men delay marriage

Table 3-2. *Labor Market Indicators by Gender and Youth, 2007*
Percent

Region	Employment-to-population ratio		Youth unemployment rate	
	Females	Males	Females	Males
Developed economies and European Union	42.8	45.6	12.5	13.8
East Asia	64.5	61.6	5.8	7.9
Southeast Asia and the Pacific	40.3	53.7	16.7	16.0
South Asia	26.2	57.2	9.9	9.8
Latin America and the Caribbean	35.3	53.4	21.6	14.0
Middle East	19.5	44.3	29.5	21.1
North Africa	14.7	39.8	32.3	21.2
Sub-Saharan Africa	49.0	63.5	13.9	13.6

Source: International Labor Organization, *Global Employment Trends for Women 2008* (Geneva, 2008).

mainly because of lack of employment opportunities and deteriorating economic conditions. In the case of women, postponing marriage in the absence of economic independence means that they remain under the authority of their father or legal guardian.[7] Yet, as women's jobs tend to be concentrated in sectors where salaries are low, this reduces their prospects for financial independence and greater say in the family.

Although NA women's low level of participation in the labor force is the result of the cumulative effect of economic, legal, and political factors, it should be understood primarily within the context of economic policies pursued since the 1960s. Owing to oil windfalls, particularly during the first and second oil booms, which allowed for high real wages for male workers and remittances from male migrant workers, the contribution of women to the market was considered unnecessary.[8] The adoption of an import substitution industrialization strategy by most Arab countries in the 1960s and1970s also worked against women's economic participation as it was inward looking, was capital intensive, and required skilled labor, all factors that favored male employment.[9]

In the mid-1980s, with collapsing oil prices and the consequent debt crisis, NA countries were compelled to change the direction of economic policies, adopting market-oriented reform programs. For a number of economic and political reasons, these policies, accompanied among other things by the retrenchment of the state from welfare services, failed to ensure well-balanced development and sufficient jobs, thus making the breadwinner model of the family less sustainable. As a result, even while NA women have been facing more constraints in accessing the formal labor market, more and more of them have sought jobs in order to augment deteriorating household budgets. At the same time, married couples have opted for smaller families.

Market-oriented policies have dampened employment prospects more for women than for men, while social and labor market policies, with the exception of microcredit programs, have tended to be biased against women.[10] The personnel reductions in the public sector, where many educated women had found jobs since the 1960s, and the implementation of privatization programs have significantly curtailed employment opportunities for them, particularly in Egypt. Trade-oriented policies in Morocco, Tunisia, and Egypt initially accelerated the employment of young uneducated women in the private sector, particularly in the textile and clothing industry, albeit for low wages and under exploitative and bad working conditions.[11] Since the mid-1990s, however, with the intensification of international competition and the consequent contraction of the manufacturing sector, particularly the textile and clothing industry, employment opportunities for Moroccan, Tunisian, and Egyptian women have declined drastically, and working conditions in this industry have degenerated further. The result of all these factors has been the emergence of very high rates of female unemployment, especially among educated women, alongside a rapid expansion of low social strata female employment in the informal economy.

Although NA economies have grown remarkably over the last decade due to the third oil boom, labor market problems, particularly among women and the educated young, have worsened dramatically. In Tunisia, from 1994 to 2007, female unemployment stagnated (from 17.5 to 17.8 percent) even though unemployment at the national level declined (from 15.8 percent to 14.1 percent).[12] In Egypt the decline in female unemployment from 1998 to 2006 reflects the fact that young women adjusted to deteriorating labor market conditions by withdrawing from the labor force. Indeed, this decline was associated with decreasing rates of participation among young women with postsecondary and university education. In other words, the lack of job opportunities for young, educated Egyptian women, reflecting the dramatic diminution in government hiring, and the large gender gap in wages in the private sector discouraged them from looking for a job.[13]

The global financial crisis has had a particularly adverse effect on women and youth in North Africa.[14] For example, in Morocco and Egypt, as the women-intensive textile and clothing industry was hit hard by the global crisis—reporting the largest number of layoffs—women, particularly young women, found it increasingly difficult to remain employed.[15] Moreover, as the case of Morocco shows, the fiscal stimulus packages implemented by the government to cope with the negative effects of the global crisis were completely insensitive to the needs of women and youth, particularly educated ones, as a large amount of public resources was devoted to infrastructure spending, and no special program directly targeted the large number of women affected by job losses in the textile and clothing industry.

Finally, while the political situations in Tunisia and Egypt, where social unrest led to the ousting of former dictators, could offer some opportunities to implement more effective and inclusive economic policies, at the time of this writing, the prospects for seriously rethinking previous economic policies in ways that respond more to the labor market problems of women and youth appear very poor. In the post-uprising phase, governments in Egypt and Tunisia have responded to past and present socioeconomic challenges by adopting measures that are in clear continuity with the past. In other words, interim authorities so far have made no attempt to review past policies critically and provide alternative and more effective solutions to cope with the labor market problems of women and youth.[16]

North African Women in the Labor Market as Agents of Change

When NA women do participate in the labor market, there are signs of positive changes in both the private and public spheres.

The Private Sphere

Within households work distribution in NA countries is strongly gender biased, with women bearing most of the burdens associated with reproduction.[17] In NA societies, more than in other regions, motherhood and marriage play a significant role in constraining the supply of women's labor to the market.[18] In Egypt, for example, many women (75 percent) who were active in 1998 still worked in 2006, as long as they remained single. If and when they married, about 60 percent dropped out of the labor force.[19]

When women enter the labor market, as quantitative evidence for Morocco shows, there seems to be no redistribution of the burden of domestic work within the family, with women either continuing to bear the main burden of domestic work or sharing it with other female members of the household, often their daughters.[20] The burden of household chores also limits the mobility of married women. This means that female entrepreneurs tend to serve local and national markets, while single women are more likely than married women to emigrate for working reasons.[21]

This limited mobility is also due to the fact that, apart from generous maternity benefits for working mothers in the public sector, the number of state-run nurseries and kindergartens in North Africa remains very low. Upper-middle-class working women, however, appear better able to reconcile family and professional life because they can resort to paid day care services.[22] Nevertheless, there is growing evidence for Tunisia and Morocco that, alongside the single and the divorced, married women also have started to emigrate, leaving their families behind, often temporarily, in their home country.[23] Caution is needed, however, in interpreting this evidence as unequivocally positive for women, as women migrating for temporary employment may face the exploitative conditions of seasonal agricultural work, as is the case for Moroccan women migrating to Spain.

While intrahousehold redistribution of domestic work is resistant to change, a few studies on NA countries suggest that working women improve their self-confidence, earn greater respect, and are more likely to intervene in various decisions within their families.[24]

The Public Sphere

Although the gender segmentation of the labor market in NA countries continues to be substantial, a number of positive, albeit still limited, developments can be observed. While women in NA countries are generally encouraged to study traditionally female disciplines such as teaching and health care, they have nonetheless started entering new fields, including engineering and science.[25] Moreover, NA women have been gradually moving into other fields of work that were previously the exclusive province of men. In Egypt women have taken the driver's seat in Cairo's cabs; in Tunisia women own shops in the *suq* (market) alongside men; in Morocco women have entered the police force, and in 2008, for the first time, nineteen women graduated as police commanders. NA women are also increasingly working in male-dominated occupations such as law, serving as judges and lawyers.

The presence of women in the media as journalists, bloggers, film producers, and the like has expanded, with positive ramifications in terms of producing alternative discourses and images about women.[26] While the share of female entrepreneurs in the NA region remains lower than in other middle-income countries, their number is reported to be on the rise, particularly in Tunisia and Algeria.[27] Interestingly, as shown in a number of recent studies on North Africa, when these women are able to establish and manage their enterprises, these are as likely as or even more likely than male-owned firms to be dynamic, stay in the market, grow, and export.[28] However, the women that emerge as successful entrepreneurs generally benefit from strategic assets (for example, belonging to wealthy families, being well educated, and having good access to social and political networks), which allow them to get around typical gender-related constraints such as lack of access to formal credit, child-care responsibilities, and so on.

Women in Decisionmaking Structures

The presence of women in decisionmaking structures (for example, political parties, parliaments, governments, and trade unions) remains low among the Arab states compared to other regions (for women's presence in the parliament, see table 3-3), although there have been important advances in recent years. Women in Algeria, Egypt, Morocco, and Tunisia have increased their participation in parliament, in government positions, local municipalities, and trade unions.[29] There are currently political parties headed by women, such as the Workers' Party led by Louisa Hanoune in Algeria, the Democratic Society Party led by Zouhour Chekkafi in Morocco, and the Parti Democratique Progressiste led by Maya Jeribi in Tunisia.[30] As discussed below, the presence of women in Islamist parties has been increasing in NA countries. Also, trade unions in Algeria, Tunisia, and Morocco have created women's committees.

However, the capacity of NA women to affect change and policymaking through these formal channels of expression has remained very limited. Because authoritarian regimes in North Africa have exercised tight and systematic control over political life, weakening the functions of parliaments and co-opting political parties and trade unions, women's agency through these bodies either has been ineffective or has reflected clientelistic interests. For example, increases in the number of female parliamentarians in the last elections in Morocco, Egypt, and Tunisia were achieved by governments through quota systems, in order to consolidate the power of ruling parties, and were therefore more symbolic than real.[31]

Also, at the level of trade unions, professional associations, and entrepreneur organizations, NA women have remained underrepresented in the upper echelons. However, the Arab Spring could open up opportunities for women

Table 3-3. *Women in National Parliaments, Regional and Country Averages,*
December 2010

Percent

Region	Women in Lower House	Women in Upper House
Nordic countries	42.1	n.a.
Americas	22.4	23.8
Europe[a]	20.1	19.9
Sub-Saharan Africa	19.6	19.7
Asia	18.2	15.3
Pacific	12.4	32.6
Arab states	11.4	7.3
North Africa		
Egypt	12.7	n.a.
Libya	7.7	n.a.
Morocco	10.5	2.2
Tunisia	27.6	15.2

Source: Inter-Parliamentary Union, "Women in National Parliaments" (www.ipu.org/wmn-e/arc/classif311210.htm).

a. Member countries of the Organization for Security and Cooperation in Europe, excluding Nordic countries.

n.a. = Not available.

to influence policy decisionmaking and occupy key positions within these institutions. After the overthrow of Ben Ali in Tunisia, for example, the Union Tunisienne de l'Industrie, du Commerce et de l'Artisanat (UTICA), the existing organization of entrepreneurs, appointed a woman, Wided Bouchemmaoui, as its interim president in an attempt to renew its image. Moreover, the vice president of the new organization of entrepreneurs, the Confédération des Entreprises Citoyennes de Tunisie, established in September 2011, is a woman, Douja Gharbi. Also, in the post–Ben Ali era, the Syndicat National des Journalistes Tunisiens nominated Nejiba Hamrouni as its new secretary. Although, following the elections held in December 2011, the new national leadership of the Union Générale Tunisienne du Travail (UGTT), the only trade union operating under Ben Ali, is still formed by men, many within the organization are seriously considering introducing a female quota system for future elections.[32] Although these changes do not always reflect a radical change vis-à-vis the old system of power, as is the case with the UTICA, they may nonetheless highlight a new positive trend toward a larger number of women in key decisionmaking positions.[33]

The Role of Women in Islamist Organizations

The presence of women in Islamist parties has been on the increase all over the Arab world. Even within an Islamist framework, women are recognized as key political actors. In Morocco, in the 2011 elections, the majority of women elected to parliament (16 percent) came from the Islamist party, Parti de la Justice et du Développment, the first party in the country to gain 27 percent of the total seats.[34] According to Nadia Yassine, founder and head of the women's branch of the Moroccan Islamist association, al Adl wa al Insan, women are claiming more and more space in the organization. Thirty percent of the movement's internal assembly, El Majlis Choura, is composed of women. Of the six members elected by the general secretariat, without a quota system, three are women. The women's section is very active and influential.[35] In the last decade in Egypt, the Islamist Muslim Brotherhood has started to recognize the importance of women. This has been reflected in the selection of women as candidates for the parliamentary and municipal elections in 2000, 2005, and 2007, as well as in the growing number of women involved in the Brotherhood's political activities. In the last decade, the party has taken an advanced position concerning women, stressing that they should have the right to strike a balance between their social duties and their work in the public sphere. It is worth mentioning that the ban against women running for the presidency maintained in the 2007 party platform led to a vigorous debate within the movement. This ongoing ban can be considered a retreat from the position previously advanced by many in the movement. A new generation of women, critical of their marginal status in the movement, are seeking ways to assert their demands for more representation and broader participation in the movement's politics.[36] Thus it is not surprising that many women from the Muslim Brothers participated in the protests that forced Hosni Mubarak to step down in February 2011.

The main Islamist party in Tunisia is al-Nahda, which was illegal until the fall of Ben Ali. It now endorses the public and political role of women, is favorable to female candidates in political competitions, and claims that it intends to respect the achievements obtained so far by Tunisian women.

From Tunisia to Egypt, Islamist women participate in political activities and religious gatherings. They are usually very active in women's groups where they discuss the sacred texts and the role of women in society and the family according to the Islamic sources. Based on their reading of the Koran and *hadith*, Islam grants women respect and rights (to property, education, political participation), but those rights have been obscured by a patriarchal reading of the sacred texts. Even if the latter claims that the main role of a woman is as a mother and educator, Islamist women are not a priori against women working and participating politically as they argue simply that these commitments should be subject to the fulfilment of family obligations. In their speeches, Islamist women particularly emphasize motherhood, which is considered the meeting point between the individual and social spheres, the personal and political domains. According to them, women make their main contribution to the welfare of humankind by engaging in the role of educators of their children, in the narrow sense, and of generations of Muslims, in the broad sense.

Women's Activism

The activism of Arab women has focused on a variety of issues, ranging from the protection of children to environment, from the fight for freedom and democracy to the fight against illiteracy. Certainly, the promotion of gender issues is a central topic. It is worth mentioning, however, that women's activism in the Arab world is not a new phenomenon. The women's movement goes back more than a century.[37] At the end of the nineteenth century, Arab women (Muslims, Christians, and Jews) started to claim the right to education and participation in the public sphere via journals, newspapers, novels, poems, and protests. It is important to underline that the early twentieth-century Arab feminist wave, characterized by nationalist and anticolonial claims, was the result of both internal changes (limited spread of women's education, the desire of middle- and upper-class women to enjoy more freedom and rights, spread of new ideas of development) and external influences (the economic and cultural penetration of Europeans in North Africa and the Middle East, European criticism of the status of women, and the travels of upper-class Arab men and women in the West). The first Arab feminist movements interacted with the activism of women in Europe and the rest of the world, albeit without losing their specificity. From the beginning of the twentieth century, in fact, women's rights activists of Arab origin, mostly Syrian, Egyptian, Lebanese, and Palestinian, exchanged views with counterparts from European movements during international conferences on women, held in various European cities. The activists from the Arab world, far from being in a subordinate position to the West, gave rise to the struggle for indigenous women's rights.

The first explicit feminist organization in Egypt, the Egyptian Feminist Union (EFU) of Hoda Sharawi, was founded at the beginning of the twentieth century. And already in the year of its constitution, 1923, three delegates participated in the Ninth Congress of the International Women's Suffrage Alliance in Rome, underlining their commitment to the right to vote. Other women's associations like the EFU were founded all over the Arab world during the last century to fight against patriarchal institutions and laws.[38] Their activism arose from a modernist perspective, in which religious discourse was marginalized. During the second half of the twentieth century, their arguments have been based on the universality of human rights and the enforcement of international agreements such as the Convention on the Elimination of All Forms of Discrimination against Women (CEDAW).[39]

Now, in the first decade of the twenty-first century, women's activism is characterized by both continuity with this secular approach and the emergence of gender activism with an Islamic perspective. In fact, since the early 1990s, a growing number of Muslim women in different parts of the Islamic world have argued that the Koran guarantees them freedom and rights but that these have been denied by the patriarchal traditions and misogynistic interpretations that have become dominant over the centuries. Scholars such as Asma Lambrabet, from Morocco, or Omaima Abou-Bakr, from Egypt, maintain that there is no justification for the subordination of women, which is done contrary to the message of Islam.[40] The new exegesis produced by women like these represents the basis on which many activists are building their cases against patriarchal laws and institutions. Their discourses and practices are called Islamic feminism.[41]

Thus the contemporary women's movement in the Arab world can be schematized into three main categories: women's organizations that work in a secular setting; associations acting in a religious sphere, referring to the discourses of Islamic feminism; and women's associations close to Islamist movements and parties. These three manifestations of the women's movement are very different from one another; in some cases they are openly and irreconcilably in conflict (especially considering the secular feminist and the Islamist activist agendas), but in other ways they are compatible. It is not always possible to draw a clear boundary between the different groups. Despite substantial differences, common cause can sometimes be made for strategic reasons, as demonstrated by the unity achieved between Islamic feminists and many secular feminists in the battles that led to reform of the Moroccan Family Code in 2004. It is noteworthy, however, that even if both Islamic feminists and Islamist women refer to Islam, they attribute different meanings to such concepts as Islam, human rights, democracy, women's issues, and *sharia*.[42] In fact, unlike the Islamic feminists, the Islamists and the women within the so-called Muslim piety movement emphasize equity rather than equality between the genders in all aspects of society. In this social construction, the man remains responsible for maintaining the family. Gender equity has to do with the complementarity of roles, which ostensibly reflects each gender's "natural inclinations"; proponents argue that men are more predisposed to the public sphere and women to the private.[43] This does not mean, however, that women should be excluded from the public sphere, or that if they participate in it, they should be considered inferior. Participation in the public sphere is considered a way to develop the Islamic concept of "common good" and fulfill one's duties toward society and God. The choice to act in the public sphere, including politics and voluntary associations, is primarily tied to the desire to adhere to the model of the pious Muslim woman who tries to strengthen her faith and go to heaven, thanks to her work on earth.[44] Thus achieving gender equity is one of the goals of these women, but it is not the only one, and certainly not the most important.

Growing Mobilization in the Last Decade: The Role of Women

The last decade has seen a wave of social and political mobilization in NA countries, reflecting the deterioration of socioeconomic conditions and political regression. In the absence of formal channels of political expression, dissent in North Africa has taken alternative and diversified forms (sit-ins, petitions, strikes), often localized and focused on particularistic demands.[45] Women have been part of this wave of mobilization, even though they have been less visible than men. For example, women actively participated in the revolt in the Gafsa Mining Basin in Tunisia in 2008, which was one of the most important protest movements seen in Tunisia since the bread revolt of January 1984. Staging sit-ins, they confronted the police and demanded the release of their sons.[46] Women have also expressed their political ideas and denounced human rights violations as bloggers or through Facebook.[47]

Egyptian women workers, mostly uneducated and young, played a leading and crucial role in the unprecedented wave of labor protests that began in 2004, reflecting the intensification of market-oriented reforms and the increased hardship experienced by large swathes of Egyptian society. Following the refusal of the prime minister to increase annual bonuses, in December

2006 female workers in the state textile factory in the industrial town of Mahalla al-Kubra initiated the largest industrial strike since 1947, demanding that their male colleagues stop production and join them in the protest.[48] During fall 2007 women workers also took part in the strikes staged by property tax workers, who mobilized the largest and most successful collective action of the labor movement since 2006.[49] Female workers, such as Aisha Abd-al-Aziz Abu-Samada at the Hennawi Tobacco factory in the Nile Delta town of Damanhur, also played a leading role in organizing workers, women and men alike.[50] These strikes were successful in pushing a number of economic demands, and the significant participation of women in the protests encouraged gender mixing in public spaces, challenging conventional gender norms and stereotypes.[51]

Women's Claims and the Arab Spring

As stated earlier, the Arab Spring was ushered in by a long process of active citizenship by women. During the protests that led to the overthrow of Ben Ali in Tunisia and Mubarak in Egypt, women were present everywhere: in the front row throwing stones and rejecting the police, in the crowds of protesters documenting what was happening with their cameras and then posting it on the Internet, in the rear distributing food and water and treating the wounded. Their action had no particular political orientation. There were women of both secular and Islamist tendencies; Muslims and Christians fought together. Some had long experience (in militant opposition groups or feminist associations), others had grown up in the opposition movements that emerged on the web during the last decade, and still others were not a part of any activist organizations. In recent years, most women and men have become involved in the antigovernment mobilizations spontaneously. Still, there is no doubt that during the protests, people from opposition parties, associations, a range of movements played an important role.[52]

It was a nonorganized civil society that made the change possible, however. The central protagonists of the Arab Spring were young men and women, mostly educated and not affiliated with political parties and movements. There was, for example, Asma Mahfouz, the twenty-six-year-old Egyptian woman who made a brave, four-and-a-half-minute "video-blog" with her own mobile phone, later posted on YouTube.[53] In the video she strongly invited Egyptians to demonstrate: "I'm making this video to give you one simple message. We want to go down to Tahrir Square on January 25. If we still have honor, and we want to live in dignity on this land, we have to go down on January 25 [...] Whoever says it's not worth it because there will only be a handful of people, I want to tell him you are the reason behind this, and you are a traitor just like the president or any security cop who beats us in the streets. Your presence with us will make a difference, a big difference!"

Like many other women in the protests, Asma Mahfouz is veiled. For many of them, *hijab* (the veil that covers the head but leaves the face uncovered) does not symbolize the transmission of traditional religion but rather is a sign of reappropriation of Islam as a religious, cultural, and often political identity; it is not necessarily an expression of political affiliation with Islamist organizations.

Women and the Transition Period

During the protests in both Egypt and Tunisia, there was an unexpected synergy between men and women. The Egyptian Mona Seif, twenty-six years old, recounts: "Pre-January 25 whenever we would attend protests, I would always be told by the men to go to the back to avoid getting injured, and that used to anger me. But since January 25 people have begun to treat me as an equal. There was this unspoken admiration for one another in the square. We went through many ups and downs together. It felt like it had become a different society."[54] In the aftermath of January 25, many women and even several men expressed similar considerations. Many were confident that they would be able to build a more just society, with no dictatorship and no female subordination established by law and reinforced by custom. Soon, however, the enthusiasm gave way to concerns and disappointments. In Egypt, since Mubarak's ouster, women have still been excluded from decisionmaking positions. Only one woman was nominated to the interim cabinet that resigned in November 2011; the eight members of the committee tasked with formulating constitutional amendments were all male; one of the proposed amendments suggested that future presidents could only be male, and the quota of sixty-four parliamentary seats for women was abolished.

Moreover, the events during the demonstration to celebrate March 8, International Women's Day, seem to suggest that the revolution, which had benefited so much from female participation, was leaving women behind. To commemorate the date, several women's associations, gender-mixed groups, and individuals who had participated in the protests held a march in Tahrir Square demanding that women have a voice in building Egypt's future and gender equality. The reaction in Tahrir Square that day was brutal, as there were only a few hundred women in the square. They were accosted by several groups of men shouting insults and much worse. They were told to go home and wash clothes, that their actions were "un-Islamic."[55] The next day, on March 9, almost a month after the resignation of Hosni Mubarak, things were even worse. During a raid by the police in Tahrir Square, seventeen young women were arrested and taken to the police station. There they were beaten, subjected to electric shocks, forced to undress and be photographed by soldiers, and finally subjected to a "virginity test" under threat of being indicted for prostitution.[56] And the military's abuse of women has not ended. For example, on November 23, 2011, the well-known U.S.-based Egyptian journalist Mona Eltahawy was arrested for twelve hours and subjected to sexual harassment by members of the Interior Ministry and military intelligence.[57] In December the image of a young female protester being harassed, beaten, and stripped naked by soldiers highlighted all the brutality of the military.

Thus post-Mubarak Egypt is going through particularly difficult times, with women paying the highest price. Excluded from decisionmaking, as stated earlier, they are having to deal with the offensive of conservative groups. The Egyptian Center for Women's Rights has collected several testimonies of women assaulted by Salafis, who ordered them to cover themselves from head to toe, get out of their cars, and go home.[58]

While the situation of women in Egypt is quite difficult, there are signs in Tunisia that give hope that the transition period can create more space for women. Although antirevolutionary forces are present in all segments of the country, and several women have complained of being attacked during demonstrations by small groups of Islamists or presumed Islamists, some important positive results can be observed. Tunisian women ensured that the lists for the election of the Constituent Assembly, held on October 23, 2011, were composed of equal numbers of men and women placed in alternating order, so that women do not find themselves confined, as often happens, to the bottom of the list. The Tunisian activist Sihem Bensedrine commented: "It was not easy, even the old progressive parties were opposed, saying that reform was impossible, that there would not be enough women to make up the lists. For them, women were there only to go to the streets, to take beatings, to formulate slogans for the revolution. It is still the opportunism of parties led by men who consider the public space a male prerogative. By having imposed equal candidacies, it will be a success: whatever happens, at least one quarter of the deputies in the future Constituent Assembly will be women. Developing a new constitution without women would be a danger: what kind of democracy is one that marginalizes half of society?"[59]

And the elections resulted in a large presence of Islamist women in the Constituent Assembly. In the 217-member Assembly, there are 49 women— 23 percent of total seats. Forty-two of them are from al-Nahda, meaning that within the Islamist party, women occupy 47 percent of total party seats.[60]

Concluding Remarks

This chapter has shown that, over the decades, NA women have increasingly entered the public sphere. As far as economic participation is concerned, NA women have gradually been moving into fields of work that were previously monopolized by men, while the number of female entrepreneurs is reported to be on the rise, at least in some NA countries. Moreover, growing numbers of women in the region have been voicing their concerns publicly, in diverse ways, from being active in women's organizations and Islamist groups and political parties to participating in less structured expressions of dissent. In spite of this growing presence of women in the public sphere and the considerable achievements in terms of education, NA women have continued to be marginalized from the economic and political spheres as well as almost absent from the high-level positions where decisions are made.

In the long run, the changing political context in Tunisia and Egypt could provide women with new opportunities for implementing a more gender-sensitive agenda and influencing policymaking. However, in the post-revolt phase, the evidence in this regard has been conflicting. In Tunisia women have been able to play a more influential role and make some advances, but in Egypt women have been excluded from the decisionmaking process and subjected to growing harassment by military forces. Yet, beyond these differences, under the changing political context, women in both countries have continued to face grave challenges, and progress toward more inclusion in the political and economic arenas appears difficult and uncertain, at least in the short term.

A major factor of concern is that women in both countries, albeit to varying degrees, seem to have limited opportunities to influence future decision-making processes. In Tunisia, thanks to the provision that women and men be equally represented on electoral lists, women were able to obtain about 23 percent of total seats during the October 23 elections, which is a significant proportion compared to other NA countries. However, the electoral result was far below expectations owing to the limited percentage of electoral lists headed by women (about 6 percent). In Egypt, where parliamentary elections took place from November 2011 to early March 2012, female representation in the parliament is minimal, not exceeding 2 percent of the total number of elected members. Indeed, women represented only 6.2 percent of the total number of candidates, and with some exceptions, they were put at the bottom of the lists.[61] This means that, in general, women will have difficulty influencing the course of change, including the future constitution, through formal decisionmaking bodies.

Another uncertainty for the direction of change affecting women is the future role of Islamist parties. As expected, the elections in Tunisia resulted in a majority vote for the Islamist party al-Nahda, while the elections in Egypt confirmed the prominent position of the Muslim Brotherhood's Freedom and Justice Party, followed by the most conservative Salafist party, al-Nour. Also, in Morocco the Islamist party, the Justice and Development Party, won the most seats in the November parliamentary elections. The electoral success of Islamist parties across North Africa is causing great concern in many parts of these societies and could lead to regression or stagnation with regard to women's issues. However, the trajectory of gender role change is likely to vary with each country, given that Islamist parties are diverse and heterogeneous. Moreover, the role and impact of women activists in Islamist parties, particularly the most moderate ones, should not be underestimated. In Tunisia, for example, under the changing context, women Constituent Assembly members who belong to al-Nahda could play important roles in redefining the Islamist party's agenda and practice, particularly with regard to gender issues, eventually proposing alternative views. Even among female members of al-Nahda, there appear to be different positions on and readings of Islam. Alongside the controversial figure of Souad Abderrahim, the unveiled candidate of al-Nahda who, after her election, released strong words against single mothers, there are other women such as Mehrezia Laabidi, vice president of the Constituent Assembly, who is notorious for having proposed reformist interpretations of Islam.

Notes

1. It is worth mentioning that our analysis is based on the idea that the gender role changes occurring in the economic and political arenas in North Africa have been the product of indigenous dynamics, which have been influenced by external factors but

not determined by them. For us this means that the gender role changes of the last few decades are not the result of Western political and economic impositions.

2. See, for instance, Sanja Kelly and Julia Breslin, *Women's Rights in the Middle East and North Africa* (Lanham, Md.: Rowan and Littlefield, 2010); Ann Way and Fatma El-Zanaty, *Egypt Demographic and Health Survey 2008* (Cairo: Ministry of Health and El-Zanaty and Associates, 2009); Ragui Assaad, "Labor Supply, Employment and Unemployment in the Egyptian Economy, 1988–2006," Working Paper 0701 (Cairo: Economic Research Forum, 2007); Philippe Fargues, "Women in Arab Countries: Challenging the Patriarchal System?" *Reproductive Health Matters* 13, no. 25 (2005): 43–48. In Morocco, for example, the nuclear model has come to represent 60 percent of all families; meanwhile, the proportion of unmarried women went up from 17 percent in 1960 to 34 percent in 2004. More than 20 percent of households in 2007 were headed by women. See Milouda Kerrouache, "The Moroccan Context," April 27, 2010 (www.arab-reform.net/spip.php?article3187).

3. République Algérienne, *Emploi en Algerie* (Algiers: Office Nationale des Statistiques, 2010).

4. Population Council, *Survey of Young People in Egypt: Preliminary Report*, February 2010 (www.unicef.org/egypt/SYPE_Preliminary_Report.pdf [March 2012]).

5. See, for instance, Kelly and Breslin, *Women's Rights*; Myriam Catusse, Blandine Destremau, and Eric Verdier, *L'Etat face aux débordements du social au Maghreb. Formation, travail et protection sociale* (Paris: Karthala, 2009); Amirah El-Haddad, "Labor Market Gender Discrimination under Structural Adjustment: The Case of Egypt," Working Paper 003 (American University in Cairo Social Research Center, November 2009).

6. Fargues, "Women in Arab Countries."

7. Assaad, "Labor Supply."

8. Massoud Karshenas, "Structural Obstacles to Economic Adjustment in the MENA Region: The International Trade Aspects," in *The State and Global Change: The Political Economy of Transition in the Middle East and North Africa*, edited by Hassan Hakimian and Ziba Moshaver (Richmond, Surrey: Curzon, 2001), pp. 59–80.

9. In Tunisia and Morocco, where dependence on oil revenues was more limited and a manufacturing export-oriented strategy began earlier than in other Arab countries, women's labor force participation rates have been historically higher. See Valentine M. Moghadam, *Women's Livelihood and Entitlements in the Middle East: What Difference Has the Neoliberal Policy Turn Made?* (Geneva: United Nations Research Institute for Social Development [UNRISD], 2005).

10. See, for instance, Mohammed Bougroum and Aomar Ibourk, "The Effects of Job-Creation Schemes in Morocco," *International Labour Review* 142, no. 3 (2003): 341–71; Catusse, Destremau, and Verdier, *L'Etat face aux débordements*.

11. Rahma Bouriqia, "Gender and Employment in Moroccan Textile Industries," in *Women's Employment in the Textile Manufacturing Sectors of Bangladesh and Morocco*, edited by Carol Miller and Jessica Vivian (Geneva: UNRISD, 2002), pp. 71–102; Blandine Destremau, "La protection sociale en Tunisie. Nature et coherence de l'intervention

publique," in *L'Etat face aux débordements*, edited by Catusse, Destremau, and Verdier, pp. 129–72; Solidarity Center, *Justice for All: The Struggle for Worker Rights in Egypt* (Washington, February 2010).

12. Azzam Mahjoub, "Labour Markets Performance and Migration Flows in Tunisia," in *Labour Markets Performance and Migration Flows in Arab Mediterranean Countries: Determinants and Effects*, vol. 2: *National Background Papers Maghreb (Morocco, Algeria, Tunisia)*, Occasional Papers 60 (Brussels: European Commission, Directorate-General for Economic and Financial Affairs, 2010), chap. 3.

13. Assaad, "Labor Supply."

14. Maria Cristina Paciello, "L'impact social de la crise financière au Maroc," *Maghreb-Machrek* 206 (Winter 2010–11): 73 –98; Arne Klau, *Impact of the Economic Crisis on Trade, Foreign Investment, and Employment in Egypt* (International Labor Organization [ILO], February 2010).

15. Ibid.

16. For a review of the economic measures taken in the post-uprising phase in Egypt and Tunisia, see Maria Cristina Paciello, "Youth Exclusion in North African Countries: Continuity or Change?" in *Reversing the Vicious Circle in North Africa's Political Economy: Confronting Rural, Urban, and Youth-Related Challenges*, edited by M. C. Paciello and others, GMF Paper Series, 2012 (www.gmfus.org/publications).

17. Royaume du Maroc, *Enquête nationale sur le budget temps des femmes 1997–1998*, vol. 1 and 2 (Rabat: Direction de la Statistique, 1999); Population Council, *Survey of Young People.*

18. United Nations Economic Commission for Africa, "The Economic Participation of Women in North Africa," 2005 (www.uneca.org/sros/na/Women.pdf [March 2012]); Royaume du Maroc, *Enquête nationale*; Stephanie Willman Bordat, Susan Schaefer Davis, and Saida Kouzzi, "Women as Agents of Grassroots Change: Illustrating Micro-empowerment in Morocco," *Journal of Middle East Women's Studies* 7, no. 1 (2011): 90–119; Rana Hendy, "Rethinking Time Allocation of Egyptian Women: A Matching Analysis," Working Paper 526 (Cairo: Economic Research Forum, June 2010).

19. Hendy, "Rethinking."

20. Royaume du Maroc, *Enquête nationale.*

21. Regarding female entrepreneurs, see World Bank, *The Environment for Women's Entrepreneurship in the Middle East and North Africa Region* (World Bank, 2010). On female migrant workers, see Ibtihel Bouchoucha, "'Gender Relations' as a Factor in Determining Who Migrates and Why: The Case of Tunisia," in *Migration and the Maghreb* (Washington: Middle East Institute, May 2010), pp. 20–25.

22. See, for instance, Mona Yahia, "Tunisian Parents Choose Day-Care over Grandma," *Magharebia.com*, November 26, 2010 (www.magharebia.com/cocoon/awi/xhtml1/en_GB/features/awi/reportage/2010/11/26/reportage-01 [March 2012]). In Cairo the number of private crèches has expanded in recent years.

23. Camille Schmoll, "Femmes et migrations. Pratiques spatiales transnationales et stratégies de mobilité des commerçantes tunisiennes," *Jura Gentium* 3 (2007)

(www.juragentium.org/topics/med/fr/schmoll.htm); Mohamed Khachani, *Les nouveaux défis de la question migratoire au Maroc* (Geneva: ILO, 2010).

24. See, for instance, Royaume du Maroc, *Enquête nationale*; Bordat, Davis, and Kouzzi, "Women as Agents"; International Foundation for Electoral Systems, "The Status of Women in the Middle East and North Africa. Focus on Morocco: Paid Work and Control of Earnings," June 2010 (www.ifes.org/Content/Publications/Papers/2010/Focus-on-Morocco-Paid-Work-and-Control-of-Earnings.aspx); Way and El-Zanaty, *Egypt Demographic and Health Survey 2008*; Jose R. Pin, Angela Gallifa, and Lourdes Susaeta, *Microcredit in Tunisia: Enda Inter-Arabe* (University of Navarra, January 2008); Schmoll, "Femmes et migrations."

25. Kelly and Breslin, *Women's Rights*.

26. Loubna H. Skalli, "Communicating Gender in the Public Sphere: Women and Information Technologies in the MENA Region," *Journal of Middle East Women's Studies* 2, no. 2 (2006): 35–59; Carol Malt, "Women, Museums, and the Public Sphere," *Journal of Middle East Women's Studies* 2, no. 2 (2006): 115–36.

27. For Algeria, see Mohand Ouali, "Algeria: Algerian Women Expand Business Opportunities," *Magharebia.com*, December 19, 2010 (http://magharebia.com/cocoon/awi/xhtml1/en_GB/features/awi/features/2010/12/19/feature-01 [March 2012]), reporting a study by the National Business Register Center released in March. For Tunisia, see Jamel Arfaoui, "Tunisia NGOs Promote Women-Run Businesses," *Magharebia.com*, November 22, 2010 (www.magharebia.com/cocoon/awi/xhtml1/en_GB/features/awi/features/2010/11/22/feature-02 [March 2012]).

28. See, for instance, Arfaoui, "Tunisia NGOs"; World Bank, *Environment for Women's Entrepreneurship*; Sahar Nasr, *Egyptian Women Workers and Entrepreneurs: Maximizing Opportunities in the Economic Sphere* (Washington: World Bank, 2010); Center of Arab Women for Training and Research, *Women Entrepreneurs in the Middle East and North Africa: Characteristics, Contributions and Challenges* (Tunis, June 2007).

29. Kelly and Breslin, *Women's Rights*.

30. Louisa Hanoune was the only woman to run for president in Algeria in 2004 and 2009, taking roughly 1 percent and 4 percent of the vote, respectively.

31. Kelly and Breslin, *Women's Rights*.

32. Interview by M.C. Paciello with various members of the UGTT in Tunis, September 2011.

33. Wided Bouchemmaoui was elected as a member of the UTICA's executive bureau under Ben Ali.

34. See Issandr El-Amrani, "Great Chart of Morocco's Election Results," *The Arabist.net*, December 2, 2011 (www.arabist.net/blog/2011/12/2/great-chart-of-moroccos-election-results.html [March 2012]). It is worth noting that in the 2007 election in Morocco, seven out of thirty-four women elected to parliament already came from the Islamist party, Parti de la Justice et du Développement. See Amina Barakat, "Status quo pour les femmes au parlement," *Inter Press Service*, September 20, 2007 (http://ipsinternational.org/fr/_note.asp?idnews=3807 [March 2012]).

35. Nadia Yassine, "Modernité, femme musulmane et politique en Méditerranée," *Quaderns de la Mediterrània* 7 (2006): 105 –10.

36. Omayma Abdel-Latif, "In the Shadow of the Brothers; The Women of the Egyptian Muslim Brotherhood," Carnegie Papers no. 13 (Washington: Carnegie Endowment for International Peace, October 2008).

37. Margot Badran, *Feminists, Islam and Nation: Gender and the Making of Modern Egypt* (Princeton University Press, 1995); Renata Pepicelli, "Il movimento femminista nel mondo arabo," *Filosofia e Questioni Pubbliche* 1 (2008): 43–52.

38. Margot Badran, *Feminism in Islam; Secular and Religious Convergences* (London: Oneworld, 2009).

39. CEDAW was adopted in 1979 by the UN General Assembly and ratified by the majority of Arab countries, even if with reservations. Described as an international bill of rights for women, it defines what constitutes discrimination against women and sets up an agenda for national action to end such discrimination.

40. Asma Lambrabet, *Aicha, épouse du prophète ou Islam au féminin* (Lyon: Tawhid, 2004); Asma Lambrabet, *Le Coran et les femmes: Une lecture de libération* (Lyon: Tawhid, 2007); Omaima Abou-Bakr, "Islamic Feminism: What's in a Name? Preliminary Reflections," *Middle East Women's Studies Review* 15 and 16 (Winter/Spring 2001), 1–4.

41. See Margot Badran, "Islamic Feminism: What's in a Name?" *Al-Ahram Weekly Online*, January 17–23, 2002 (http://weekly.ahram.org.eg/2002/569/cu1.htm [March 2012]); Renata Pepicelli, *Femminismo islamico. Corano, diritti, riforme* (Rome: Carocci, 2010).

42. Leon Buskens, "Recent Debates on Family Law Reform in Morocco: Islamic Law as Politics in an Emerging Public Sphere," *Islamic Law and Society* 10, no. 1 (2003): 70–131.

43. Houria Alami M'chichi, *Genre et politique au Maroc: Les enjeux de l'égalité hommes-femmes entre islamisme et modernisme* (Paris: L'Harmattan, 2002).

44. Lara Deeb, *An Enchanted Modern: Gender and Public Piety in Shi'i Lebanon* (Princeton University Press, 2006).

45. See Joel Beinin and Frèdèric Vairel, eds., *Social Movements, Mobilization, and Contestation in the Middle East and North Africa* (Stanford University Press, 2011); Sarah Ben Nefissa and Blandine Destremau, *Protestations socials, revolutions civiles: Transformations du politique dans la Méditerranée arabe* (Paris: Armand Colin, 2011).

46. Eric Gobe, "The Gafsa Mining Basin between Riots and a Social Movement: Meaning and Significance of a Protest Movement in Ben Ali's Tunisia," 2010 (http://halshs.archives-ouvertes.fr/docs/00/55/78/26/PDF/Tunisia_The_Gafsa_mining_basin_between_Riots_and_Social_Movement.pdf [March 2012]).

47. See Lina Ben Mehenni in her blog "A Tunisian girl" (http://atunisiangirl.blogspot.com/). Another example is Esraa Abdel Fattah Ahmed Rashid, a thirty-year-old Egyptian woman who was one of the founders of the April 6 Facebook group and among the main organizers of the general strike of April 6, 2008, after which she was arrested.

48. Joel Beinin, "A Workers' Social Movement on the Margin of the Global Neo-Liberal Order, Egypt 2004–2009," in *Social Movements, Mobilization, and Contestation*, edited by Beinin and Vairel, pp. 181–201; Solidarity Center, *Justice for All*.

49. *Ibid.*

50. Solidarity Center, *Justice for All*.

51. *Ibid.*

52. In Egypt these movements included Kifaya and the April 6th movement. In Tunisia they included historical opposition organizations such as the Ligue Tunisiennes des Droits de l'Homme, Conseil National pour le Respect des Libertés en Tunisie, and Association Tunisienne des Femmes Démocrates.

53. Available at www.youtube.com/watch?v=SgjIgMdsEuk [March 2012].

54. Fatma Naib, "Women of the Revolution," *Al Jazeera.com*, February 19, 2011 (www.aljazeera.com/indepth/features/2011/02/2011217134411934738.html [March 2012]).

55. Sheema Khan, "Egypt's Revolution Is Leaving Women Behind," *Globe and Mail*, April 7, 2011 (www.theglobeandmail.com/news/opinions/opinion/egypts-revolution-is-leaving-women-behind/article1973918/ [March 2012]).

56. Amnesty International, "Egitto: manifestanti costrette a fare il 'test di verginità,'" March 23, 2011 (www.amnesty.it/flex/cm/pages/ServeBLOB.php/L/IT/IDPagina/4652).

57. Melissa Bell, "Egyptian-American Columnist Mona Eltahawy Tweets of Sexual Assault, Beating by Police," *Washington Post Blog Post*, November 24, 2011 (www.washingtonpost.com/blogs/blogpost/post/egyptian-american-columnist-mona-eltahawy-tweets-of-sexual-assault-beating-by-police/2011/11/24/gIQAz8X4sN_blog.html [March 2012]).

58. Khan, "Leaving Women Behind."

59. Marina Forti, "La vera minaccia è l'Ancien régime," *il Manifesto*, June 10, 2011, p. 9.

60. See Anouk Ledran, "Tunisie—49 femmes dont 42 islamistes élues à la Constituante," *MaghrebEmergent.com*, October 29, 2011 (www.maghrebemergent.com/actualite/maghrebine/5974-tunisie-49-femmes-a-lassemblee-constituante-42-sont-islamistes.html [March 2012]).

61. Democratizing the New Egypt, "Which Egyptian Parties Represent Women and Copts and Young People?" Blog post, November 15, 2011 (http://democratizing egypt.blogspot.com/2011/11/which-egyptian-parties-represent-women.html [March 2012]).

GARY R. BUNT

4

Mediterranean Islamic Expression and Web 2.0

Just prior to 9/11, I completed writing a piece entitled "Islam Interactive: Mediterranean Islamic Expression on the World Wide Web" for the journal *Mediterranean Politics,* subsequently published in the book *Shaping the Current Islamic Reformation.* This was written shortly after my book *Virtually Islamic* was published.[1] The events of 9/11, coupled with the technological developments of the succeeding decade, make that period seem like a different world compared to today—one that was relatively unconnected digitally. The main driving elements of the Internet at that time were FTP (file transfer protocol), e-mail, Usenet groups, and prototype web pages. It was an era with limited online activity in languages other than those using roman script. Internet use back then was characterized by slow connection speeds and limited online multimedia. It may be difficult for today's "digital natives" to recall an era when there were no blogs, Twitter, or social networking; MySpace and Facebook were on the distant horizon (Facebook co-creator Mark Zuckerberg was still in high school). Hardware for Internet access was primarily desk bound: there were no iPods, BlackBerrys, e-books, smartphones, or iPads. It was an era dominated by Internet Explorer, Mosaic, and Netscape browsers, used on versions of Windows and Apple operating systems that might be seen as antique by contemporary standards. Search engines were limited: Yahoo was a dominant brand crawling the web, and Google had only been running a couple of years. The leaps in technological and Internet development within a relatively short period have transformed communication patterns and methods on a global scale, and the impact has been felt throughout the Mediterranean microcosm.

In the 1990s, when I started research in this area, there was a great deal of scepticism from some quarters about the relevance of observing, chronicling, recording, and analyzing Islam on the Internet. My perspective was shaped by an interest in religious authority and—although multidisciplinary in scope—by religious studies frameworks. The reason I found the Internet relevant was because Muslim scholars and activists had begun communicating and networking globally online, and those pulses of digital activity were starting to have an impact at grassroots levels. So in 1996 I established the Islamic Studies Pathways site as a platform to monitor these developments.[2] In addition, my undergraduate students were coming to seminars with web materials. This raised questions about the veracity of the online content presented, how or whether it was representative of a specific worldview, and how digital discourse was starting to underpin significant contemporary discussions on Islam and Muslims.[3]

Observations during the succeeding decade may now provide some answers to these questions. Of course, the answers are contextual, in that they depend on the situation, location, and issue being studied. Issues may be global, national, or local in nature. It is still possible to focus on the Mediterranean sphere with the proviso that the input of globalizing influences is more profound than a decade ago. It would be naive to suggest that the Internet was changing all boundaries of knowledge and authority. One would also have to explore other channels of Internet-driven and -related activities, of which the World Wide Web is but one component. The current digital milieu is characterized by integrated cross-media platforms and dialogues accessed through a variety of devices and methods, an online environment in which even previously sceptical parties are now fully engaged.

The Cyber Islamic Environment

I continue to utilize the term cyber Islamic environments (CIEs), while recognizing that the conceptual framework has shifted somewhat since I first introduced it in *Virtually Islamic* in 2000. It encompasses digital online media content developed with an "Islamic" emphasis, however subtle or overt that might be. CIEs refer to a variety of contexts, perspectives, and applications of the media by those who define themselves as Muslims and who represent elements of specific worldviews and notions of exclusivity, combined with regional and cultural understandings of the Internet and its validity. CIEs have demonstrated the ability to transform aspects of religious understanding and expression within

Muslim contexts. A complex spectrum of access, dialogue, networking, and application of the media has emerged. The term's original definition as an online Internet space with an Islamic religious orientation has evolved to incorporate elements of so-called Web 2.0 tools, as well as alternate interfaces with different forms of functionality, such as web-enabled smartphones, gaming interfaces, and televisions with net access.[4] It can include online services such as blogs, social networking sites, media distribution channels, and interfaces in which the web is integrated into "traditional" media delivery (for example, media channels using online delivery in real-time and storage modes). I stress elsewhere that for some users Islam is "always on," whether being accessed online or through traditional channels. Just as different levels of religiosity and Islamic activity can be distinguished, depending on the beholder, the same holds true for levels of Islamic activity and usage of online materials. Different reading styles, diverse media frameworks, and varying user attention spans mean that consumption of web content can differ from that of other media forms.

For some individuals and organizations, the effect of this online activity has been transformative, and that includes those within the Mediterranean Muslim sphere. Those "iMuslims"—a term I use to represent diverse online users with Muslim identities—can feel obligated to be online regularly, in order to maintain and reinforce online affiliations, networks, and relationships. They may do so at the expense of traditional networks. The development of Islamic Internet products, such as IslamicTube, HalalTube, IslamicTorrents, and MuslimSpace, has added a perception of safety and permissibility to Internet use.[5] The elements of everyday online Islamic activities, including business, shopping, chat, and social networking, may fall under the radar of international press coverage, but in many ways they are just as significant as *jihadi* sites or online *fatwa* services. For example, consider the relevance on personal and community levels of the abundance of "Islamically approved" sites for arranging marriages.[6] The varieties of Islamic religious expression and orientation online range from the orthodox to the esoteric and the marginalized, and appear in a variety of contexts, drawing upon many facets of the Internet, including Web 2.0. The World Wide Web, social networking sites, chat rooms, video blogs, Facebook, Twitter, Flickr, collaborative wiki sites, podcasts, and video upload sites such as YouTube are just some of the multimedia venues that have been used to present aspects of Islam and Muslim expression. For those with access, computer use is an integrated component of contemporary Muslim political-religious-cultural expression, facilitating networking and understanding across generations.

There is a broad range of "authoritative" Islamic opinion available on the Internet, and it promotes a variety of agendas, from advising on the mundane issues of everyday life through providing commentary (and inspiring action) in relation to world affairs. Some Islamic websites seek to project religious authority via the Internet. The phenomenon of the online fatwa has become commonplace online, with petitioners e-mailing questions to authorities for a scholarly response. The utilization of the Internet, and in particular the World Wide Web, in the name of Islam has necessitated a reconsideration and reconfiguration of Muslim networks. While elements of historical networking patterns and concepts apply, there are also new issues to address. An innovative online knowledge economy, focused on peer-to-peer networking, has become a challenge to traditional top-down authority models. Islamic platforms, organizations, and Muslim individuals are competing for attention in the Internet *suq* (marketplace)—amid numerous distractions—and have established an abundance of online materials promoting their understandings of Islam.

The fact that individuals or small groups present online content about Islam in an informative and authoritative manner—and acquire the same or greater readerships than traditional, governmental authorities—has not gone unnoticed. The representation of aspects of Islam on the Internet also influences the perceptions of "outsiders," whether they are non-Muslims or Muslims from other social and cultural contexts. By creating attractive portals and online services, various shades of the Islamic spectrum have sought to channel their readers and "manage" the knowledge associated with their belief perspectives. Products include translations of the Koran, commentaries, chat rooms, free e-mail services, women's and children's web sites, and online community services. There can be commercial elements to these services, with digital entrepreneurs recognizing markets with specific interests and requirements for Islamic online content. In some cases, these entrepreneurs and technical innovators have collaborated with traditional authorities to develop and promote products. Thus during an extended developmental phase, there remains a jostling for position within CIEs at local and global levels, and this is especially true in the Mediterranean microcosm.

Cellular CIEs

Telecommunications are a critical factor in Muslim contexts, with serious differences in access across a multilayered digital divide. The level of Internet access can vary from the basic telephone line, enabling simple dial-up access, to the high-speed ADSL (asymmetric digital subscriber line) connectivity, integrated with wireless technology and 3G(+) smartphone high-speed mobile access. The digital divide widens further when discussing the international coverage of broadband ADSL penetration. There is a spectrum of access, so it is not possible to generalize regarding Internet access within and across Muslim countries. There are technology-rich locations within urban environments, providing a multitude of entry points and connections to the Internet, and rural environments with limited or no telephone service, where inhabitants cannot access the most basic of Internet services.[7] Location, cost, and digital literacy are significant generic factors that also influence Internet access, along with religious factors, such as the barriers imposed by those still perceiving the Internet (or aspects of it) as "un-Islamic."

Mobile phone service is another channel for Internet networking and information distribution, and its growing use shows no signs of slowing down as networks expand, access increases, and technology becomes cheaper. Service providers have moved into the area of content provision, while competition to obtain licences to operate in various territories has intensified, and the markets have become more regulated. All this has implications for Internet access within Muslim contexts. The types of users have also evolved: it is a cliché to consider generational divides between Internet users, but it is also true to say that there are generations for whom the Internet and cell phone use (and technology in general) are more natural modes of communication, including access to news, commerce, entertainment, and knowledge. Such communication can include the development and exchange of packets of data about Islam, although it is recognized that religiously oriented transactions form only a small component of overall net use by web users who define themselves as Muslim. Determination of web surfing habits, especially in Muslim contexts, can be speculative at best, Internet use being a highly personalized activity with participants unwilling to enter the public domain to describe their activities. Those who have experienced cultural and religious barriers to self-expression— for example, in some contexts, Muslim women— have used the Internet medium to articulate their concerns. This has opened up possibilities for networking and communication that have had an impact on Muslim Mediterranean societies. Although it is not possible to generalize about Muslim Internet surfing habits, there are emerging trends that may also apply outside of Muslim spheres.

Mobile devices have played a major role in opening up Internet access in a variety of Muslim contexts. For several years Islam-oriented applications and programs have been devised for phones, and these have been enhanced with multimedia and Flash elements as technology has developed further. Significantly, the development of information and communication technology has been linked to the rise in mobile phone use in a number of contexts. The expansion of cellular technology into previously marginalized markets has enabled not only basic phone access for many but also some Internet access as well. Many Muslim regions have high mobile phone use and ownership; one mobile phone may be used by several people within a family or community— or even as a small business where the phone's owner charges others for it use. This level of cell phone use was reflected in the events of the Arab Spring in Egypt and Tunisia (discussed below) and is evident in events occurring in Syria and Yemen as of this writing.

As with the early growth of Islamic websites, there is now competition to promote Islamic apps and other programs for the mobile computing and mobile phone markets, which may further expand the Internet's influence on matters of religion. As with other areas of Internet consumption, Islamic content developers have seen that the future for Internet access is less restrained to the desktop, and with that in mind, they have focused on developing mobile phone–specific applications. Web design for mobile phones is a critical undertaking, for effectiveness depends on successful integration of content accessibility, bandwidth restraints, clarity, and navigation for mobile phones.

The dissemination of Islamic apps and phone products has a number of important impacts: for phone manufacturers seeking to promote their brand in a crowded marketplace, the integration of preinstalled Islamic apps, if not unique, may still be a potent selling point. The cell phone market has become substantially more sophisticated in the past decade, with improvements in memory, audiovisual quality, and network coverage. This has stimulated the creation of multimedia applications, in particular for the iPhone, BlackBerry, and Android smartphones—and for tablet devices such as iPads. Such innovation has also generated a number of ethical and religious issues in association with mobile device use.[8]

Online Censorship

Governments in Muslim contexts have had to adjust to the consequences of the Internet as a phenomenon. With the growth in Internet access and use, especially through blogs, comes the issue of censorship, which can take many forms, in an attempt to prevent apparent transgressions in societal and religious norms.

Muslim political discourse, where paradigms for Islamic political activism have been presented online or in other media, has been one area of consistent censorship. Transgressions of religious values or attacks against state policy are dominant rationales for some form of censorship, even by those who otherwise claim that they uphold "freedom of speech." Parameters for freedom of speech vary in different Muslim contexts, with some critics suggesting that the concept is a misnomer. The freedom of speech platform embraces a number of different themes and causes, not all of which are mutually compatible within an Islamic context. This is, of course, not just an Internet-related issue. Advocates of freedom of Islamic political and religious expression may seek to censor others espousing values deemed incompatible with their worldview. The issue itself is indicative of an intensified awareness of the potential and realized impact of the Internet on Islamic values and societies, as well as its capacity to fulfill a variety of political and religious agendas.

Accusations that some governments in Muslim contexts have used sophisticated software to index and filter out political opposition on the Internet point to complex attendant issues associated with the online information flow from jihadi and other entities perceived as "destabilizing."[9] Governments have tried to use the Internet to observe dissident activities online.[10] However, more sophisticated encryption programs have obstructed governmental attempts to control many aspects of online communication, for example, by censoring e-mail exchanges. In fact, online advice is available on how to evade controls over Internet usage, for instance, by retaining anonymity.[11]

There have also been complaints from diverse Islamic perspectives about apparent anti-Islamic materials published online. Not all objectionable materials were necessarily produced or published in the complainants' own countries, making censorship and restrictions problematic.

Jihadi Discourse

The use of the web as a strategic jihadi tool predated 9/11, with a relatively sustained level of activity—albeit among small groups given the low levels of web literacy and access. There were campaigns in and about the United Kingdom, Palestine, Lebanon, Kashmir, and Chechnya. Previously disparate campaigns were united online under a single banner, enhancing familiarity with causes in different global contexts. I found dialogues about *jihad*-oriented issues in the mid-1990s, primarily on mailing lists, discussion groups, and FTP platforms that enabled the up- and downloading of files. Files were small, text only, and often sent in mass mailings. The emergence of the browser led to graphical interfaces presenting various Islamic perspectives, including online campaigns that had forms of jihadi discourse integrated into them.[12]

In online discourse the term jihadi has largely been applied to the protagonists and supporters of the lesser jihad (militaristic in nature). While theoretically the term jihadi could be applied across conflicts and interpretations, it is narrowed down here to refer to those groups and individuals ideologically affiliated with the entity and networks known as al Qaeda. The latter is itself an amorphous entity: there is no single headquarters or structure, and while Osama bin Laden and his immediate associates (especially bin Laden's successor and long-term deputy Ayman al-Zawahiri) were ostensibly al Qaeda's leaders, its loose structure mutated into separate but affiliated identities within different zones.

Jihadi discourse also constitutes part of the cyber Islamic equation: concepts associated with electronic jihad or "e-jihad" have been utilized in cyber contexts in combination with classical interpretations of the term jihad.[13] Defining jihad is a significant issue, and one would not want to produce a homogeneous umbrella definition of jihadi activity that cannot be nuanced and contextually oriented. "Jihad" in its lesser form may have a militaristic emphasis, but its sense of "striving" in its greater form relates to spiritual matters.[14]

Online distribution of content is an essential element of jihadi strategy. Those advocating militaristic interpretations of jihad have benefited from improvements in Internet access, a reduction of the digital divide, and increased web literacy. Videos and online magazines have been augmented by Web 2.0 applications to enhance the effectiveness of their message. Media campaigns used the Internet as an effective method to garner support, intimidate opponents, develop logistical planning, and facilitate fundraising to support military campaigns.

Participants and supporters may represent militaristic jihadi actions as "Islamic." However, there are long-standing issues associated with the stereotyping of Muslims in this regard, which came into sharp focus after 9-11. Some Muslim observers, scholars, opponents, and apologists have reacted by stating that activities justified by this militaristic interpretation of jihad are criminal acts or forms of "terrorism," having no connection with or being contradictory to Islam.

After 9-11 the principal focus on e-jihad shifted from Palestine to al Qaeda. Computer technology not only had logistical value for al Qaeda, it has been a key tool for communicating various agendas, aims, objectives, and results to audiences in a nuanced and, in many cases, creative, structured, and professional fashion. Online content focused on Osama bin Laden, the Taliban, and the al Qaeda configuration(s). Supporters of al Qaeda used the Internet to disseminate statements from bin Laden and others, spreading al Qaeda's influence in (aspects of) jihadi networks in various locations. The connections among disparate campaigns were emphasized online, suggesting the "global" reach and cellular nature of al Qaeda. Publicity on campaigns and statements was transmitted through web sites, chat rooms, and e-mail listings.

Technological developments in the Internet and computers in general have been reflected in the evolving nature of jihadi online sites. For example, the martyrdom pages of websites have transformed from text only to graphics to poster style photos to downloadable audio recordings to slickly edited videos. Increasing emphasis has been placed on the production of online manuals as a means of propagation to targeted audiences. Linguistic diversity has increased; for example, the preponderance of manuals generated during 2010–11 were in English (notably through *Inspire* magazine and the activities of Anwar al-Awlaki and Samir Khan).[15] Within the Islamic Maghreb, al Qaeda's media strategy centered on multimedia productions, such as videos, magazines, and a stream of news and pronouncements. Affiliates and supporters of al Qaeda in Egypt, Palestine, Lebanon, Syria, and Turkey have been similarly productive. It is thus apparent that the Internet is fully integrated into the strategies of al Qaeda within global and regional contexts, keeping supporters and media informed and logistically networked through development of productions focused on specific markets and interests.

Social Networking and the "Arab Spring"

Many political and social platforms and campaigns, far beyond the jihadi sphere, have used the Internet to facilitate the promotion of agendas and coordination of activities. In 2010–11 attention was particularly drawn to the Arab Spring and the ways in which social networking tools such as Twitter and Facebook were used to contribute to activism in Tunisia, Egypt, Syria, Libya, Bahrain, Yemen, and elsewhere. Participation in Facebook is, according to statistical analysis by the *Arab Social Media Report*, an activity primarily undertaken by people between the ages of fifteen and twenty-nine, who constitute three-quarters of Facebook users in the Arab region.[16] The report noted substantial regional increases in the number of Facebook and Twitter users during the first quarter of 2011, in part as a response to the Arab Spring.[17] It also noted that "most information on Twitter is generated by a minority, while the majority uses Twitter to consume news as more of a newsfeed than a microblog."[18] While there can be inherent difficulties with statistics about Internet use, these figures provide an indicator of trends and activities relating to Twitter and Facebook during this formative period.[19]

It is not possible to reduce these issues to a single paradigm, although there are some shared factors. Social networking tools undoubtedly had a role to play in the events of this period—which are still ongoing at the time of this writing—and clearly each location has diverse contextual factors to consider. It is not necessarily helpful to generalize regarding "Facebook revolution(s)" or similar epithets, given the combination of social, economic, cultural, religious, and other factors: "There is no doubt that social media played a major role in the recent revolts but equally looking at the current events unfolding there are clear indicators that social media will only ever be a tool of organising. The streets are the place where revolutions can create facts on the ground."[20]

Long-standing issues of regional economic and social deprivation, dissatisfaction with government and national leadership, lack of political accountability and representation, and human rights issues combined with the growing influence of diverse regional media to create momentum for activism. The WikiLeaks exposure of sensitive U.S. government documents, including cables and e-mails from embassies discussing regional and local intelligence on specific countries, amplified discontent—particularly since these materials were discussed, edited, and reposted by news media and through social networking sites.[21]

This coincided, in turn, with the steep growth in access to digital technology and broadcast media and recognition of the potential of these tools to promote and mobilize campaigning. For example, the use of these tools in Iran during the "Green Revolution" in 2009 provided a template for social network activism.[22] Coverage of relatively small protests achieved rapid circulation locally, nationally, and internationally; this included "conventional" domestic and satellite television broadcasts (for instance, by Al Jazeera and Al Arabiya) and reportage gathered from cell phone clips and online posts. A symbiosis between these two sources meant that satellite broadcasters drew upon these alternative materials, rebroadcasting them on their own networks, while the grassroots activists also reposted and publicized broadcasters' reports. The reporting by satellite broadcasters had a profound effect on the Arab Spring sequence of events; the organization, mobilization, and publicizing of protests was facilitated in a significant part through social networking tools such as

Facebook, Twitter, YouTube, blogs, photo sharing sites, and generic websites. These tools were mashed together and accessed at an unprecedented level online through cell phone and computer use.

While the events have their origins in the social and cultural histories of the region—with long-standing factors— the "Jasmine Revolution" in Tunisia is considered the starting point in this sequence of events.[23] It developed from on- and offline protests following events on December 17, 2010, in the town of Sidi Bouzid: street trader (and university graduate) Mohamed Bouazizi immolated himself, apparently frustrated after a conflict with local officials relating to trading permits and restrictions. The accounts of these events were subsequently disputed, but what was clear was that Bouazizi had updated his Facebook status beforehand with an indication of his suicide plans.[24]

The suicide is controversial within Muslim contexts, being forbidden according to Islamic authorities. However, whatever the ethical dimensions of Bouazizi's actions, small protests in Tunisia rapidly gained a national momentum, as images of Bouazizi's death spread through the Internet. They were fueled not only by Bouazizi's horrific death but also by chronic concerns about food prices, the economy, and dissatisfaction with perceived government corruption. Footage of a heavily bandaged Bouazizi being visited by President Zine El Abidine Ben Ali, apparently prior to Bouazizi's death on January 4, 2011, were followed by the uploading of clips showing Bouazizi's well-attended funeral. The Tunisian authorities tried to suppress this coverage, but it was subsequently rebroadcast on satellite media, garnering international attention. Protests were galvanized through the use of social networking tools by participants and the uploading of mobile phone clips online. This was accompanied by protest through the popular culture, notably the rap track "Rais Lebled"— performed by El Général and circulated via YouTube—which achieved wide circulation due to its lyrics attacking the government and its ready access by predominantly youthful protesters.[25] Twitter hashtags such as "#sidibouzid" trended.[26] The protesters' organization could not be effectively suppressed or censored by Tunisian state agencies, contributing to the departure of Ben Ali in January 2011.[27]

Key activists did not necessarily use their own identities to promote campaigns. Anonymity and collective approaches to activism mean that highlighting one individual in events may be considered inappropriate. One prominent online campaigner, whose name emerged during protests in Egypt in 2011, was Wael Ghonim, a Middle East executive for Google. In a personal capacity, Ghonim organized (initially anonymously) the "We are all Khaled

Said" Facebook page, which became the locus for articulating discontent and organizing protest in Egypt: "It became and remains the biggest dissident Facebook page in Egypt, even as protests continue to sweep the country, with more than 473,000 users, and it has helped spread the word about the demonstrations in Egypt, which were ignited after a revolt in neighboring Tunisia toppled the government there."[28]

Khaled Said was a victim of Egyptian state security. Police murdered him after he exposed corruption and posted evidence of it online. Photos of Said's battered body were posted on the Internet, leading Ghonim and others into a flurry of protest. This happened concurrently with newly formed initiatives seeking to reconcile conflicts between Coptic Christians and Muslims in Egypt and calling for a united Egyptian identity. Reports and updates on Said's death, the subsequent protests, and dialogue initiatives between different interest groups rapidly circulated on Twitter and Facebook, referencing videos on YouTube and blog postings.[29] The Internet became a natural and dynamic platform and meeting point for mobilization and discussions on the situation in Egypt. The protests were effectively streamed to regional and global audiences, resulting in a panicked response from Egyptian authorities, who were unsure about how to respond to this online discourse.

Ghonim's own participation combined digital media with appearances at protests; he was arrested on January 28 and released ten days later. He was probably the most prominent of the arrested online activists. Ghonim later addressed protestors at Tahrir Square, the central protest point in Cairo. Throughout the sequence of events in Egypt, Twitter was utilized, in particular through hashtags including #Egypt, #Jan25, and #25Jan.[30] "The most popular trending hashtags across the Arab region in the first quarter were #egypt (with 1.4 million mentions in the tweets generated during this period), #jan25 (with 1.2 million mentions), #libya (with 990,000 mentions), #bahrain (640,000 mentions), and #protest (620,000)."[31]

These hashtags enabled Twitter users (via cell phones and other entry points) to keep pace with the hundreds of thousands of tweets that emerged on Egyptian issues, from within and outside of the country.[32] The websites of high-profile bloggers on Muslim issues, such as Mona Eltahawy (a U.S. citizen of Egyptian origin), became hubs for the reposting of Facebook and other web content and were drawn upon by other media.[33] This information was augmented by dramatic protest footage posted on YouTube, which was subsequently rebroadcast and reposted worldwide. The role of broadcasters such as Al Jazeera, reporting live (and posting live on their websites) from Cairo in

English and Arabic during this turbulent period, cannot be underestimated. Despite attempts at censorship by Egyptian authorities, web users were able to circumvent restrictions. When online access was cut, protesters were able to post audio reports of events in Tahrir Square and elsewhere by landline phone, through services such as Alive In Egypt or Tweet2Speak. "The service has been used to express outrage, indignation, fear, exhilaration and pleas for help in the fight to oust Mubarak. 'This corrupt regime must be eliminated,' said one of the translated tweets on Alive In Egypt. Another said: 'For all our Arab Brothers, for all the men in Tahrir Square. Please help us, stand with us, if you abandon us we will die.'"[34]

Efforts by Egyptian authorities to counter online pronouncements through their own online output were unsuccessful.[35] Internet censorship was seen as a sign that President Hosni Mubarak's hold on power was becoming increasingly tenuous, especially when Egypt "disappeared" from the Internet.[36] "Twitter was an early casualty. Then Facebook access became spotty. But when the Internet itself went down, Egyptian pro-democracy activists knew their protests were having an effect."[37] Bloggers and social networkers were clearly aware of the implications of censorship and Internet closure: "'While the Egyptian government believed that shutting down the Internet would quiet the protests, the exact opposite happened,' said Tarek Amr, an Egyptian blogger and computer programmer. 'The protests became bigger and bigger without the Internet,' Amr said during a webcast hosted by Access, a nonprofit digital rights advocacy group."[38]

The departure of President Mubarak from office was heralded on- and offline by networks of supporters in and outside of Egypt. Clips of Ghonim embracing Khaled Said's mother in Tahrir Square appeared on YouTube and across social media sites of supporters.[39] Ghonim was feted by the international media for his role, although he did not necessarily embrace this new status, tweeting, "The real hero is the young Egyptians [sic] in Tahrir square and the rest of Egypt #Jan25." He was one of thousands using social networking tools as part of the protests during this period.[40] The departure of Mubarak on February 10, 2011, did not end the problems for Egypt, with subsequent protests and activism continuing online, including demonstrations from Tahrir Square that continued through 2011.

In a prescient comment (at least in terms of bin Laden's subsequently revealed location), Abubakar Siddique noted, "It's not difficult to imagine Al Qaeda leaders Osama bin Laden and Ayman al-Zawahri huddling together listening to Arabic-language broadcasts inside some nondescript house in a teeming Pakistani city. Like their enemies in the West, they are probably grappling with one fundamental question: how to manipulate the popular revolt on the 'Arab Street'?"[41]

One critical point about all this, however, is that these campaigns were not "Islamic" in orientation. Key participants had Muslim identities (on a number of levels)—although many would identify themselves as secular, agnostic, or atheist—but a number were not Muslim. Some Muslim entities held back from full participation in demonstrations at that time: the Muslim Brotherhood in Egypt was a prominent example of this. Its members are web literate, and its infrastructure draws on the Internet to coordinate and publicize the group's activities, as well as to air internal disputes and quests for reform within the movement.[42] Regional and national hubs linking to social networking sites provide a broad digital infrastructure for the Muslim Brotherhood, and they have also developed their own networking tools, notably IkhwanBook, based on the Facebook social networking paradigm.[43]

The sequence of events in Tunisia and Egypt stimulated further protests in other, very different contexts—notably, in the Mediterranean zone, in Libya and Syria. This adds further layers of complexity to analysis, given that at the time of this writing protest and reaction were very much ongoing. What can be said at this stage is that despite the different milieu in Syria and Libya, digital media were still very much part of their processes. Reports and footage from protests in Syria were immediately uploaded onto YouTube, despite censorship, drawing the attention from networks of activists. The Syrian Revolution 2011 Facebook page was one significant hub, presenting news from conventional media as well as cell phone footage from demonstrations in Damascus and elsewhere; often there was a blurring between the news sources.[44] Libyan protests had a different edge, given the military campaign that occurred and the involvement of Western powers through NATO against Muammar Qaddafi. Movements in Libya used YouTube to upload footage of combat from the front lines and also used Facebook to mobilize support.[45] Digital content was very much integrated—albeit with different emphases—into protest and conflict in these regions of the Mediterranean microcosm.

Concluding Comments

The bulk of this chapter was written in July 2011. Protests (and their suppression) continued in various forms after this—particularly in Libya and Syria (in relation to the Mediterranean; they also continued in Bahrain and Yemen). By

November 2011 the situation in a number of contexts had undergone changes that had profound digital linkages. Libya had experienced the demise of Muammar Qaddafi, whose death (and surrounding events) was captured by cell phone. The resulting videos were rapidly distributed on YouTube, publicized through social media channels, and broadcast worldwide. In Syria cell phone videos continued to record protests and their aftermath (particularly the regular Friday demonstrations after prayers), chronicling the actions of the Syrian Army against demonstrators in Homs and elsewhere. In Egypt military prosecutors detained the prominent blogger Alaa Abd El Fatteh, inspiring a protest in Tahrir Square and a rapid social media campaign centered on the Twitter hashtag #FreeAlaa; he was subsequently released from custody.[46] In Tunisia the election processes had been dominated by the use of online media by campaigning parties of all hues and were widely scrutinized through social media sites. Digital content about these and other issues generated at "street level" was transmitted by satellite and other broadcasts, demonstrating the symbiosis between diverse media forms. Given these subsequent events, one could say that "Arab Spring" had perhaps become a misnomer since its impact stretched across the year.

In light of the events in 2011, it could be useful to expand the scope of discussion to include the impact of social networking tools and their influence on religious issues and discourse within other Muslim Mediterranean contexts, such as Algeria, Morocco, Palestine, Lebanon, and Turkey.[47] It could conceivably be extended to cover Muslim concerns within minority contexts, for example, in France, Italy and Spain. Exploration of issues such as media representation, gender roles, sexuality, intergenerational communication, economics, and education and their online analysis in relation to Islam would further highlight the dynamic impact of the Internet on diverse Muslim societies.[48] In the Muslim Mediterranean microcosm (and elsewhere), governmental, political, and religious organizations and individuals continue to face new challenges in managing the Internet medium and responding to rapid shifts in levels of access and technological sophistication.[49] Those platforms that have failed to respond appropriately to social media developments have, in some cases, damaged their profiles and levels of influence. Adaptive responses may include participation in social networking contexts or use of the Internet to present specific documentation or worldviews. It may also include—in governmental contexts—the use of monitoring tools in order to observe opponents.[50] This can be a two-way process, resulting in a circuit of mutual monitoring and observation online between various players.[51]

Given the brief overview within this chapter, what can be said, at this early stage, is that developing a comprehensive understanding of the role of the Internet in social activism is a critical element within the study of Islam and Muslims in the modern world. While not all online activity is focused on Islam and Muslim issues, Internet-based communication clearly has a role in societal development and exerts a mediating influence in the articulation of approaches toward contemporary religious issues in Islamic contexts—especially in the Mediterranean microcosm. Based on a dynamic period of digital usage in 2011, which acted as a "test bed" for applying digital technology during a period of change and upheaval, one can say that social media use became more granular and integrated in order to promote and sustain the diverse movements of societal change arising from the many actors in the region.

Notes

1. See Gary R. Bunt, *Virtually Islamic: Computer-Mediated Communication and Cyber Islamic Environments* (University of Wales Press, 2000); Bunt, *Islam in the Digital Age: E-jihad, Online Fatwas and Cyber Islamic Environments* (London: Pluto Press, 2003); Bunt, "Mediterranean Islamic Expression on the World Wide Web," in *Islam and the Shaping of the Current Islamic Reformation*, edited by Barbara Allen Roberson (London and Portland: Frank Cass and Co., 2003), pp.164–86.

2. Gary R. Bunt, "Islamic Studies Pathways" (www.islamicstudies.tumblr.com [March 2012]).

3. Gary R. Bunt, "Studying Islam after 9-11: Reflections and Resources," *PRS-LTSN Journal* 1, no. 1 (2002): 156–64; Bunt, "Mediterranean Islamic Expression."

4. Web 2.0 is an umbrella term that encompasses social media applications and a strong element of interaction, with Wikis, blogs, and RSS elements integrating with multimedia tools in an interoperable synthesis, which integrates long-standing protocols of the Internet. The term Web 2.0 cannot be rigid and is somewhat ambiguous, and may itself become outmoded as further refinements to web architecture emerge.

5. See HalalTube (www.halaltube.com), IslamicTube (http://islamictube.net), IslamicTorrents (www.islamictorrents.net), and MuslimSpace (www.muslimspace .com).

6. See, for instance, Single Muslim (http://uk.singlemuslim.com), Muslim and Single (www.muslimandsingle.com), and Muslim Match (http://muslimmatch.com). The spectrum also includes conventional dating sites.

7. For country-specific data on information technology penetration, see International Telecommunications Union, "Measuring the Information Society 2011" (www. itu.int/ITU-D/ict/publications/idi [March 2012]).

8. Further elements of the discussion on phones can be found in Gary R. Bunt, "Surfing the App Souq: Islamic Applications for Mobile Devices," *CyberOrient: Online*

Journal of the Virtual Middle East 4, no. 1, 2010 (www.cyberorient.net/article.do?article Id=3817 [March 2012]).

9. Jonathan Zittrain and Benjamin Edelman, "Documentation of Internet Filtering in Saudi Arabia," 2002 (cyber.law.harvard.edu/filtering/saudiarabia/ [March 2012]). Also see Hal Roberts and others, "International Bloggers and Internet Control," 2011 (cyber.law.harvard.edu/publications/2011/International_Bloggers_Internet_Control [April 2012])

10. For country-specific data on censorship, see OpenNet Initiative, "Global Internet Filtering Map," 2012 (http://map.opennet.net [April 2012]); see also Reporters Without Borders, "Internet Enemies Report 2012" (http://en.rsf.org/IMG/pdf/rapport-internet2012_ang.pdf [April 2012].

11. For example, see resources provided by online anonymity advocates the Tor Project (www.torproject.org [April 2012]). Also see Ultrareach, "Ultrasurf" (http://ultrasurf.us [April 2012]. Advice was provided for online activists in Reporters Without Borders, "A Handbook for Bloggers and Cyber Dissidents," 2005 (http://en.rsf.org/spip.php?page=article&id_article=33844 [March 2012]).

12. Bunt, *Virtually Islamic.*

13. See the discussions on e-jihad in Gary R. Bunt, *iMuslims: Rewiring the House of Islam* (University of North Carolina Press and London: C. Hurst, 2009); Bunt, *Islam in the Digital Age.* Also see Roel Meijer, "Re-reading al-Qaeda: Writings of Yusuf al-Ayiri," *ISIM Review* 18 (Autumn 2006): 16–17 (https://openaccess.leidenuniv.nl/bitstream/handle/1887/17089/ISIM_18_Re-Reading_al-Qaeda_Writings_of_Yusuf_al-Ayiri.pdf?sequence=1 [March 2012]); Rohan Gunaratna, *Inside al Qaeda: Global Network of Terror* (London: C. Hurst, 2002); Brynjar Lia, *Architect of Global Jihad: The Life of Al-Qaeda Strategist Abu Mu'sab Al-Suri* (London: C. Hurst, 2007).

14. Definitions of jihad are discussed in Bunt, *Islam in the Digital Age,* pp. 25–36.

15. Discussed in Gary R. Bunt, "#Islam, Social Networking and the Cloud," in *Islam in the Modern World,* edited by Jeffrey Kenney and Ebrahim Moosa (New York: Routledge, forthcoming).

16. Racha Mourtada and Fadi Salem, "Facebook Usage: Factors and Analysis, " *Arab Social Media Report* 1, no.1 (2011): 4. The data captured here go beyond the Mediterranean sphere but remain useful in providing an indication of trends and activities.

17. Racha Mourtada and Fadi Salem, "Civil Movements: The Impact of Facebook and Twitter," *Arab Social Media Report* 1, no. 2 (2011): 9.

18. Ibid., pp. 15–16.

19. For further discussions on statistics in relation to social media, see Jillian C. York, "Arab World: How Much Does Internet Access Matter?" *Global Voices Online,* March 9, 2011 (http://globalvoicesonline.org/2011/03/09/arab-world-how-much-does-Internet-access-matter/ [March 2012]); Jeffrey Ghannam, "In the Middle East, This Is Not a Facebook Revolution," *Washington Post,* February 20, 2011; Jeffrey Ghannam, Social Media in the Arab World: Leading up to the Uprisings of 2011 (Washington: Center for International Media Assistance, February 2011) (http://cima.

ned.org/publications/social-media-arab-world-leading-uprisings-2011 [March 2012]).

20. Sohail Dahdal, "How Social Media Changed Arab Resistance," *newmatilda.com*, March 4, 2011 (http://newmatilda.com/print/9319 [March 2012]).

21. See WikiLeaks archives at http://wikileaks.org.

22. Gary R. Bunt, "Gary Bunt on the 2009 Iranian Presidential Elections …," *University of North Carolina Press Blog*, June 22, 2009 (http://uncpressblog.com/2009/06/22/gary-bunt-on-the-2009-iranian-presidential-elections/ [March 2012]).

23. Timelines of postings and links relating to the events discussed in this section can be found in the relevant archives (listed by date) of Gary R. Bunt, "Virtually Islamic Blog" (http://virtuallyislamic.blogspot.com/).

24. See, for instance, "The Last Facebook Status Update of Bouazizi Who Set Him Self on Fire Starting the Tunisian Revolution," *Arabcrunch.com* (http://arabcrunch.com/2011/01/the-last-facebook-status-update-of-bouazizi-who-set-him-self-on-fire-marking-starting-the-tunisian-revolution.html [March 2012]). Bouazizi was perhaps representative of many (digitally literate) graduates in low-level jobs in Tunisia.

25. El Général, "Rais Lebled" (http://www.youtube.com/watch?v=IeGIJ7OouR0 [January 2011]). "El Général" was Hamada Ben-Amor, who was detained following his critical track's release. See "Tunisia Rapper Critical of Government Freed amid Riots,"*Al Arabiya*, January 10, 2011 (www.alarabiya.net/articles/2011/01/10/132866.html [March 2012]). On a similar theme, see the Egyptian release "Thawrgya," on Revolution Records (www.facebook.com/revrecordz [March 2012]).

26. Mourtada and Salem, "Civil Movements," p. 22.

27. Nate Anderson, "Tweeting Tyrants Out of Tunisia: Global Internet at Its Best," *Wired.com*, January 14, 2011 (www.wired.com/threatlevel/2011/01/tunisia/all/1 [March 2012]); Tim Lister, "Tunisian Protests Fueled by Social Media Networks," *CNN*, January 12, 2011 (http://articles.cnn.com/2011-01-12/world/tunisia_1_protests-twitter-and-facebook-tunisian-government?_s=PM:WORLD [March 2012]); Alexia Tsotsis, "A Twitter Snapshot of the Tunisian Revolution: Over 196K Mentions of Tunisia, Tweeted by over 50K Users," *TechCrunch.com*, January 16, 2011 (http://techcrunch.com/2011/01/16/tunisia-2/ [March 2012]); Firas Al-Atraqchi, "Tunisia's Revolution was Twitterized," *thedailynewsegypt.com*, January 16, 2011 (www.thedailynewsegypt.com/columnists/tunisias-revolution-was-twitterized.html [March 2012]).

28. Jennifer Preston, "Facebook and YouTube Fuel the Egyptian Protests," *New York Times*, February 5, 2011(www.nytimes.com/2011/02/06/world/middleeast/06face.html?pagewanted=all [March 2012]).

29. Phoebe Connelly, "Curating the Revolution: Building a Real-Time News Feed about Egypt," *The Atlantic* (www.theatlantic.com/technology/print/2011/02/curating-the-revolution-building-a-real-time-news-feed-about-egypt/71041/ [March 2012]). For a selective narrative of Twitter posts in relation to Egypt, see Nadia Idle and Alex Nunns (eds.), *Tweets from Tahrir* (New York: OR Books, 2011).

30. Hashtags (denoted with a # sign) are a means of highlighting trending topics on Twitter that aid in the categorization of and searching for key stories and themes.

31. Mourtada and Salem, "Civil Movements," p. 16.

32. Author's analysis of data traffic from Google Realtime Twitter archive search, using Timeline #Egypt site: twitter.com 2.2.11. Due to the conclusion of an arrangement between Twitter and Google, the Google Realtime Twitter archive was suspended in July 2011. An archive of Twitter content became available in June 2011 at www.r-shief. org (accessed June 11, 2011). There is scope for more extensive interdisciplinary studies of the hundreds of thousands of tweets that emerged during this period.

33. See her blog at www.monaeltahawy.com.

34. Michael Liedtke, "How Google Removed the Muzzle on Twitter in Egypt," *Associated Press*, February 4, 2011 (www.usatoday.com/tech/news/2011-02-04-google-egypt-twitter-tool_N.htm [March 2012]). See also Alive In Egypt (http://alive.in/egypt/ [March 2012]); Speak2Tweet (http://twitter.com/#!/speak2tweet [March 2012]); "Some Weekend Work That Will (Hopefully) Enable More Egyptians to Be Heard," *Google Blog*, January 31, 2011 (http://googleblog.blogspot.com/2011/01/some-weekend-work-that-will-hopefully.html [March 2012]). For background on the service, see Voice of America, "Egyptians Gain a Voice with Social Media Service Used by Stars," *VOANews.com*, February 6, 2011 (www.voanews.com/learningenglish/home/How-a-Social-Media-Service-Used-by-Stars-Gave-Egyptians-a-Voice-11543 0564.html [March 2012]).

35. See, for instance, the Facebook page of Hosni Mubarak, "President Mohamed Hosny Mubarak" (www.facebook.com/pages/President-Mohamed-Hosny-Mubarak/14512914651), which had 10,000 fans in February 2010 (last accessed February 10, 2010).

36. "Egypt Disappears from Internet Entirely—Final ISP Connection Severed," *TechEye*, February 1, 2011 (www.techeye.net/internet/egypt-disappears-from-internet-entirely [March 2012]).

37. Cam McGrath, "Mubarak Regime Shuts Down Internet in Futile Attempt to Stop Protests," *Electronic Intifada*, January 28, 2011 (http://electronicintifada.net/v2/article11759.shtml [March 2012]). Also see "Facebook Reported Inaccessible in Egypt," *AFP*, January 26, 2011 (www.google.com/hostednews/afp [January 2011]); Ryan Singel, "Threat Level: Egypt Shut Down Net with Big Switch, Not Phone Calls," *Wired.com*, February 10, 2011 (www.wired.com/threatlevel/2011/02/egypt-off-switch/ [March 2012]).

38. Grant Gross, "Egyptian Activist: Internet Shutdown Backfired," *IDG News*, February 3, 2011 (www.pcworld.com/businesscenter/article/218630/egyptian_activist_internet_shutdown_backfired.html [March 2012]).

39. It was widely published; see, for example, "The Photo of the Day: At Last They Met," *Egyptian Chronicles*, February 8, 2011 (http://egyptianchronicles.blogspot.com/2011/02/photo-of-day-at-last-they-met.html [March 2012]). For a video of Ghonim's speech, see "Wael Ghonim's Speech in Tahrir Square," *YouTube*, February 8, 2011 (www.youtube.com/watch?v=jqESVmC1YI4 [March 2012]). See also "Wael

Ghonim Is Free," *YouTube*, February 7, 2011 (www.youtube.com/watch?v=Cq2b FgvvtYE [March 2012]).

40. Timothy M. Phelps, "Egypt and Mubarak: Mubarak Resigns," *Los Angeles Times*, February 11, 2011 (www.latimes.com/news/nationworld/world/la-fg-egypt-mubarak-20110212,0,3072259.story [March 2012]).

41. Abubakar Siddique, "Charting a New Way Forward in the Middle East," *Radio Free Europe/Radio Liberty*, February 13, 2011 (www.rferl.org/content/commentary_charting_new_way_forward_middle_east/2307878.html [March 2012]).

42. "Arab Youth—Changing Worldwide Perceptions," *Ikhwanweb.com*, April 16, 2011(www.ikhwanweb.com/article.php?id=28411 [March 2012]); Zvi Bar'el, "Where Is Egypt's Muslim Brotherhood Headed?" *Ha'aretz*, April 6, 2011 (www.haaretz.com/print-edition/features/where-is-egypt-s-muslim-brotherhood-headed-1.354353 [March 2012]).

43. Ikhwan Book (www.ikhwanbook.com). See also Matt Bradley, "Muslim Brotherhood Launches Its Own Version of Facebook," *The National*, July 2, 2010 (www.thenational.ae/news/world/africa/muslim-brotherhood-launches-its-own-version-of-facebook [March 2012]).

44. "The Syrian Revolution 2011" (www.facebook.com/Syrian.Revolution [March 2012]). See also Abdullah Omar, "Donkeys Take over from DSL as Syria Shuts Down Internet," *The Media Line, Jerusalem Post*, May 15, 2011(www.jpost.com/MiddleEast/Article.aspx?id=220763 [April 2012]); Liam Stack, "Activists Using Video to Bear Witness in Syria," *New York Times*, June 18, 2011 (www.nytimes.com/2011/06/19/world/middleeast/19syria.html?pagewanted=all [March 2012]).

45. One example of this was the Libyan Youth Movement Facebook page: "Libyan Youth Movement" (www.facebook.com/LibyanYouthMovement [March 2012]). See also "@shabablibya" (http://twitter.com/#!/shabablibya [March 2012]).

46. Twitter, "#FreeAlaa." See also Manal Hussein and Alaa Abd El Fattah's blog, "*Manal and Alaa's Bit Bucket*" (www.manalaa.net [March 2012]); Alaa Abd El Fattah (http://shorouknews.com [March 2012]).

47. Ghada Alakhdar, *Cyber Culture Studies: Palestinian E-Resistance: New Scopes for Cultural Political Intervention* (Saarbrücken: VDM Verlag Dr. Müller, 2011); Yves Gonzalez-Quijano and Christophe Varin (eds.), *La société de l'information au Proche-Orient: Internet au Liban et en Syrie* (Beirut: Presses de l'Université Saint-Joseph, 2006).

48. With regard to gender roles, see chapter 3 in this volume.

49. See chapter 5 in this volume.

50. For example, in the Libyan context, see Paul Sonne and Margaret Coker, "Firms Aided Libyan Spies: First Look Inside Security Unit Shows How Citizens Were Tracked," *Wall Street Journal*, August 30, 2011 (http://online.wsj.com/article/SB10001424053111904199404576538721260166388.html [March 2012]).

51. See chapter 11 in this volume.

GONZALO ESCRIBANO *and* ALEJANDRO LORCA

5

Modern Commercial and Social Entrepreneurship as a Factor of Change

Classical modernization and political economy approaches both consider a wide array of economic agents as potential drivers for change. These actors include international agents such as foreign companies (not only transnational corporations but also smaller companies), international organizations, and nongovernmental organizations (NGOs), and local agents such as national public companies, entrepreneurs, bureaucrats, and segments of civil societies involved in economic or social activities (professional associations, trade unions, and local NGOs). Several authors have highlighted the linkages between entrepreneurs and Mediterranean political systems, but their analyses have tended to focus on the role of large entrepreneurs.[1] In fact, nobody could have anticipated that the self-immolation of a humiliated and frustrated street fruit vendor, Mohamed Bouazizi—who exemplified the overtrained, informal microentrepreneur—would catalyze the most profound upheaval seen in the Arab world since its independence. This chapter tries to fill this gap in the literature by analyzing entrepreneurship as a driver for social transformation, focusing on the role of small and medium enterprises (SMEs). While mainly dealing with the southern Mediterranean region, this discussion also includes some contextual references to the wider Middle East.[2]

The first section briefly presents the current situation of SMEs and entrepreneurship in North Africa. In the second section, we try to conceptually address the role of entrepreneurship as a driver for social change in North African countries. This is followed by an exploration of how SMEs and entrepreneurship are linked with other factors for change covered in this volume.

96

The final section concludes with some implications and suggestions for U.S. and EU relationships with the region, as well as for transatlantic relations.

SMEs and Entrepreneurship in North Africa

The nature of the North African productive fabric has largely been shaped by the historical evolution of its economic strategies, which in turn have resulted from continuous bargaining between the state and the economic actors that emerged out of those strategies. This process has been well documented in the region's political economy literature.[3] After independence, state-led growth and import-substituting industries generated a class of public company managers and rent-seeking entrepreneurs. The collapse of this model in the 1980s led to liberalization policies that resulted in the economic elites obtaining most of the privatized assets thanks to their political connections; the upshot was a more sophisticated model of rent seeking. In fact, corporatist capitalism, through privilege and cronyism, is the main entry barrier to new entrepreneurs and the development of entrepreneurship.[4]

However, recent efforts directed toward diversification and export orientation have created a new class of micro, small, and medium-size entrepreneurs integrated into transnational industrial networks, which coexist with a more traditional class of small and very small merchants and traditional services providers. Today, SMEs, including micro- and often informal or semi-formal entrepreneurs, are the more dynamic economic actors in the southern Mediterranean region: they grow faster, are more flexible and are more innovative than big companies, and are far more labor intensive.[5] According to the Middle East and North Africa (MENA)–OECD Investment Program, SMEs contribute to more than two-thirds of total formal employment in the region and a very significant share of value added. To this figure the whole informal sector, mostly microentrepreneurs, should be added. For instance, according to the Direction de la Statistique in Morocco, 97.4 percent of companies have fewer than ten employees, and very small enterprises, including semi-formal ones that pay the professional tax, account for more than 80 percent of companies. While there are no rigorous and homogeneous statistics for North African countries, it is estimated that SMEs account for 70 percent of GDP, while the contribution of the informal sector ranges between 20 to 30 percent of GDP.[6]

Today, Mediterranean (and Middle Eastern) non-oil economies are no longer driven by the public sector. Even resource-rich economies such as Algeria, Syria, and Libya (or Iran in the Middle East) with significant state ownership are now dominated by the private sector, which averages 80 percent of GDP across the MENA region, a share similar to that of Eastern Europe or Asia. However, in spite of producing most of the region's value added, the share of the private sector in total investment for the MENA region is the lowest in the world: around 60 percent for non-oil-exporting and 50 percent for oil-exporting MENA countries. Between 1995 and 2006, the share of private investment only increased in Egypt, Morocco, and, to a lesser extent, in Tunisia, while it rose sharply in most of the developing world. The private sector has a strong dualistic structure: some companies have adopted modern management techniques, but most SMEs remain traditional and are family managed. In addition, SMEs suffer more than their larger counterparts from lack of access to credit, anticompetitive practices (including informality), corruption, and administrative burdens.[7]

According to World Bank enterprise surveys, the industrial sector in the region is disproportionally dominated by older firms, which are able to survive all kinds of reforms, "capturing" them to their own profit. The median age for local manufacturing firms in the MENA is nineteen years, the same as in mature OECD economies and twice the average for East Asia and Eastern Europe, indicating that the renewal of the industrial structure is slower than elsewhere. This lack of renewal among the business elite parallels the one described by political scientists for the political elite and has profound implications for social mobility and political change in the region. Businessmen also tend to be older than in other developing regions (fourteen years of average experience compared with around eight years for Latin America and South Asia), a striking fact for countries where the youth represent the majority of the population. Furthermore, and despite efforts to increase the number of university graduates, the educational level of MENA businessmen is still consistently lower than in other developing regions: 13 percent of MENA manufacturing business owners have not completed secondary education, the highest share across the world.

The generational gap is even higher when semi-formal microenterprises are compared to formal SMEs. Data from Morocco show that the median experience in formal SMEs is between sixteen and eighteen years, while for microenterprises the median is eight years, and the average age of their owners is thirty-two years.[8] These data easily explain the widespread unrest and frustration among young graduates who are unable to climb the social ladder in spite of being better prepared, more dynamic, and more internationally oriented than the old business elite. They feel overtrained (at a high economic and personal cost) for the kind of jobs they obtain and develop a deep sense of injustice when facing the old entrepreneurial elite and its heirs, who profit from their political connections to monopolize quality jobs in the labor market. Anyone visiting the cities of the region can easily observe a vibrant established business sector alongside a myriad of young microentrepreneurs trying to overcome deeply entrenched entry barriers.

The capacity of the economic elites to capture capital and labor rents, together with the paucity of economic institutions in the region, has led to low entrepreneurship levels by international standards. Entrepreneurship can be proxied by average business density (the number of businesses per 1,000 working-age people). The World Bank entrepreneurship database shows that the average business density in the MENA region is among the lowest in the world, with the average firm density in Algeria, Egypt, Jordan, Lebanon, Morocco, Syria, and Tunisia being between a third to a quarter of the figures for Latin America or Eastern Europe and Central Asia. Table 5-1 shows a more dynamic indicator for entrepreneurship, firm entry density (newly registered limited liability firms per 1,000 working-age people), in some selected countries. As a group, MENA countries have the second-lowest entry density in the developing world for the 2004–09 period (0.63), slightly more than the sub-Saharan Africa ratio (0.58) but lower than the entry densities in Asia (around 0.8), Latin America (1.31), or Europe and Central Asia (2.26); for high-income countries, average entry density was 4.21.

However, within the region firm entry density has greatly increased in some countries such as Jordan, Morocco, and Tunisia, while Algerian and especially Egyptian data reflect very low and decreasing firm entry density. Table 5-1 data on new firms in Morocco and Tunisia for 2009 are impressive and are probably related to the slow but cumulative process of economic opening and modest upgrading of the business environment. This points to the fact that when entry barriers are relaxed or become less effective in a more diversified and internationalized economic system, new entrepreneurs enter the market, in both new and existing activities.

Another challenge to entrepreneurship is the inadequacy of most business associations in the region: they are weakly institutionalized and tend to preserve the status quo thanks to tacit alliances between large incumbent firms and political elites. In most cases they do not represent SME interests at all but rather pursue rent-seeking strategies for the benefit of incumbents. SMEs have encountered several obstacles to developing their own organizations because in many MENA countries, independent associations are directly forbidden or de facto lack the capacity to advocate their interests or criticize economic policies. A 2007 survey of the principal business associations in the

Table 5-1. *Firm Entry Density, Selected Countries and Selected Years, 2004–09*
Units as indicated

Country	Year	New firms[a]	Entry density[b]
Algeria	2004	11.252	0.53
	2009	10.544	0.44
Egypt	2004	6.303	0.14
	2008	6.291	0.13
Jordan	2004	1.104	0.37
	2009	2.737	0.74
Morocco	2004	9.852	0.53
	2009	26.166	1.28
Tunisia	2004	4.917	0.73
	2009	9.079	1.23
Turkey	2004	40.819	0.87
	2009	44.472	0.87
Non-Muslim Countries			
Brazil	2009	315.645	2.38
Czech Republic	2009	21.717	3.00
Israel	2008	19.758	4.46
Republic of Korea	2008	60.039	1.72

Source: World Bank entrepreneurship database (http://econ.worldbank.org/research/entrepreneurship).
a. Number of newly registered limited liability firms during the calendar year.
b. Number of newly registered limited liability firms per 1,000 working-age people (ages fifteen to sixty-four).

MENA region showed that their demands usually mismatched the needs identified by the majority of companies, which are predominantly SMEs. Because they have a rent-seeking agenda and are dominated by incumbents, these associations ignore the pressing constraints faced by SMEs, which mostly relate to economic governance and the quality of institutions. However, with the opening and diversification of economic activity, and where allowed to do so, new business organizations have been created that voice the concerns of new young entrepreneurs (Algeria and Syria), specific regions or sectors (Algeria, Jordan, and Morocco), SMEs (Egypt), and even Islamic-oriented businesses (Musiad in Turkey).

Despite this progress, entrepreneurs are still fragmented into several associations that tend to be weak and divided. The Algerian case illustrates this situation, with at least four business organizations and other associations of managers and agricultural owners. One is the Union des Commerçants et Artisans Algériens, representing about 200,000 SMEs, whose main issue is unfair competition from the informal sector, but it has not been involved in policy reform discussions, and its influence is marginal. The situation is very similar in the agricultural domain, represented by two organizations: l'Union Nationale des Paysans Algériens, which inherited the structures of the agricultural arm of the old single-party government but lost all its influence in the policymaking process and today is very compliant with government decisions; and the Union des Agriculteurs Indépendents, established during the 1990s restitution of lands nationalized in the 1973 agrarian revolution, whose influence and representativeness are very small. In practice, most agricultural and agrofood producers channel their demands through the regional agricultural chambers, created at the beginning of the 1990s, whose directors are appointed by the government. The absence of functioning and representative business institutions has left a void filled by hidden clientelistic networks mostly dominated by big companies closely associated with the regime.[9]

Entrepreneurship and SMEs as Drivers of Change

Classical modernization and economic development theories stress the importance of achieving some economic prerequisites before transitioning from authoritarian to democratic regimes. Economic development should fulfil basic economic needs, market institutions need to be in place, and a bourgeois middle class has to emerge.[10] This theoretical framework has been challenged by some who see it as an argument to support those authoritarian leaders who are supposedly pro-development. As Carothers put it, "Despite some commitment to socioeconomic progress, such leaders may also be fixated on enriching themselves, protecting certain privileged groups . . . and undercutting potential political rivals."[11] This argument applies not just to authoritarian leaders or political elites: economic actors, both local and foreign, pursue different agendas according to their (often narrow) interests. Business associations, for instance, tend to follow the "distributive coalition" model to capture rents, as first described by Olson in 1965.[12]

As mentioned earlier, literature on the southern Mediterranean political economy has documented how incumbent firms and regime-controlled business associations managed to preserve the status quo by capturing not only state rents but also the benefits of economic reforms—such as privatization and liberalization—that often were pushed from abroad. Foreign investors have exhibited a more mixed behavior: when confronted with local economic and political elites, they had to choose between accommodation and defiance. In the first and most common case, they clearly became a part of the status quo–preserving coalition. A clear example was the entrenched network of interest between EU companies and Tunisian companies with close ties to Ben Ali's clan; but similar cases can be found in most countries in the region.

When foreign companies' interests have clashed with those of the ruling elites, they have opted for calculated exit strategies that allowed them to optimize the returns on their investments. A recent example is Telefónica, a Spanish telecom company that allegedly sold its Moroccan business to local investors when the royal milieu decided to enter its business. Hibou describes a similar experience in the Tunisian insurance market: the insurance group Allianz was unable to become the majority holder in the local company Astrée by increasing its participation after the departure of other foreign investors; Allianz decided then to leave Tunisia and sell off the totality of its shares, part of which went to local investors.[13]

So whatever their merits in modernizing the domestic economy, neither local incumbents nor foreign companies have been helpful as drivers of political change by significantly altering the equilibrium of political economy.[14] Foreign companies have been useful in promoting social mobility through their more merit-based management of human resources, but their need for employees or counselors with local political connections has eroded to some extent the effects of such transformational policies. By contrast, SMEs often are unable either to come to terms with the ruling elites, who rely on patronage and do not need to compromise, or to implement optimal exit strategies. In the absence of reforms allowing them to exploit their comparative advantages, they are trapped in a low-level equilibrium leading to mere survival strategies or going informal. In both cases productivity and innovation suffer, and so does their potential for fostering social mobility and therefore societal transformation.[15] In order to prosper, SMEs have to find a way to advocate for reforms that alter the status quo, and by doing so, they can eventually become drivers of change, challenging the entrenched alliance between economic and political elites.

What entrepreneurs are not doing, at least not in an open and collective manner, is to participate in the recent protests that, at the time of this writing, have led to the stepping down of Ben Ali and Hosni Mubarak from the presidencies of Tunisia and Egypt and the assassination of Qaddafi in Libya. In a recent account of the protest movements that have emerged in the Arab world during the last years, Hamzawy and Ottaway stress the importance of labor unions, youth movements, leftish and Islamist movements, and bloggers, but not entrepreneurs.[16] However, they also highlight the participation in the protests of professional associations (mainly lawyers' organizations), which formally are not business organizations but in some cases represent liberal professionals that in fact are often small entrepreneurs. Bayat also has stressed the role of middle-class professionals in democracy movements, dating back to the 2004 Egyptian demonstrations catalyzed by Kefaya ("Enough"; officially, the Egyptian Movement for Change), as well as the massive participation of the "middle-class poor" forced into the informal sector and civil servants who must take second or third jobs in the informal sector, which now employs between one-third to a half of the urban population.[17]

The absence of business organizations in protest movements is hardly surprising and is in fact a common trait of most democratic transitions. There are several reasons for this. First, as has been shown in the previous section, existing business organizations are controlled by incumbents and lack independence from the regimes in place. Second, in most countries in the region, associations for SMEs (not to mention informal or semi-formal microentrepreneurs) simply do not exist, and therefore such entrepreneurs have to participate in protests as individuals. Finally, entrepreneurs are probably very sensitive to retaliation by the regimes in place, which can easily deprive them of their livelihood. Interestingly enough, while entrepreneurs tend to be economic risk takers, they show much higher levels of politically induced risk aversion. In this regard, the regimes consistently implement cooptation strategies toward entrepreneurs, either by inclusion or exclusion from economic reforms.[18] As Grim explains for the Algerian case, the emerging entrepreneurial class is fragmented "by the punches that the power has inflicted upon all these businessmen . . . in order to impoverish or to salvage them."[19] In Egypt, businessmen who want to donate funds to human rights NGOs, another channel for entrepreneurs to promote democracy, "are systematically harassed, and [in] many cases this has led to withdraw[ing] the funds."[20]

This is not to say that businessmen are absent from protest movements. Given their lack of voice or absence of representative associations, the only way they can find to express their preferences is to join the protests; however, they participate as citizens rather than as entrepreneurs or managers. A good example is the case of the Google marketing executive Wael Ghonim, who has become one of the most prominent figures of the Egyptian protest movement. However, the principal role of entrepreneurs seems to lie more in changing the equilibrium of the political economy by expanding the middle class and the private sector, and by advocating for institutional and economic policy reforms.

While both the Tunisian and Egyptian revolutions have attained a wide social base, the participation of middle-class professionals and middle-class poor has been widely highlighted.[21] Martínez alludes to this when he describes the Tunisian paradox: "How can a well-educated society, employed in a diversified economy, composed of middle classes, coexist for a long time with a police regime as brutal as it is corrupt ? "[22]

There are other ways that entrepreneurs can induce political changes. In some cases, they can deliver demonstration effects by reforming the procedures of business associations so that they are more open and democratic, and by pushing for greater freedom and independence from incumbents and their patrons in the regime. The troubled 2009 election for president of the Algerian Forum des Chefs d'Entreprises (an association of CEOs) illustrates this demonstration effect. A young and reform-oriented entrepreneur, Slim Othmani, ran for the presidency of the forum, challenging the government-supported incumbent who had previously backed the reelection of long-term Algerian president Abdelaziz Bouteflika. While Othmani ultimately lost the election, he successfully introduced electoral competition, changed voting rules from open vote to secret ballot, and attracted considerable public attention through debates, conferences, and other public events. Despite the limited scope, by setting such a precedent in the region, he was able to not only positively influence the association's operations but also offer a model for other organizations to follow and a widely publicized example of democratic governance. Foreign assistance to professional associations for artisans or small merchants, as well as support for start-ups and exporters, may be a highly effective way to spread a participatory and democratic culture.

Such demonstration effects have not been a salient feature of the Tunisian experience thus far. Hédi Djilani, president of the country's main business organization, l'Union Tunisienne de l'Industrie, du Commerce et de l'Artisanat, was forced to resign, after twenty-three years of leadership, only after Ben Ali left the country. He was the father-in-law of Belhassen Trabelsi, the strongman of the Trabelsi clan, and had always supported Ben Ali, to the point that he directed the latter's 2009 campaign and announced that he would support Ben Ali's candidacy for the 2014 elections. Djilani's removal had been a long-standing demand by the Centre des Jeunes Dirigeants, which represents the aspirations of a new generation of entrepreneurs, but they only managed to force him to step down once Ben Ali disappeared from the scene.

The Egyptian case shares several similarities with Tunisia. The popular anger against cronyism found its target in the person of Ahmad Ezz, whose fortune was frozen shortly after Mubarak's resignation. He is a steel magnate and was the ruling party leader; he funded Mubarak's campaigns and was a close associate of his son Gamal, having played a major role in the last fraudulent parliamentary elections. Less regime-contaminated Egyptian businessmen have accommodated the wave of change and distanced themselves from the Mubarak regime in an ex-post manner, like the Coptic owner of Orascom Group, Naguib Sawiris. As Goldberg has argued, the merit of the Egyptian revolution should accrue to the people who risked their lives by demonstrating against the regime, thus allowing businessmen "to come out in the open and demand structural changes."[23] While SMEs have gained more of a voice lately, their history of exclusion from policymaking and lack of representation mean that most private sector influence remains in the hands of big businesses.[24]

These experiences suggest that SMEs' main potential contribution to political change in the southern Mediterranean region lies in promoting social mobility by expanding the middle class and adding fresh blood to entrepreneurial elites. Their activities can help alter the political economy equilibrium within societies by diversifying and decentralizing economic power away from the big entrepreneurs and public companies that tend to support entrenched regimes. SMEs also can advocate for institutional reforms that weaken the economic elite's capacity to capture the benefits of economic reforms. Such efforts, in turn, could erode the political elites' capacity to exert social control through patronage and nepotism and thus contribute to social transformation. SMEs can also deliver demonstration and learning effects by implementing more transparent and democratic procedures within business associations, which can spill over into other civil society organizations and, eventually, the whole political system.

Of course, there are other kinds of entrepreneurship in the MENA region, notably social entrepreneurship, usually defined as the "other way of entrepreneurship" (*entreprende autrement*). For the sake of simplicity, this can be exemplified by cooperatives, associations, foundations, and benefit societies devoted to providing social services. A wider approach could include all civil society organizations, which historically have been repressed in several countries in the region, especially Egypt.[25] In the southern Mediterranean region, social entrepreneurship has a long history and is often linked with religious movements (up to half of existing associations in Egypt).[26] However, there are other social entrepreneurship institutions that date back to spontaneous mutual help and solidarity mechanisms in agriculture (*Maouna*) or to delivery of social services (public *waqfs*), as well as the modern institutions introduced by colonization (cooperatives). Their trajectories vary from country to country and are sector specific. Given the lack of studies on their economic and entrepreneurial activities, they are mentioned here just in recognition of their existence. The lack of comparable data about Islamic social entrepreneurship in North Africa, beyond the fact that its influence is prevalent in the provision of nongovernmental social services, prevents us from further elaboration.

Returning to non–religiously oriented associations, in Tunisia, for instance, agricultural cooperatives were instruments of the state for its collectivization efforts in the 1960s. Some of them still depend upon the agriculture and economy ministries. According to 2006 data, they represented 20 percent of Tunisian agricultural producers and 5.5 percent of agricultural production. There are also nonagricultural cooperatives, about which very little information is available. Tunisian socially oriented associations are mostly local in nature and play a very important role in the social economy or "third sector"; they are financed mainly by the state, having a very poor governance structure. Foundations have no legal status in Tunisian law, which suppressed public waqfs in 1956 and private ones in 1957. In general, the whole sector remains very fragmented, lacks human resources and a governance framework (very few have internal statutes), and is highly dependent on financing from the state.[27] In Morocco the situation seems more dynamic, especially regarding social institutions devoted to socioeconomic development, but foundations there share the Tunisian problems of state dependence and lack of human resources.[28]

From a more general perspective, while many countries in the region may claim to have a "vibrant" civil society when measured by the number of registered organizations, those entities working on democracy promotion and human rights tend to face administrative obstacles for registration and access to foreign financing. However, these measures do not seem able to undermine the influence of civil society actors, especially in the context of increasing social needs (and demands), which lead to a "more disenfranchised citizenry, less willing to cooperate with their governments and rulers."[29]

In sum, what we find in the region is a typology of business with different potential to induce social change across a range of divides.[30] First, there is the public-versus-private sector category, which actually is a fuzzy distinction given that regimes co-opt big entrepreneurs by giving them seats on public company councils and benefits from monopolistic administrative concessions. Second, within the private sector, there is the big company–SME divide, with the latter concentrating most of labor and value added but being underrepresented in business associations. Finally, within the SME category there are traditional versus modern firms that to some extent reflect the same, aforementioned generation gap between large and small enterprises. Traditional firms are usually family-led companies that rely on traditional and unskilled management; they would include *bazaris*, providers of traditional services, and agriculturalists, many of them operating on an informal or semi-formal basis. However, the economic reforms implemented in the region during the last three decades, though slow and fragmentary, have generated a new group of industrial and modern service SMEs owned or managed by younger and more dynamic, innovative, and internationally oriented entrepreneurs. These firms probably have more transformative potential, but their ability to prosper suffers the most from corruption, lack of financing, and absence of business infrastructures. They are potential Schumpeterian entrepreneurs with the capacity to induce social change through political and social externalities related to the values and preferences embedded in their entrepreneurship. However, such political and social spillovers are limited by path-dependent and political economy–generated institutional constraints, which hamper the social projection of their values and preferences.[31] Despite many obstacles and being local and fragmented in nature, social entrepreneurship is finding an outlet in numerous associations struggling for independence from the state. While many of these may be in a precarious situation, they could pave the way for a less dependent and more open and participatory model of society.

Linkages between Entrepreneurship and Other Drivers of Change

Entrepreneurship does not develop in a vacuum. As a social phenomenon, it will interact with the other drivers of change described in this volume. The business diasporas are linked with the issue of migration, entrepreneurship offers women an opportunity to gain autonomy and political influence, information and communications technologies (ICTs) can widen and transform business relations, and religious (Muslim) values have the potential to foster entrepreneurship. This section of the chapter builds upon the findings of the other chapters to assess entrepreneurship's linkages and synergies in promoting social transformation.

In chapter 1, Philippe Fargues speaks of the "birth of the individual" and analyzes the phenomenon of migration in the MENA region. The former would seem to be a fundamental driver for transformation since it favors the emergence of entrepreneurs. Regarding migration, business diasporas are one of the most analyzed links between migration and transformative entrepreneurship. In our discussion here we concentrate on the relationship of migration and entrepreneurship in the context of sociopolitical change.

Migration can influence entrepreneurship in several ways. The "brain drain" paradigm tends to view migration as a mechanism that deprives emigrant countries of their more entrepreneurial and creative individuals, whereas the "circular migration" model emphasizes codevelopment, mainly via monetary remittances. These, however, tend to finance consumption, housing improvements, and health care and education; they seem to play only a limited role in financing economic activity and, consequently, in fostering entrepreneurship. The "brain circulation" paradigm, by contrast, focuses on the mobility of competences and skills through a network that serves as a gateway for knowledge and innovation through mentoring, coaching, intercluster missions, and productive externalization in the home country.[32]

Inspired by the experience of Asian immigrants in Silicon Valley, the last diaspora model is more complex, implying neither the need for emigrants to return to the home country nor exclusively a massive flow of monetary remittances but rather the creation of business networks, acting as corridors through which goods and services as well as financial and human capital are exchanged and integrated. The Chinese diaspora, for instance, has woven a dense network of commercial, financial, and productive links both with its home country and among its different communities abroad. However, such multifaceted corridors have not been built in the southern Mediterranean to the same extent as in the Asian region.[33] For instance, the Lebanese diaspora, despite being spread all over the world, has not maintained such a productive nexus in Lebanon.

Among the three paradigms for migration, the circulating diaspora model seems to have the most potential to bring about real societal transformation, at least with regard to spreading entrepreneurship. Social, not financial, remittances—including ideas and behaviors—play a significant role in promoting entrepreneurship.[34] For our purposes, social remittances in the form of encouraging entrepreneurship can have a higher transformative potential than financial ones.[35] While countries like Morocco, Egypt, or Lebanon receive very significant flows of monetary remittances, they seldom generate a well-structured, bidirectional corridor of goods, services, production factors, and, most important, new ideas and entrepreneurial behavior patterns.

It is true that the southern Mediterranean political economy currently does not facilitate such a productive integration of resources and ideas. A poll among Moroccans both living abroad and having returned to Morocco gives some insight into the gaps between their aspirations and accomplishments.[36] While contributing to the development of their home country ranked as the main reason to return among foreign residents (25 percent of those polled), it was the first reason for satisfaction for only 7.7 percent of those who had returned. The main obstacle to return according to 82.7 percent of foreign residents was an unfulfilling professional environment, due to its archaic character (lack of professionalism and excessive administrative burdens) and arbitrariness (absence of meritocracy, clientelism, and abuse of hierarchical power). This same issue was the main cause of dissatisfaction for 92 percent of those who had already returned. However, the majority of foreign residents still considered creating a new business, while only a few wanted to enter the public sector. Interest in entrepreneurship was highest among those aged thirty-six to forty, men, and U.S. residents.

The significant barriers to return have not discouraged some emigrants from attempting to replicate the brain circulation model. One example is the Association Maroc Entrepreneurs, which was created in 1999 with the aim of contributing to the country's economic development by encouraging Moroccans living abroad, especially in France, to establish a new business in their home country and by offering incentives to talented Moroccans to return. The association offers information on investment and job opportunities, organizes seminars for prospective entrepreneurs, and holds an annual business plan competition.

In recent years many other initiatives have come from the southern Mediterranean region's diasporas, to which the ANIMA Investment Network has devoted a recent study.[37] Many of these initiatives are not focused on the physical return of emigrants, but rather encourage their technical and entrepreneurial "remittances." The TechWadi network was launched in 2010 to draw the attention of the Arab American diaspora working in Silicon Valley to the need to improve technological capacities in their country of origin. Another example is the Algerian Startup Initiative, a network created in 2010 to engage ICT professionals living in Silicon Valley and Europe in coaching activities and organizing a business plan competition directed toward young, innovative Algerian entrepreneurs.

The ANIMA-MedDiasporas directory has identified 470 networks related to southern Mediterranean diasporas between January and September 2010. The principal diaspora countries were the United States (155 networks), France (47), Canada (45), the United Kingdom (32), and Germany (29), while the main origin countries were Morocco (72), Lebanon (66), Algeria (51), Egypt (42), and Israel (40). ANIMA conducted a mini-audit of networks' web pages and concluded that while some of them were "fallen stars," most have remained active. Among them, 50 percent belonged to the business community, 37 percent to civil society (mainly associations and think tanks), and 13 percent to the scientific and technical community. Many of the business and scientific networks were devoted to the development of ICTs while some of the civil society networks promoted gender-based programs.

As described by Gary Bunt in chapter 4, the spread of ICT has acted as a "game changer" in North African politics, but it does not necessarily follow Western models. Regarding entrepreneurship, it offers new business opportunities and changes the way businesses are managed. Beyond the big public contracts for mobile telecommunications and the privatization of the old state monopolies, there is a plethora of SMEs emerging in the field of ICT-related services. Most of them may be unsophisticated service providers or equipment sellers, whose activities have few technological or international spillovers. But countries like Morocco or Tunisia have structured strategies for the promotion of offshore ICT services, and as mentioned earlier, entrepreneurial diasporas are quite active in this sector. In any case, ICT should be valued as an opportunity to develop a new segment of middle-class professionals and entrepreneurs.

While widespread scepticism exists about the possibility of such countries developing an ICT-related service sector comparable to, say, the Indian one, it would be helpful to remember that the Indians also started with call centers and other unsophisticated services that were subsequently scaled up to higher-value activities. But there is no direct link between being a Twitter or Facebook activist and start-up programming. North African countries currently have too few engineers and applied science students for this to be the case. But ICT offers new opportunities to develop a range of economic activities that by their very nature are decentralized and difficult to stifle with traditional entry barriers. In particular, it allows small firms to obtain information on international markets and to establish international connections. Also, by definition, ICT professionals could be viewed as more cosmopolitan and better informed—but this is not necessarily so.

In the short run, perhaps the most valuable ICT input is that the sector's expansion could support and consolidate some of the social attributes of middle classes, such as a capacity to stay informed and participate in political decisions, for instance, regarding economic policies. In this sense, ICT both reduces information costs and increases the opportunity to voice and project social preferences, and its role along these lines in recent revolts has been widely acknowledged.

The comprehensive chapter by Paciello and Pepicelli describes the potential of entrepreneurship to transform women's roles in both the household and the public space. Their conclusions are cautious on the effectiveness of several tools on the grounds that men are somehow able to capture part of the benefits of gender equality measures. It is difficult to add much more to their in-depth analysis of the economic impact of women or to the transformative role of women's entrepreneurship. In fact, many of their findings are in line with ours: businesswomen face additional entry barriers, but once these barriers are either relaxed or painfully surmounted, they play a more significant transformative role in both the economic and political arenas than is the case for businessmen.

The changes induced by drivers such as demographics, ICT, and expanding roles for women are not linear and do not necessarily conform to the preferences of the West or Western-oriented Arab citizens, as the aforementioned chapters have pointed out. This uncertain outcome is perhaps magnified even more when one considers the religious context. Islamic economics is a rather unconsolidated theoretical corpus. More important, when one attempts to reconcile these often contradictory theoretical frameworks with economic policy decisions, it seems that almost anything goes. Free trade and protectionism, interventionism or laissez-faire policy, Arab socialism or IMF-backed reforms can all be defended on the grounds of Islamic economics. Of course, there is a strong sense of social justice in all the Islamic approaches to economics, but it can be attained via different pathways that are often influenced by political economy equilibriums rather than religious beliefs.

Concerning religious movements, there is an entrepreneurial dimension of Islam that in some cases aspires to offer an alternative to the Weberian protestant model.[38] The paradigm of "green capitalism" portrays an Islamic entrepreneur with most of the Schumpeterian attributes but whose ethical set of values is influenced by Islamic religious references rather than Protestantism.[39] This segment of businesses has grown considerably over the last decades, especially in Turkey but also in some Maghreb countries, and is somehow path dependent on the traditional alliance between mosque and bazaar. According to Roy, the transformative role of the Islamic entrepreneur is quite ambivalent. On the one hand, the modeling of honesty, transparency, and business success is doubtless a vigorous driver for change. However, religion-based preferences also can lead to unrealistic social demands that pursue social justice by the means of unsustainable fiscal policies or to advocacy of a social conservatism that is hostile to international opening, which could undermine the potential for economic growth through tourism, foreign investment, and trade.

In recent months most North African countries except Libya (due to civil war) have adopted fiscal packages to increase public wages and employment, food or energy subsidies, and public works. While these measures are not exclusively attributable to Islamist preferences but rather reflect the wishes of a majority of Arab citizens, they have been presented as an effort to advance social justice. Whether such measures are a nod to Islamist movements or are part of a strategy to erode their influence by appropriating the most socially attractive components of their social agenda, it seems that socioeconomic inclusiveness has finally come to the fore.

It is too early to evaluate the economic record of the recently elected Islamist majorities in countries like Tunisia, Morocco, and Egypt. In their electoral programs, they have emphasized economic and human development, support to SMEs, social justice, transparency and accountability, and an increase in public spending and salaries. While these and other promises are too numerous and varied to constitute a consistent and well-specified economic policy agenda, they are broad enough to allow pragmatism and compromise to play a role. This might moderate the adoption of restrictive measures regarding social behavior that could harm tourism or foreign investments, as well as the already declared continuity in external economic relations with traditional partners. Whether both trends will be sustained in the long run is difficult to assess. However, from an economic perspective, pragmatism would favor economic growth in order to achieve the promises made during the campaigns. While some rhetorical concessions are probably going to be made regarding traditional social norms, economic autonomy from the West, or the need to increase intra-Arab economic integration, none of these platforms has the potential to spur significant economic growth.

What is relevant for our purposes is that pious entrepreneurs could act as the most effective brake on counterproductive economic policy measures aimed at an ill-conceived, short-term concept of social justice. No group is more aware of the trade-offs between religious values and a thriving economy. As businessmen they are expected to have a pragmatic, bottom-line approach, which would allow them to advocate for compromise and alliances with other economic agents. They are also the main source of local financing for Islamist social entrepreneurs, who, as mentioned earlier, may constitute by far the most efficient and extended network for the provision of nongovernmental social services. This reinforces the influence of businesspeople when confronting socioeconomic policy decisions. By moderating political radicalism and projecting a set of ethical economic values—even if they do not always practice in their businesses what they preach abroad—they can act as important agents of change and thus should be the focus of any strategies emanating from the West. The results of the recent elections in Morocco, Tunisia, and Egypt suggest that there is an urgent need for both the EU and the United States to identify the new interlocutors within Islamist parties, associations, and movements who are in charge of economic issues and try to interact with them.

Final Remarks: Toward More Comprehensive EU, U.S., and Transatlantic Perspectives on Entrepreneurship in North Africa

Up to this point we have tried to offer some insights on the transformative role of entrepreneurship in North Africa. Our findings can be summarized by saying that businesses, especially small and very small (often individual or family) companies, constitute a potential driver for economic, social, and, ultimately, political change. This relationship is neither unequivocal nor mechanical and leaves ample room for unexpected consequences, a common occurrence given the complexity of social dynamics. But if we agree on the transformative potential of entrepreneurship, then the policy debate is not about whether to promote entrepreneurship but rather about how small entrepreneurs can be supported. This final section briefly evaluates the responses of the EU and the United States to this challenge and attempts to provide some insights for targeting policy design.[40]

Have past and current EU and U.S. economic relations generated positive externalities for nascent social and political transformation processes? Perhaps the most representative answer can be found by evaluating the long-run sociopolitical effects of free trade agreements, for which the Euro-Mediterranean Free Trade Area offers a broad time frame. In spite of their shortcomings, which are dealt with below, free trade areas have generally had a gradual but cumulatively significant impact by fostering and anchoring microeconomic reforms and macroeconomic stability. As a consequence, some entry barriers have been relaxed, easing market competition in sectors that used to be closely controlled by incumbents. The integration into the world economy implicit in such agreements also entails the diversification and decentralization of economic power.

It is not realistic to infer that the EU's Mediterranean policy by itself "caused" the socioeconomic transformations analyzed in this study, which are of a broader and longer-term nature. But in some way it could have helped to gradually configure a somewhat different business environment, one more conducive or at least receptive to change. How much this strategy has delivered over the long run and how it could be upgraded and made more consistent should be borne in mind when considering the challenges ahead.

In this regard, four different points may be noteworthy for the EU and the United States in their efforts to promote North African entrepreneurship and SMEs in a consistent, effective manner.

First, both EU and U.S. relations with North African countries are afflicted by a de facto lack of inclusiveness regarding microentrepreneurs and SMEs. They are rarely considered, consulted, or even informed in the design of policy measures that may affect them greatly, such as the signing of free trade agreements, whose negotiation procedures are often opaque and not readily available. The EU and the United States tend to assume that the preferences of SMEs are included in the set of negotiation positions adopted by North African governments, but as we have tried to show, this is seldom the case. If the EU and the United States want to empower small and medium entrepreneurs, and offer more opportunities to develop transformative entrepreneurship, they should start by including them more fully in their bilateral negotiations with governments. Inclusion would cover the full array of private and social entrepreneurial actors: different business and professional associations, cooperatives, social entrepreneurs, and other representatives of civil society, including religiously inspired ones. For example, invite traditional, small farmers, and consumer associations to participate, at the very least informally, in agricultural trade liberalization negotiations. In a similar vein, include neighborhood associations in the process of designing a sanitation project.

A second consideration is the need to support initiatives that promote SMEs. This requires making a subtle distinction between measures directly targeting SMEs and implementing more horizontal policies to improve the economic and legal institutions and infrastructures intended to benefit micro- and small businesses the most. The effectiveness of the latter approach can be limited unless it is accompanied by a detailed accounting of measures and sectors; but on the whole, horizontal policies to encourage liberalization and institutional and administrative upgrading allow SMEs more space to operate and should therefore be fostered.

Direct promotion of SMEs has become a mantra of recent EU initiatives in the region. There are partnerships devoted to this task, and direct promotion of SMEs is the focus of one of the six projects in the Union for the Mediterranean (one put forth by the Italian and Spanish delegations). In addition, direction promotion of SMEs has been given priority in the recently delivered package of measures included in two European Commission and High Representative communications.[41] Unfortunately, as of this writing, those measures remain vague at the policy level.

In fact, the record of the EU and the United States in promoting SMEs and entrepreneurship is at best modest: there have been several meetings between entrepreneurs on both sides of the Mediterranean, but they usually have focused on big, well-established firms rather than SMEs, not to mention the absence of initiatives targeting the informal sector. While there have been some exceptions, they probably have not made a noticeable difference. Euro-Mediterranean relations, for instance, focus on governments and big policy designs, and SMEs have often been marginalized. The best example is the Union for the Mediterranean, a partnership engaged in huge projects whose impact on inclusiveness is doubtful. However, the exclusion of SMEs is a general shortcoming of Euro-Mediterranean relations.[42] In their analysis of how U.S. and international financial institutions can engage civil society organizations (CSOs), Abdou and others identify some approaches that are much in line with our suggestions for SMEs and economically oriented CSOs: include them in policy dialogue, help successful undertakings scale up, provide more money for institution building and local entities, and support efforts to improve legal frameworks.[43] Regarding SMEs, this also can include targeted measures such as trade facilitation and training programs and a dedicated financial facility managed either by a regional bank or the European Investment Bank (EIB). These mechanisms have been discussed for years within the framework of Euro-Mediterranean relations, but both the EU and its southern partners have thus far failed to implement them.

A third issue refers back to horizontal policy reforms. North African countries are facing very difficult economic situations that require tough policy decisions. The cronyism and capture of previous reforms by economic elites have discredited the reforms themselves, together with their proponents, rather than the way they were implemented. While some reforms, such as those addressing corruption, may be in line with social demands, others are not necessarily so, such as subsidy reductions and targeting, containment of fiscal imbalances, or trade liberalization, to mention just a few. In the midst of both national and international economic difficulties, keeping North African economies on the path to reform is crucial for the survival and expansion of the SME productive fabric. To anchor economic reforms, the EU and the United States should consider offering a consistent package of incentives, including financial assistance and better access to their markets for North African goods, services, and workers.

While it is probably not the best of times to undertake such an effort, the opportunity cost of not doing so would probably be higher. SMEs are usually the weakest link of North African productive systems: they have no voice or representative associations to effectively advocate for them, are defenseless against corporatist interests and lobbies, and encounter serious problems accessing financing and overcoming institutional entry barriers. As the World Bank has recently highlighted, recent events in the region have halted economic activity and seriously affected SME activities in several countries.[44] Horizontal policy reform is necessary for economic recovery, but its design must consider the needs of SMEs, ensuring that they do not bear an unfair burden of economic adjustments.

A final point concerns the troubled relationship between business and democratization. As Youngs puts it, "The one sector rarely included in democracy initiatives is the business sector."[45] NGOs often overlook businesses as a part of civil society worth targeting. Business representatives are seldom invited to civil society meetings; when they are, discussions focus on narrow economic issues. Business associations are not considered capable of organizing themselves in a participatory manner and leading by example. They only occasionally engage with other civil society actors, both local and international, and therefore are usually not obliged to develop a stance on sociopolitical issues and defend it. Inclusion of the business sector, especially SMEs, in democracy promotion programs seems to be an unexploited opportunity to empower both small entrepreneurs and elicit their support for other civil society actors.

These four issues suggest several possibilities for cross-fertilization with the other drivers of change considered in this volume—bearing in mind that the complexity of the social interactions involved may generate ambivalent outcomes and unexpected consequences. Demographic transition to a younger population paves the way for more individualistic approaches, which in principle are more in line with private than social entrepreneurship, though self-realization can be achieved both ways. Migration can lead to the building of entrepreneurial bridges between diasporas and their origin countries. ICT has the potential to reduce transaction costs and lower entry barriers by increasing access to information and expanding communication to all social agents, not just businesses. Women's autonomy and influence in the public and private spheres can improve with their inclusion in the labor market and entrepreneurship. The role of pious entrepreneurs in shaping the preferences of religiously inspired political or social movements may also be important, and the EU and the United States urgently need to engage with this sector of business owners. But in order to profit from these linkages, SMEs and economically oriented CSOs must be more fully included in civil society, and both the EU and the United States must incorporate SMEs' and CSOs' preferences more seriously.

Convergence toward this inclusion of SMEs and related CSOs can be built upon existing and past initiatives, but a new impetus is needed. Supporting SMEs and entrepreneurship can serve several key objectives for the region, such as job creation, economic growth, social stability, and the decentralization of economic power structures. At the same time, it complements the usual large-scale political paradigm for transatlantic relations with a more pragmatic economic narrative that may align better with the bulk of North African citizens' demands. Of course, this would not balance all the asymmetries and gaps observed in transatlantic relations in the region.[46] However, a commitment to SMEs and related CSOs can be a relatively depoliticized undertaking, one enabling a convergence of interests among the EU, the United States, and North African societies that could, in turn, generate significant transformative political externalities in the medium to long run.

Moreover, an emphasis on smaller enterprises would send a positive signal by contrasting with the approaches of other external actors such as China or the Gulf countries, whose main strategy in the region has been to do businesses with traditional elites. For the latter countries, the electoral success of Islamist parties in Tunisia, Morocco, and Egypt is seen as a promising opportunity to extend their influence over the region; this is also the case for Turkey. In this context, transatlantic cooperation to promote SMEs offers a balancing influence, one more aligned with both the needs of the region's citizens and the values and interests of the EU and the United States. It also provides an avenue for better mutual understanding and closer interaction between Western countries and the new economic actors emerging in North Africa, at both the entrepreneurial and economic policy level.

Notes

1. See, for instance, Olivier Roy, *L'Islam mondialisé*, 2d ed. (Paris: Seuil, 2004); Myriam Catusse, *Le temps des entrepreneurs? Politique et transformations du capitalisme au Maroc* (Paris: Maisonneuve et Larose, 2008); Scott Greenwood, "Bad for Business? Entrepreneurs and Democracy in the Arab World," *Comparative Political Studies* 41, no. 6 (2008): 837–60.

2. Several observations made in these pages derive from interviews conducted by Gonzalo Escribano. For Algiers (February 2008 and May 2011), see Gonzalo Escribano, "Las relaciones económicas hispano-argelinas y el desarrollo de Argelia," in *¿Somos coherentes? España como agente de desarrollo internacional*, edited by Iliana Olivié (Madrid: Marcial Pons y Real Instituto Elcano, 2008), pp. 113–70. For Istanbul (February 2008), see Gonzalo Escribano, *Turquía y la internacionalización de la empresa española* (Madrid: Real Instituto Elcano de Relaciones internacionales-ICEX-ICO, 2008). For Rabat and Casablanca (December 2009), see Gonzalo Escribano, *Marruecos y la internacionalización de la empresa española* (Madrid: Real Instituto Elcano de Relaciones Internacionales-ICEX-ICO, 2010).

3. See, for instance, Sufyan Alissa, "The Political Economy of Reform in Egypt: Understanding the Role of Institutions," Carnegie Paper 5 (Washington: Carnegie Endowment for International Peace, October 2007); Myriam Catusse, "Ordonner, classer, penser la société: Les pays arabes au prisme de l'économie politique," in *La politique dans le monde arabe*, edited by Elizabeth Picard (Paris: A. Colin, 2006), pp. 215–38; Gonzalo Escribano and Alejandro Lorca, "Economic Reform in the Maghreb: From Stabilization to Modernization," in *North Africa: Politics, Region, and the Limits of Transformation*, edited by Yahia H. Zoubir and Haizam Amirah-Fernandez (London: Routledge, 2008), pp. 135–58; Greenwood, "Bad for Business ?"; Steven Heydemann (ed.), *Networks of Privilege in the Middle East: The Politics of Economic Reform Revisited* (London: Palgrave, 2004); Alan Richards and John Waterbury, *A Political Economy of the Middle East*, 3d ed. (Boulder: Westview Press, 2007).

4. Roberto Toscano, "A Premature Spring," July 1, 2011 (www.wilsoncenter.org/article/premature-spring [March 2012]); Maria Cristina Paciello, "Egypt's Last Decade: The Emergence of a Social Question," in *Transition to What: Egypt's Uncertain Departure from Neo-Authoritarianism*, edited by Daniela Pioppi and others (Washington: German Marshall Fund, May 2011), pp. 7–28.

5. Pierre Henry and Benedict de Saint-Laurent, "Appui aux PME pour investir en Méditerranée," Presentation at Colloque du CJD, Marseille, March 19, 2010 (www.animaweb.org/uploads/bases/document/Inv_AppuiPME_CJD_19-3-2010.pdf [March 2012]); Alissa, "Political Economy of Reform."

6. OECD, "Middle East and North Africa Initiative on Governance and Investment for Development" (www.oecd.org/pages/0,3417,en_34645207_34645466_1_1_1_1_1,00.html).

7. World Bank, *MENA Development Report: From Privilege to Competition; Unlocking Private-Led Growth in the Middle East and North Africa* (Washington: World Bank, 2009).

8. World Bank, *Morocco Investment Climate Assessment* (Washington: World Bank, 2008).

9. Interviews in Algiers. See also Forum Euroméditerranéen des Instituts de Sciences Économiques, *"Profil pays Algérie"* (Marseille, 2006), and Kristina Kausch, "Morocco: Negotiating Change with the *Makhzen,"* Working Paper 54 (Madrid: Fundación para las Relaciones Internacionales y el Diálogo Exterior [FRIDE], February 2008). These authors reach similar conclusions regarding the Moroccan business community's lack of interest in institutionalizing dialogue on economic reforms or accountability mechanisms.

10. Seymour M. Lipset, "Some Social Requisites of Democracy," *American Political Science Review* 53, no. 1 (1959): 69–105; Seymour M. Lipset, "The Social Requisites of Democracy Revisited," *American Sociological Review* 59, no.1 (1994): 1–22; Walt W. Rostow, *The Stages of Economic Growth: A Non-communist Manifesto* (Cambridge University Press, 1960).

11. Thomas Carothers, "How Democracies Emerge—The Sequencing Fallacy," *Journal of Democracy* 18, no. 1 (2007): 12–27, p. 15.

12. Mancur Olson, *The Logic of Collective Action: Public Goods and the Theory of Groups* (Harvard University Press, 1965).

13. Beatrice Hibou, "Discipline and Reform—I," *Sociétés politiques comparées* 22 (February 2010) (www.fasopo.org/reasopo/n22/art_bh.pdf [March 2012]).

14. See Richard Youngs, "Misunderstanding the Maladies of Liberal Democracy Promotion," Working Paper 106 (Madrid: FRIDE, January 2011), p. 7. Youngs argues that multinationals' actions regarding democratization vary enormously, but when referring to the Middle East, he notes their lack of commitment to democracy promotion.

15. Hibou, "Discipline and Reform—I," shows, however, some ambivalence about the role of the Tunisian informal sector, which acts as a driver of modernization while at the same time reinforcing the status quo.

16. Amr Hamzawy and Marina Ottaway, "Protest Movements and Political Change in the Arab World," *Carnegie Endowment Policy Outlook*, January 28, 2011 (www.carnegieendowment.org/files/OttawayHamzawy_Outlook_Jan11_ProtestMovements.pdf [March 2012]).

17. Asef Bayat, "A New Arab Street in Post-Islamist Times," *Foreign Policy: Middle East Channel*, January 26, 2011 (http://mideast.foreignpolicy.com/posts/2011/01/26/a_new_arab_street [March 2012]).

18. Holger Albrecht and Oliver Schlumberger, "'Waiting for Godot': Regime Change without Democratization in the Middle East," *International Political Science Review* 25, no. 4 (2004): 371–92.

19. In the original French, "par tous les coups de boutoir que le pouvoir a assénés à tous ces cadres ... en les appauvrissant ou en les récupérant." Nordine Grim, "Quels rôles pourraient jouer les classes moyennes algériennes?" *El Watan*, January 25, 2011.

20. Kristina Kausch, "Defenders in Retreat. Freedom of Association and Civil Society in Egypt," Working Paper 82 (Madrid: FRIDE, April 2009).

21. See Bayat, "A New Arab Street"; Hamzawy and Ottaway, "Protest Movements."

22. In the original French, "Comment une société éduquée, employée dans une économie diversifiée, composée d'une classe moyenne, peut-elle cohabiter durablement avec un régime policier aussi brutal que corrompu?" Luis Martinez, "La leçon tunisienne," *ISS Opinion*, January 2011 (www.iss.europa.eu/uploads/media/La_lecon_tunisienne.pdf [March 2012]).

23. Ellis Goldberg, "Egyptian Businessmen Eye the Future," *Foreign Policy: Middle East Channel*, February 10, 2011 (http://mideast.foreignpolicy.com/posts/2011/02/10/egyptian_businessmen_eye_the_future [March 2012]).

24. World Bank, *MENA Development Report*.

25. Ehaab Abdou and others, "How Can the U.S. and International Finance Institutions Best Engage Egypt's Civil Society?" Policy Paper 2011-06 (Brookings, June 2011) (www.brookings.edu/~/media/Files/rc/papers/2011/06_egypt_civil_society/06_egypt_civil_society.pdf [March 2012]).

26. Kausch, "Defenders in Retreat."

27. Ouled A. Belaïd, "Rapport sur l'économie sociale en Tunisie," in *L'Économie Sociale au Maghreb* (Madrid: Confederación Española de Economía Social [CEPES], 2010), pp. 171–218.

28. Touhami Abdelkhalek, "L'économie sociale au Maroc: État des lieux et perspectives d'avenir," in *L'Économie Sociale au Maghreb*, pp. 115–70.

29. Club de Madrid, *Strengthening Dialogue and Democratic Discourse through Freedom of Association in the Mediterranean and the Middle East Region* (2009), p.14.

30. Gonzalo Escribano, interviews in Algiers (November 2008 and May 2011), Istanbul (February 2008), Rabat and Casablanca (December 2009), and Tangier (June 2011).

31. See Timur Kuran, "The Scale of Entrepreneurship in Middle Eastern History: Inhibitive Roles of Islamic Institutions," in *The Invention of Enterprise: Entrepreneurship from Ancient Mesopotamia to Modern Times*, edited by David S. Lanes, Joel Mokyr, and William J. Baumol (Princeton University Press, 2010), pp. 62–87; Richards and Waterbury, *A Political Economy*.

32. Ann L. Saxenian, *Brain Circulation: How High-Skilled Immigration Makes Everyone Better Off* (Brookings, 2002) (www.brookings.edu/articles/2002/winter_immigration_saxenian.aspx [March 2012]).

33. Wai Mun Hong, Alejandro Lorca, and Eva Medina, "Population Growth and Economic Development in Southern Mediterranean Countries: A Comparative Focus," *Mediterranean Review* 3, no. 2 (2010): 41 –72.

34. Peggy Levitt, "Social Remittances: A Local-Level, Migration-Driven Form of Cultural Diffusion," *International Migration Review* 32, no. 124 (1998): 926–49.

35. Ibrahim El Nur, "Chasing Modernities: On the Mobility-Development Nexus— the Challenges of Harnessing Transformative Potential," CARIM Analytic and Synthetic Notes 2010/52 (San Domenico di Fiesole: Robert Schuman Center for Advanced Studies, 2010) (http://cadmus.eui.eu/bitstream/handle/1814/14407/CARIM_ASN_2010_52.pdf?sequence=1 [March 2012]).

36. Association Maroc Entrepreneurs, *Grande enquête Maroc entrepreneurs sur le thème du "Retour au Maroc*," December 2006 (www.marocentrepreneurs.com/file admin/files/autres/enquete/Enquete-Retour-Maroc-Entrepreneurs.pdf [May 2012]).

37. ANIMA Investment Network, "Diasporas: Gateways for Investment, Entrepreneurship and Innovation in the Mediterranean," Study 20, December 2010 (www.animaweb.org/uploads/bases/document/diasporas_ENG.pdf [May 2012]).

38. Roy, *L'Islam mondialisé.*

39. Emin B. Adas, "The Making of Entrepreneurial Islam and the Islamic Spirit of Capitalism," *Journal for Cultural Research* 10, no. 2 (2006): 113–37.

40. When referring to the EU, we include both the European institutions and the policies that member states put before the EU to be implemented at the EU level.

41. See European Commission and High Representative of the Union for Foreign Affairs and Security Policy, *A Partnership for Democracy and Shared Prosperity with the Southern Mediterranean*, March 8, 2011 (http://eeas.europa.eu/euromed/docs/com 2011_200_en.pdf [March 2012]); European Commission, *A New Response to a Changing Neighbourhood*, May 25, 2011 (http://ec.europa.eu/world/enp/pdf/com_11_303_en.pdf [March 2012]).

42. Gonzalo Escribano and Alejandro Lorca, "The Mediterranean Union: A Union in Search of a Project," Working Paper 13 (Madrid: Real Instituto Elcano, 2008).

43. Abdou and others, "How Can the U.S.?"

44. World Bank, "MENA Facing Challenges and Opportunities," World Bank Middle East and North Africa Region Regional Economic Update (Washington, May 2011) (http://siteresources.worldbank.org/MENAEXT/Resources/EDP_MNA_2011.pdf [March 2012]).

45. Youngs, "Misunderstanding," p. 6.

46. Roberto Aliboni, "The Mediterranean and the Middle East: Narrowing Gaps in Transatlantic Perspective," Mediterranean Paper (Washington: German Marshall Fund, March 2010) (www.iai.it/pdf/mediterraneo/GMF-IAI/Mediterranean-paper_01.pdf [March 2012]).

CAROLINE FREUND *and* CARLOS A. PRIMO BRAGA

6

The Economics of Arab Transitions

Lack of economic freedom in the southern Mediterranean countries played an important role in the revolutions of 2011. At the onset of the Arab Spring, the economies were characterized by high unemployment, especially among youth and women; large public sectors; bloated subsidies on food and fuel; and a weak investment climate. While the revolutions were primarily motivated by a demand for dignity, voice, and government accountability, the absence of economic opportunity fueled the population's frustration with the long-standing political systems.

The Middle East and North Africa (MENA) countries now face serious short-term challenges because of the uncertainty, business disruptions, and in some countries security concerns brought about as a result of change. Growth declined sharply in Egypt, Libya, and Tunisia, while unemployment soared and fiscal expenditures expanded. In the short run, the most urgent need is a return to economic and political stability and to growth. But the long-run prospects are now better, assuming that new governments will answer the public's demand for better governance.

This chapter explores the social compact before the Arab Spring, the ensuing economic challenges, and the key areas for change in the long run. We also examine the history of relations in trade and foreign direct investment between Europe and the MENA countries (with emphasis on the North African countries) in order to explore ways that outsiders can contribute to economic growth and inclusive development through economic integration.[1]

Before the Spring

Trends in democracy indexes show that the MENA region was trailing all other regions by a large margin before 2011. Figure 6-1 shows a simple average of an index of democracy across regions, with 0 being autocracy and 10 being democracy.[2] Gains made in Latin America in the 1980s and in Africa, Asia, and Eastern Europe later on were notably absent in the region. MENA regimes made only small steps at opening up their political systems. For example, from 1988 to 1992, Jordan improved by two points according to this index, with the legalization of political parties. It failed to evolve further, however, as the executive branch of government retained power over the legislature. As of 2010 only Lebanon in the MENA region was rated as a democracy.

To promote stability and minimize political dissent, governments in the region provided extensive benefits to the population. These included large food and fuel subsidies, government jobs, and in some cases housing and cash transfers. This social compact, however, was not sustainable, as economies stagnated and governments did not have the necessary revenues to employ a growing youth population in the civil service. The recent spikes in global food prices added pressure, as subsidies could no longer keep domestic prices stable.[3]

The fiscal cost of subsidies has been and continues to be sizeable in many countries in the region. For example, in 2009 Algeria spent 13.5 percent of GDP on food and fuel subsidies; Egypt, over 8 percent, and Tunisia and Morocco, about 2 to 3 percent—and all of these countries have increased benefits since the revolutions began. While the population views these subsidies as essential, the reality is that in addition to the large budgetary expenditures, which could have been allocated to support health, education, or infrastructure instead, subsidies are not an efficient way of providing benefits. Subsidies distort prices, and hence too much of the subsidized good is used by consumers and producers because it is relatively cheap. Despite being perceived as equalizing, subsidies actually accrue largely to the wealthy who spend a greater absolute amount on most goods. In addition, there is often leakage through smuggling to neighboring nations. Fuel subsidies are especially egregious because they encourage excessive fuel consumption, which is bad for the environment and distorts the critical energy market. They also push resources into production of capital-intensive goods, a major distortion in labor-rich countries. The size and expansion of subsidies, especially for fuel and energy, pose a complex problem. On the one hand, they are demanded by the majority of

Figure 6-1. *Democracy and Autocracy across Regions, 1960–2011*

Polity score (index of democracy)

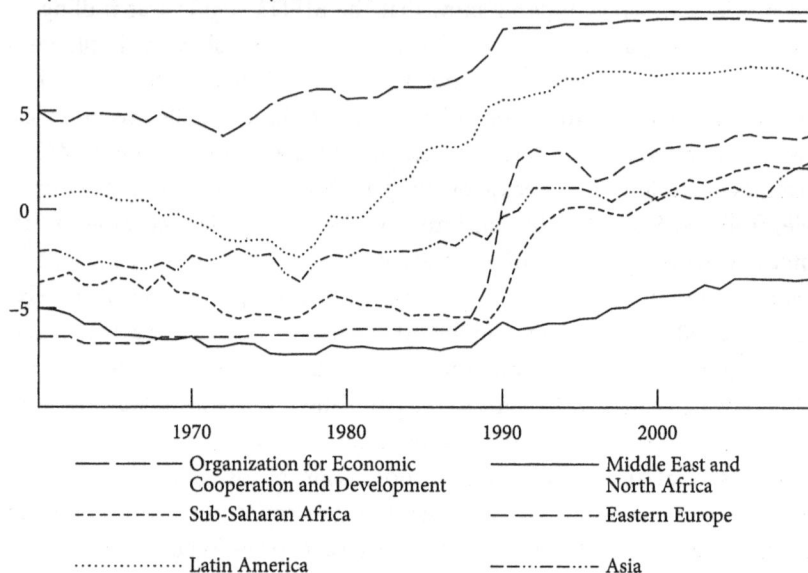

Source: Simple averages of polity score from Polity IV database (user's manual available at www.systemicpeace.org/inscr/p4manualv2010.pdf). The index is based on the difference between the democracy score and the autocracy score. According to the polity index, –10 to 0 are autocracies, where a more negative score represents a more authoritarian regime, and 0 to 10 are democracies, where a higher score represents a more democratic regime.

the population that has become accustomed to receiving them. On the other hand, they are very costly and create severe economic distortions.

In addition to subsidies, MENA governments also have used public sector jobs to expand or maintain employment in the past. As a result, the government services sector's share of total employment in a typical North African country tends to be relatively large. For example, government services in Algeria employ about 30 percent of the active workforce, 25 percent in Egypt, and 14 percent in Morocco. Only Morocco compares favorably with major developing economies such as Brazil (18 percent), Malaysia (18 percent), Turkey (16 percent), and Indonesia (9 percent).[4] Moreover, the figures for the MENA region are an underestimate, as they do not include workers in state-owned enterprises. This situation also burdens the state with a high wage bill, which for the MENA region is 8.5 percent of GDP, higher than all in other developing regions.[5]

The large government sector is intricately linked to the high unemployment rate that has characterized many MENA countries. It is in part a response: as jobs have been hard to find in many countries, the public sector expanded to fill the gap. As it expanded, it distorted the labor market, with entrants queuing for relatively "good" government jobs, in turn pushing the wage bill up. An additional issue is that with a goal of securing a public sector job, people are often receiving the wrong type of training for a productive private sector. So the long-term consequence has been a significant misallocation of resources. Moreover, over time the government expansion became fiscally unsustainable in the resource-poor countries, and the lack of jobs became one of the primary complaints of the growing population.[6]

Unemployment rates in North Africa have been especially high for young people, with about one-quarter of those seeking work unemployed in recent years. Youth unemployment is typically higher than overall unemployment, as it includes first-time job searches among new entrants to the labor force (figure 6-2). This is magnified in countries with rapidly growing populations because of the ever-increasing number of entrants competing for jobs each year. Female unemployment has also been high and labor force participation has been very low, as compared with countries of a similar income level from other regions (see figures 6-2 and 6-3). A forthcoming World Bank report on gender inequality in the region attributes this to social norms and slow economic growth.[7]

Proximate Factors

The old social compact was one of high government spending on public sector jobs and generous subsidies in exchange for acquiescence to autocratic regimes and limited government accountability. But as populations grew, these policies contributed to high structural unemployment and slow economic growth. Moreover, because of strong central control by the government and limited accountability, efforts to stimulate the private sector encouraged the development of a business community that was allied with the government; as a consequence, corruption became widespread and concerns about unfair practices and favoritism (typical attributes of "crony" capitalism) increased over time.

An additional contributing factor to political unrest was the aforementioned spike in global food prices, which surged nearly 50 percent from June 2010 to February 2011. The MENA region is the largest importer of wheat in

Figure 6-2. *Unemployment by Group across Regions, Decadal Average, 1999–2008*

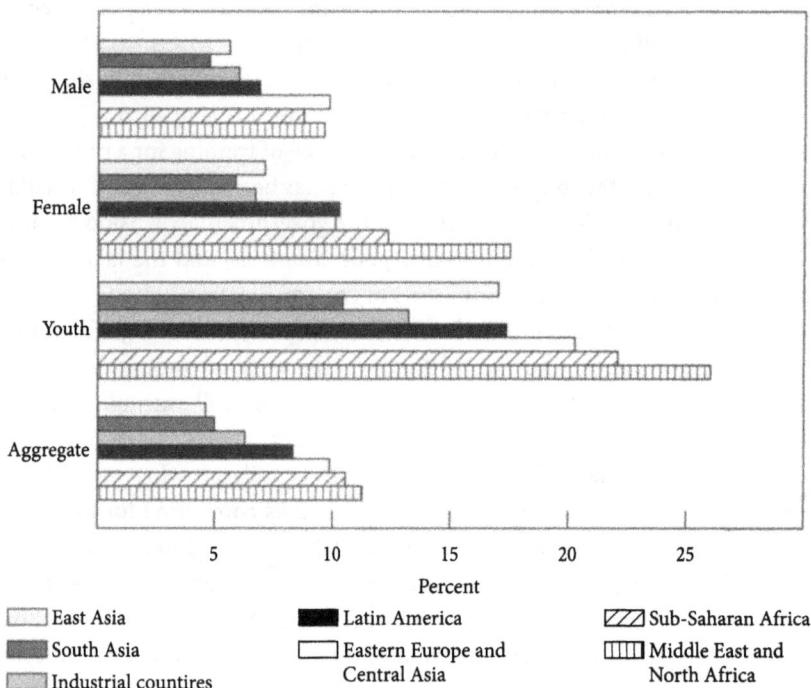

Source: World Bank, World Development Indicators.

the world. The importance of wheat is illustrated by the Arabic word for bread in Egypt—*aish*—which is also the world for life. Despite governmental subsidies, evidence shows a sizable pass-through to domestic prices, especially in Egypt where the food consumer price index rose 18 percent over this period.[8] This had a significant impact on the poorest segments of societies in the region.

Lack of jobs, in turn, has been the major concern facing the young population. That the private sector has failed to thrive and grow jobs is related to the large government sector, as noted above, but is also a result of a weak business climate. Enterprise surveys show that firms in the Middle East and North Africa list corruption and tax rates as their top two concerns. In addition, these surveys show that firms are not treated uniformly. There is wide variation in the time it takes firms to accomplish regulatory tasks. This has reinforced a type of crony capitalism where connected firms are favored by the

Figure 6-3. *Labor Force Participation in the Middle East and North Africa, Decadal Average, 1999–2008*

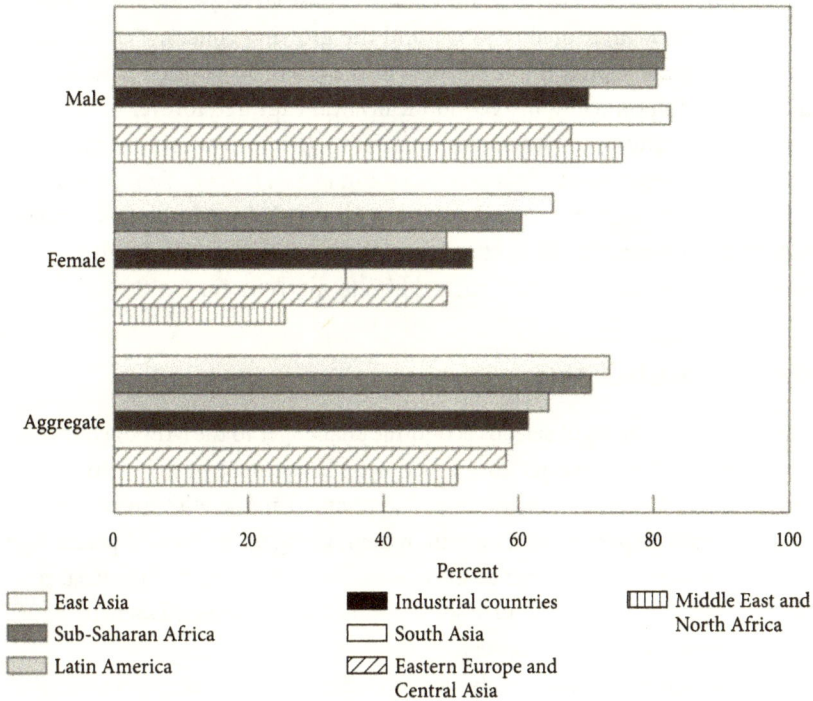

Source: World Bank, World Development Indicators.

bureaucracy, making it difficult for new firms to survive and expand. Evidence of this shows up in the median age of firms, which in the Middle East and North Africa is nearly twice that of firms in East Asia and Eastern Europe.[9] In most economies young firms account for a large share of job growth, but in MENA countries they have been stifled by favoritism toward older, connected firms. Adding to the loss of faith in business, a number of privatizations over the last decade were perceived as being affected by corrupt practices, with firms often sold at less than market value to friends of the ruling regime.

Finally, the global economy likely played a role in determining the timing of the revolutions. With the 2008–09 financial crisis, global growth slowed sharply, and while the MENA region did better than much of the rest of the world—because these countries were not as integrated into the global system—there were still repercussions.

In short, in addition to political concerns about voice and human rights, economics played a role in heightening the frustration of the population, and people eventually rejected a continuation of past failed policies. The lack of jobs—especially high-quality jobs—and the growing concerns about crony capitalism underscored the unfairness also evident in politics. This lack of freedom, both politically and economically, was captured forever in the catalyst of the revolutions: Mohamed Bouazizi's self-immolation in response to government harassment of his produce stand in Sidi Bouzid, Tunisia. According to reports from family members, it was economic frustration that brought him to the governor's office, after his wares were confiscated, but it was the humiliation by the police that pushed him to martyrdom.

Short-Term Challenges

The revolutions brought serious economic challenges to the MENA countries. The unrest and uncertainty abruptly slowed investment in the region. GDP growth for 2011 came in near zero in Egypt and Tunisia, with tourism dropping by about 40 percent and unemployment going up by about 3 percentage points. The economic impact in Libya was the most severe as industrial production came to a near halt during the conflict, and continued security issues have hindered restrained recovery.

The growth slowdown has also led to declining government revenues and additional budgetary problems. As noted above, the recent uprisings resulted in expanded spending on subsidies and government wages. In all of the North African countries, some combination of increased food and fuel subsidies, higher public sector salaries, and more civil service jobs was instituted after the uprisings began. Egypt and Tunisia significantly expanded their public sectors: the former regularized about 450,000 temporary government contractors, and the latter recruited 20,000 new civil servants; both countries increased existing subsidies.[10] The idea behind this spending is to ease difficult times while in some countries also placating a population that is demanding more political and economic freedom. The immediate problem is the high fiscal cost of the programs, and over time a further issue arises as these decisions become difficult to reverse. Firing civil servants, lowering their wages, and removing subsidies are all deeply unpopular.

The relatively smooth elections in Tunisia and the ongoing political process in Egypt have helped alleviate some of the uncertainty. But investors are still primarily waiting on the sidelines to see how the new governments will function before investing further.[11] Research on political transitions shows that private investment typically takes longer to resume than does income growth.[12]

In the short run, political and economic stability as well as security are key concerns in the transition countries. Showing a clear move away from past policies toward more transparency and accountability in governance is also important. Economic growth may wane, but strong political achievements can go a long way toward maintaining support for the revolutions.

One thing that remains unclear in the aftermath of the regime changes, however, is the economic direction that the new governments will take, either toward a more market-driven economy or a more state-driven capitalism. In Egypt there have been a number of popular renationalizations of companies that were privatized by the Mubarak regime. At the same time, the Freedom and Justice Party, the big winner in the 2011–12 Egyptian parliamentary election, has embraced privatization in its economic platform. It remains to be seen how these contrasting trends will play out.

Long-term Challenges

In the medium to long term, three related economic challenges stand out: improving governance, including voice and accountability, service delivery, and the regulatory environment; stimulating the private sector to grow and create jobs for the large and youthful population; and increasing inclusion across economic lines and for women and minorities.

Governance is what the revolutions were about, but better governance also leads to higher economic growth, as it provides the foundation for efficient resource allocation. The political transitions in Tunisia and Egypt, as well as promises of deep reform by incumbents in some of the other countries, have increased the likelihood of comprehensive institutional and regulatory reforms. A large body of work shows that improvements in rule of law have sizable positive economic returns. For example, there is evidence that differences in the quality of institutions are the main reason for differences in prosperity across countries.[13] Related to the institutional argument is the concept that excessive regulation serves to protect rents and guide resources to special interests. Indeed, research shows that more burdensome regulatory systems lead to more corruption and lower income.[14] If the MENA countries take seriously their populations' demands for more accountable and transparent governance, and change their structures to promote competition and a level playing field, this will stimulate robust growth in the region and generate many more opportunities for the young population over the medium to long term.

It is worth noting that the MENA region's growth performance was respectable in the early 2000s, but it just was not good enough. Growth averaged around 5 percent and unemployment around 10 percent. Contrast that with China, which recorded growth of 10 percent and unemployment below 5 percent in the same period. Growth and private sector development are key to meeting the employment challenges of the region. In many ways this is the most standard of the three challenges, but it still remains elusive in many countries and is complicated by the role of the private sector in the past. Corruption and crony capitalism have led to a strong distrust of the private sector as a job creator.

Especially important in this context is the business climate. Many MENA countries rank quite low on ease of doing business according to the Doing Business indicators, including Algeria at 148, Egypt at 110, and Morocco at 94.[15] Tunisia, by contrast, has improved significantly in this area and now ranks 46, between countries such as Spain and Slovakia. But equally important to the laws on the books is their fair implementation. As World Bank research shows, rules are not uniformly applied, so what is on the books does not accurately reflect the regulations that countries enforce.[16]

The real exchange rate is an additional factor affecting growth. Nearly all of the MENA countries have fixed exchange rates, either tied to the dollar or to a composite, typically with a large weight on the euro. The problem is that in many countries exchange rates have become overvalued, which reduces competitiveness and growth prospects. Nabli and Veganzones-Varoudakis show that MENA currencies in a number of countries were characterized by significant overvaluation during the 1970s and 1980s, which retarded diversification and export growth.[17] Some countries in the region adopted more flexibility in the 1990s, which improved competitiveness, but in others significant overvaluation persists, as evidenced by large trade deficits and limited diversification.

Improving economic inclusion is also a key economic challenge. While income inequality in the MENA region is not nearly as high as that in Latin America and Eastern Europe, there appears to be a large and seemingly growing inequality of opportunity. For instance, a study using household data from Egypt finds that despite education becoming more equalized across socioeconomic groups over the last thirty years, young men have become less socially mobile in terms of the job they obtain. Specifically, twenty-eight-year-old men whose fathers did not have white collar jobs are less likely to have a white collar job today than same-age men in a similar situation in the 1980s.[18] What these results show is that the type of work that people are doing now is more connected to their social strata than it was in the past.

Exclusion is also highlighted in the large divide between the formal and informal sector, and in the differences in labor participation and employment between men and women and the young and old. The informal sector employs two-thirds of workers in the region and accounts for one-third of GDP, yet these workers lack job security and social protection.[19] While it is important that this sector be unrestricted because it is an important employer, it would be better if the business climate were such that more firms could be formalized. This would be fostered by lower taxes, leaner regulatory environments, and better access to finance.

Despite improvements in female-versus-male education levels, such that the MENA countries match or exceed others with similar income, employment for women has failed to materialize. As previously pointed out, the MENA region has the lowest female labor participation rate (24 percent as a whole and about 30 percent in Egypt and Tunisia and 15 percent in Morocco) and the highest level of female unemployment in the world, at nearly 40 percent.[20] Improving opportunities for women will be fundamental to ensuring inclusive growth. Active labor market policies, such as subsidies and training that encourage the hiring of women, may play a role in this process.

Against this background, it is worth analyzing what has been the international economic response to the challenges raised by the Arab Spring. The next section focuses, in particular, on the response of European countries and institutions.

International Response

The initial reaction from major economic partners (particularly EU countries and the United States) to the Arab Spring could be summarized by one word: surprise. There were many analyses of the existing economic shortcomings in MENA countries, including detailed evaluations of how jobs lagged population growth and how inefficient are existing social programs. But the conventional wisdom in the West focused mainly on the unfulfilled economic promise of the region rather than on the role of economic imbalances as something that could help spark dramatic political change, such as the three regime changes and two armed conflicts ushered in by the Arab Spring in 2011.

European countries, in view of their long-standing economic and strategic relations with the region, reacted to the upheavals in the MENA region by becoming the main advocates of a new partnership (the Deauville Partnership), framed in the context of the G-8 (which was led by France in 2011). Before discussing the prospects for international responses to foster positive economic change in the region, this section briefly reviews the patterns of international economic relations with MENA countries since the 1990s.

Trade and Foreign Direct Investment Trends

Table 6-1 summarizes the trends in international trade for MENA countries. It illustrates the different patterns of trade displayed by resource-rich and resource-poor countries. The first group is composed of countries for which hydrocarbon (oil and natural gas) exports represent, on average, often more than 80 percent of total exports. These countries typically achieved higher rates of growth (although with higher volatility) in the 2000–10 period.[21] Resource-poor countries, in turn, although displaying lower levels of economic growth, showed a more diversified export profile and were less affected by economic volatility. Among resource-poor MENA countries, Europe remains a major export destination (in some cases accounting for more than 60 percent of total exports).

The region has become much more open and integrated with the world economy over the last three decades, as illustrated by the figures in table 6-2. Trade barriers have declined, reflecting unilateral liberalization, preferential trade agreements, and in a few cases (Jordan, Oman, and Saudi Arabia) the outcome of World Trade Organization accession negotiations. Non-oil export growth, however, has lagged behind the performance of most other developing regions. Moreover, the impact of EU-driven preferential liberalization, in the context of the bilateral free trade agreements (FTAs) associated with the Barcelona Process (see below), was limited. Actually, the EU share in total exports for several countries of the region has declined since1995 (see table 6-1).

With respect to foreign direct investment (FDI), traditionally the bulk of these flows have been directed to high-income, resource-rich countries such as Saudi Arabia, Qatar, and the United Arab Emirates. Developing resource-poor countries (such as Egypt, Jordan, Morocco, and Tunisia), however, witnessed a significant increase in FDI inflows in the first years of the new millennium. The global financial crisis reversed this trend, and the political disturbances of 2010–11 contributed to additional declines in FDI inflows. Although in most MENA countries intra-MENA investments are responsible

Table 6-1. *Exports from MENA Countries, Various Years, 1995–2010*[a]

Units as indicated

Countries	1995	2000	2005	2006	2007	2008	2009	2010
Resource-rich countries								
Algeria								
Total exports (FOB, in US$ billion)	9.4	21.9	46.0	54.5	59.2	79.3	45.2	57.1
Manufacture (percent of exported goods)	3.7	2.3	1.3	1.2	1.5	1.6	1.6	1.8
Fuel (percent of exported goods)	94.6	97.2	98.0	97.9	97.8	97.6	97.7	97.3
Goods exported to EU (percent of exported goods)	66.5	63.4	55.6	52.6	44.3	52.0	51.3	49.1
Bahrain								
Total exports (FOB, in US$ billion)	4.2	7.7	15.9	20.0	24.4	29.1	23.2	29.8
Manufacture (percent of exported goods)	18.1	9.8	6.1	5.2	8.0	11.8	12.5	21.9
Fuel (percent of exported goods)	53.1	n.a.	78.2	80.6	80.8	69.1	68.8	n.a.
Goods exported to EU (percent of exported goods)	3.1	4.9	3.9	3.2	4.5	4.1	2.3	2.4
Iran, Islamic Republic of								
Total exports (FOB, in US$ billion)	18.4	27.0	55.2	75.8	89.4	119.5	74.2	99.3
Manufacture (percent of exported goods)	n.a.	7.1	8.8	10.1	n.a.	n.a.	n.a.	15.6
Fuel (percent of exported goods)	n.a.	88.7	82.6	82.8	n.a.	n.a.	n.a.	70.8
Goods exported to EU (percent of exported goods)	42.2	26.3	23.6	21.7	19.8	17.9	16.2	17.3
Iraq								
Total exports (FOB, in US$ billion)	0.4	14.9	17.6	27.5	35.2	56.8	36.2	46.6
Manufacture (percent of exported goods)	n.a.	0.4	0.2	0.2	0.1	0.0	0.2	n.a.
Fuel (percent of exported goods)	n.a.	97.1	96.4	99.6	99.7	33.8	98.6	n.a.
Goods exported to EU (percent of exported goods)	0.3	33.2	22.9	21.0	24.4	21.9	22.5	17.3

(continued)

Table 6-1. *Exports from MENA Countries, Various Years, 1995–2010*[a] (Continued)
Units as indicated

Countries	1995	2000	2005	2006	2007	2008	2009	2010
Kuwait								
Total exports (FOB, in US$ billion)	12.9	18.8	35.9	46.9	54.2	78.4	47.4	61.4
Manufacture (percent of exported goods)	4.7	4.5	n.a.	3.2	3.3	3.2	6.2	n.a.
Fuel (percent of exported goods)	94.7	94.3	n.a.	96.5	96.3	96.5	93.2	n.a.
Goods exported to EU (percent of exported goods)	0.2	13.8	10.2	9.7	9.6	9.0	7.6	6.0
Oman								
Total exports (FOB, in US$ billion)	6.0	10.7	18.5	21.5	23.5	35.1	23.9	32.6
Manufacture (percent of exported goods)	13.9	12.4	4.7	5.7	7.5	7.3	10.3	12.5
Fuel (percent of exported goods)	78.7	82.5	91.8	91.4	89.1	86.4	79.0	81.3
Goods exported to EU (percent of exported goods)	0.9	1.3	2.5	1.4	2.5	1.3	2.8	1.6
Qatar								
Total exports (FOB, in US$ billion)	3.7	11.6	25.3	33.6	41.5	55.7	46.3	67.3
Manufacture (percent of exported goods)	17.5	8.6	5.6	7.0	8.5	4.5	5.3	n.a.
Fuel (percent of exported goods)	82.0	91.2	85.1	90.9	90.7	93.8	72.8	n.a.
Goods exported to EU (percent of exported goods)	1.3	1.0	2.0	3.6	4.5	5.5	8.7	13.5
Saudi Arabia								
Total exports (FOB, in US$ billion)	50.0	74.8	154.8	196.1	209.3	304.5	172.8	232.4
Manufacture (percent of exported goods)	10.2	7.2	8.2	8.0	8.7	6.0	8.1	11.2
Fuel (percent of exported goods)	88.5	92.1	90.9	91.0	90.1	91.2	87.6	87.5
Goods exported to EU (percent of exported goods)	20.4	17.7	16.3	13.8	11.1	9.7	8.6	8.2

Syrian Arab Republic								
Total exports (FOB, in US$ billion)	4.0	4.8	9.8	11.4	12.9	16.3	11.4	15.6
Manufacture (percent of exported goods)	17.4	7.8	13.8	32.0	34.8	33.0	n.a.	n.a.
Fuel (percent of exported goods)	62.5	76.4	67.7	40.4	41.1	38.6	n.a.	n.a.
Goods exported to EU (percent of exported goods)	60.8	62.8	34.0	34.9	32.9	29.6	26.1	27.5
United Arab Emirates								
Total exports (FOB, in US$ billion)	24.1	40.8	96.3	118.6	136.2	194.6	121.6	175.4
Manufacture (percent of exported goods)	n.a.	2.3	2.6	n.a.	3.1	4.0	n.a.	n.a.
Fuel (percent of exported goods)	n.a.	93.8	57.8	n.a.	65.3	64.8	n.a.	n.a.
Goods exported to EU (percent of exported goods)	4.0	5.1	10.8	5.5	6.0	4.1	3.9	3.4
Yemen								
Total exports (FOB, in US$ billion)	1.9	4.1	5.6	6.7	6.8	9.5	4.9	8.1
Manufacture (percent of exported goods)	0.6	0.3	1.6	1.1	3.0	2.1	1.7	n.a.
Fuel (percent of exported goods)	95.3	96.9	93.8	94.4	91.2	92.4	92.2	n.a.
Goods exported to EU (percent of exported goods)	1.1	1.2	0.9	2.3	4.0	1.0	0.8	4.0
Resource-poor countries								
Egypt, Arab Republic of								
Total exports (FOB, in US$ billion)	3.4	6.4	10.6	13.7	16.2	26.2	24.1	26.6
Manufacture (percent of exported goods)	40.4	38.4	23.6	21.2	18.8	36.5	43.8	43.4
Fuel (percent of exported goods)	37.2	41.9	51.3	56.4	52.5	44.4	28.9	29.8
Goods exported to EU (percent of exported goods)	48.1	48.1	34.1	33.9	29.1	35.4	28.2	30.2
Jordan								
Total exports (FOB, in US$ billion)	1.4	1.3	4.3	5.2	5.5	6.2	5.0	5.9
Manufacture (percent of exported goods)	48.7	69.0	69.7	71.2	76.3	75.4	73.3	73.6
Fuel (percent of exported goods)	0.0	0.0	0.2	1.0	0.8	0.2	0.6	1.1
Goods exported to EU (percent of exported goods)	7.2	4.3	3.6	3.3	3.3	4.1	3.0	3.7

(continued)

Table 6-1. *Exports from MENA Countries, Various Years, 1995–2010*[a] (Continued)
Units as indicated

Countries	1995	2000	2005	2006	2007	2008	2009	2010
Lebanon								
Total exports (FOB, in US$ billion)	0.7	0.7	2.2	2.5	3.3	4.0	3.3	3.9
Manufacture (percent of exported goods)	n.a.	70.7	69.3	69.1	67.0	71.5	72.5	63.6
Fuel (percent of exported goods)	n.a.	0.2	0.4	0.4	0.2	0.4	0.5	0.2
Goods exported to EU (percent of exported goods)	29.2	23.2	11.4	10.4	11.8	11.9	9.9	9.4
Morocco								
Total exports (FOB, in US$ billion)	5.0	7.4	10.6	12.3	14.5	18.9	13.5	16.6
Manufacture (percent of exported goods)	51.4	64.1	65.8	67.8	66.8	63.9	64.7	66.3
Fuel (percent of exported goods)	2.2	3.7	2.4	1.9	2.3	2.2	2.3	1.1
Goods exported to EU (percent of exported goods)	59.9	75.7	71.8	74.0	73.4	60.5	64.2	58.9
Tunisia								
Total exports (FOB, in US$ billion)	5.8	5.8	10.1	11.4	14.8	18.6	14.0	15.2
Manufacture (percent of exported goods)	79.4	77.0	74.9	73.3	69.8	71.6	75.4	76.0
Fuel (percent of exported goods)	8.5	12.1	13.0	13.0	16.2	17.3	13.6	14.2
Goods exported to EU (percent of exported goods)	80.3	80.3	83.2	79.3	81.2	74.2	76.2	74.1

Sources: World Bank and International Monetary Fund databases.
a. FOB = Freight on board; n.a. = Not available.

for most of the FDI stock, Egypt, Tunisia, and particularly Morocco are outliers, with European companies controlling between 49 and 93 percent of their FDI stock.[22]

As the trade and FDI numbers illustrate, the economic links to Europe are particularly strong in the case of Algeria, Egypt, Morocco, and Tunisia. Moreover, the tourism industry (which accounts for more than 10 percent of employment in Egypt, Morocco, and Tunisia) is also significantly driven by European demand.

Economic Agreements

The modern history of trade and related economic agreements between MENA countries and Europe goes back several decades. The first generation of trade agreements focusing on exports of some manufactured products from selected MENA countries to the EU was signed in the 1960s. In 1972 the European Commission launched the Global Mediterranean Policy, which resulted in a series of cooperation agreements involving preferential access for industrial and agricultural products, although the latter remained constrained by trade restrictions associated with the Common Agricultural Policy. The cooperation agreements encompassed not only MENA countries (Morocco, Algeria, Libya, Tunisia, Egypt, Jordan, Lebanon, and Syria) but also Israel, Turkey, Cyprus, Malta, and the former Yugoslavia.[23] These agreements were further modified over the years—reflecting the EU's southern enlargement in 1986—but continued to entail unilateral tariff reductions from the EU to partner countries (the exception being Israel, which negotiated reciprocal concessions) to the extent that by 1993 the main market access restrictions to the European markets were the existing nontariff barriers under the Common Agricultural Policy.

By 1995, however, EU and MENA countries decided to pursue an even more ambitious integration process, launching the Euro-Mediterranean Partnership, often referred to as the Barcelona Process (as it was launched at the Euro-Mediterranean Conference of Ministers of Foreign Affairs held in Barcelona, November 1995).[24] It represented a change in strategy reflecting not only growing concerns from Mediterranean countries about preference erosion in view of new economic agreements between the EU and Eastern European countries, but also the objective of pursuing deeper market integration beyond trade. The Barcelona Process envisaged further cooperation in three main areas: political and security relations, economic and financial agreements, and social and cultural partnerships. The ultimate goal on the economic front was the creation

Table 6-2. *MENA Trade Indicators, Various Years, 1995–2010*[a]

	1995		2000		2005	
Countries	*Exports + imports of goods/ GDP*	*Exports of goods/ GDP*	*Exports + imports of goods/ GDP*	*Exports of goods/ GDP*	*Exports + imports of goods/ GDP*	*Exports of goods/ GDP*
Resource-rich countries						
Algeria	48.7	24.6	56.9	40.2	64.8	45.0
Bahrain	133.8	70.3	135.8	77.7	145.9	76.1
Iran, Islamic Republic of	35.5	20.2	42.1	28.4	50.1	29.3
Iraq	n.a.	n.a.	131.4	79.7	150.8	75.7
Kuwait	75.7	47.0	70.5	51.5	75.1	55.5
Oman	75.7	44.0	82.8	57.0	89.5	60.5
Qatar	86.6	44.9	83.6	65.3	83.2	59.9
Saudi Arabia	54.8	35.1	57.2	41.2	76.1	57.3
Syrian Arab Republic	72.6	31.3	43.7	24.0	67.8	30.2
United Arab Emirates	79.3	43.1	81.3	47.8	111.8	64.9
Yemen	82.8	45.7	66.5	42.3	65.6	33.5
Resource-poor countries						
Egypt, Arab Republic of	25.3	5.7	19.9	5.3	39.4	14.4
Jordan	81.2	26.3	76.7	22.4	117.6	34.2
Lebanon	69.1	7.0	40.2	4.1	54.8	10.7
Morocco	51.2	20.9	51.2	20.1	53.7	18.8
Tunisia	74.2	30.4	67.1	27.2	73.3	32.5

Source: See table 6-1.
a. n.a. = Not available.

of a Euro-Mediterranean Free Trade Area by 2010. The main novelty in this context was the idea of replacing the existing system of nonreciprocal preferences with bilateral free trade agreements. These trade agreements were supported by grants to projects under the Mesures d'Accompagnement program and by loans from the European Investment Bank. Moreover, the Euro-Mediterranean Association Agreements (EMAAs; the bilateral FTAs) were expected to be complemented by intra-MENA trade liberalization.

The implementation of the Barcelona Process proceeded slowly, with the first EMAAs being signed in 1995–96, but entry into force in most cases only occurred four to five years later. In the case of EU candidate countries (Cyprus, Malta, and Turkey), special agreements entailing a customs union with the EU were adopted, paving the way for the EU enlargement that brought Cyprus and Malta into the EU in 2004. Initiatives to promote intra-MENA trade lib-

2006		2007		2008		2009		2010	
Exports + imports of goods/ GDP	Exports of goods/ GDP	Exports + imports of goods/ GDP	Exports of goods/ GDP	Exports + imports of goods/ GDP	Exports of goods/ GDP	Exports + imports of goods/ GDP	Exports of goods/ GDP	Exports + imports of goods/ GDP	Exports of goods/ GDP
64.9	46.6	64.6	44.3	69.5	46.4	61.2	32.7	60	35.2
143.3	76.9	136.0	73.8	128.4	79.1	94.1	57.7	n.a.	n.a.
52.8	34.6	46.7	31.0	50.6	33.6	39.2	23.8	n.a.	n.a.
111.5	65.1	110.2	72.4	108.9	70.8	121.1	64.3	116	64.3
72.1	55.2	73.3	54.6	75.5	58.8	66.0	47.4	n.a.	n.a.
88.6	58.6	97.2	58.9	100.5	62.3	97.3	59.0	n.a.	n.a.
83.5	56.3	81.1	52.0	76.3	51.1	67.1	41.7	n.a.	n.a.
78.8	59.3	84.1	60.6	90.0	65.8	77.2	51.6	79.8	57.4
67.2	32.8	64.8	28.6	63.7	29.3	48.5	20.1	51.4	22.8
110.6	65.5	120.5	69.2	132.2	76.0	123.9	68.4	127.7	79.3
66.7	34.9	68.4	29.1	67.4	28.2	58.6	23.7	58.8	27.8
41.0	15.6	43.2	14.7	45.8	16.1	36.0	12.2	36.3	12.1
107.1	33.3	109.2	32.2	109.9	35.0	82.1	25.4	81.3	25.5
55.5	12.5	63.2	14.3	70.5	14.8	59.4	12.0	60.2	12.9
55.9	19.4	62.9	20.4	70.6	22.9	51.6	15.5	58.2	19.4
77.7	34.0	88.0	39.0	97.9	43.0	77.1	33.2	87.3	37.1

eralization, in turn, proceeded in an ad hoc manner until the signature of the Agadir Agreement (encompassing Egypt, Jordan, Morocco, and Tunisia) in 2004. Its implementation, however, was also delayed by a slow ratification process. In 2008 the Barcelona Process was revamped with the creation of the Union for the Mediterranean, which in addition to continuing the pursuit of the FTA objective launched a series of projects in areas such as environment, energy, health, migration, and culture.

There is an extensive literature on the implications of the EMAAs for trade among the EU and MENA countries.[25] Most of the analyses suggest that the impact of the Barcelona Process has been modest in terms of expanding trade opportunities for MENA countries. Actually, non-oil exports from MENA countries expanded at a slower pace than exports from other regions to the EU during the first ten years after the launch of the process. This is often attributed to the slow pace of implementation of the EMAAs, not to mention the erosion of preferences associated with evolving nondiscriminatory (most favored nation) trade liberalization in the EU. It is important, however, to recognize that the additional liberalization fostered by these agreements was limited; for example, access to EU markets remained restricted in the case of agricultural products, and previous cooperation agreements had already liberalized access to most industrial exports. Moreover, the "hub-and-spoke" format of the EMAAs (with the EU as the hub for the series of bilateral FTAs), the lack of progress in intra-MENA trade liberalization, and the effects of restrictive rules of origin across overlapping trade agreements all conspired to hamper the potential trade effects of the Barcelona Process. These considerations, in turn, serve as a cautionary tale for post–Arab Spring efforts toward economic integration.

After the Arab Spring

The Arab Spring rekindled international interest in supporting the process of economic and political reform in the MENA region. This renewed support was articulated in the launch by the G-8 (then under French presidency) of the so-called Deauville Partnership in May 2011. The Deauville Partnership was structured as a long-term initiative based on two pillars: support for the democratic transition (political pillar) and support to country-led strategies to promote inclusive growth (economic pillar). Kuwait, Qatar, Saudi Arabia, Turkey, and the United Arab Emirates joined the endeavor in September 2011, and the focus of the actions of the partnership was extended to five countries (Morocco, Jordan, and Libya were added to Tunisia and Egypt). International organizations and financial institutions also committed to support the partnership by creating a coordination platform and making resources available to finance suitable reform efforts, with up to $38 billion expected to be committed over the 2011–13 period.[26]

Trade and investment agreements are listed once again as critical platforms to advance the economic pillar by supporting regional integration. In the case of the EU, the European Commission was given the mandate (December 2011) to start negotiations leading to deep and comprehensive free trade areas (DCFTAs) with Egypt, Jordan, Morocco, and Tunisia. DCFTAs are expected to go beyond the removal of tariffs, covering also other regulatory issues relevant to trade relations, including investment protection and government procurement.

The experience with previous efforts to promote regional integration underscores the difficulties in achieving quick results along this front. The current generation of initiatives may have a better chance to succeed as further progress is made on agriculture and nontariff barriers (including sanitary and phytosanitary measures) under DCFTAs. Moreover, progress already achieved in the simplification and harmonization of rules of origin for trading with the EU is expected to minimize the distortions of the "hub-and-spoke" design of the Mediterranean FTAs.

Concluding Remarks

The political and economic changes ushered in by the Arab Spring are still unfolding. Countries affected face many challenges ahead. In the short term, the need to preserve macroeconomic stability against a background of high expectations of significant political and economic reforms underscores some of the difficulties faced by the new regimes. Over the medium to long term, the capacity to sustain and implement credible governance reforms will determine the final outcome of the Arab Spring. Improving transparency and accountability in government services will promote investment in the private sector while also paving the way for difficult economic reform as the population's trust in the government improves.

Actions by external partners can help, but they will not drive the process. The long-term vision of effective economic integration with the EU, for example, can provide a useful goal to anchor the process of political and economic liberalization. This is, however, an arduous process that requires mutual accountability and commitment. In the end, local buy-in and ownership of the integration process will be the key factors in determining the sustainability and economic impact of these efforts. As mentioned before, it is still too early to judge if MENA governments will embrace a more market-oriented route to sustain their processes of political reform. If that is their final option, however, the regional integration efforts may become useful levers to support the transition.

Notes

1. Assistance and comments from J. P. Chauffour, N. K. W. Jones, R. Mills, L. Mottaghi, and M. Wiatrowski are gratefully acknowledged. The views expressed here are those of the authors and do not necessarily reflect those of the World Bank Group or those of the executive directors of the World Bank or the governments they represent.

2. To access the data and for a description of the methodology, see Center for Systemic Peace, Integrated Network for Societal Conflict Research, "Data Page" (www.systemicpeace.org/inscr/inscr.htm) [March 2012]).

3. For an analysis of the impact of food price increases in the late 2000s on the MENA countries see World Bank, *Middle East and North Africa Economic Development Prospects: Investing for Jobs and Growth* (Washington, 2011).

4. Ibid.

5. Calculations based on data from the International Monetary Fund (IMF) Fiscal Affairs Department.

6. Resource-poor countries are small producers or importers of oil and gas. In the MENA region, they include Djibouti, Egypt, Jordan, Lebanon, Morocco, and Tunisia.

7. World Bank, *Opening Doors: Gender Equality in the Middle East and North Africa* (Washington, 2012).

8. World Bank, *Middle East and North Africa*.

9. World Bank, *From Privilege to Competition*, Development Report Series (Washington, 2009).

10. World Bank, *Middle East and North Africa*.

11. Multilateral Investment Guarantee Agency (MIGA), *World Investment and Political Risk* (Washington: World Bank, 2011).

12. World Bank, *Middle East and North Africa*.

13. Daron Acemoglu, Simon Johnson, and James Robinson, "The Role of Institutions in Growth and Development," *Review of Economics and Institutions* 1, no. 2 (2010): 1–33.

14. Simeon Djankov and others, "The Regulation of Entry," *Quarterly Journal of Economics* 117, no. 1 (2002): 1–37.

15. World Bank and IFC, *Doing Business 2012: Doing Business in a More Transparent World* (Washington, 2012).

16. World Bank, *From Privilege to Competition*.

17. Mustapha Nabli and Marie-Ange Veganzones-Varoudakis, "How Does Exchange Rate Policy Affect Manufactured Exports in MENA Countries?" *Applied Economics* 36 (2004): 2209–19.

18. Christine Binzel, "Decline in Social Mobility: Unfulfilled Aspirations among Egypt's Educated Youth," Discussion Paper 6139 (Bonn: Institute for the Study of Labor, November 2011).

19. World Bank, *Striving for Better Jobs: The Challenge of Informality in the Middle East and North Africa*, Directions in Development Series (forthcoming).

20. World Bank, *Opening Doors: A MENA Regional Companion to the WDR 2012* (forthcoming).

21. For further details, see MENA-OECD Investment Program, "Socio-Economic Context and Impact of the 2011 Events in the Middle East and North Africa Region," (Paris: Organization for Economic Cooperation and Development, 2011).

22. See MIGA, *World Investment and Political Risk*, p. 24.

23. For details, see Jan Hagemejer and Andrzej Cieslik, "Assessing the Impact of EU-Sponsored Trade Liberalization in the MENA Countries," MPRA Paper 17721 (University Library of Munich, October 2009).

24. The Mediterranean partners included Algeria, Cyprus, Egypt, Israel, Jordan, Lebanon, Malta, Morocco, Syria, Tunisia, Turkey, and the Palestinian Authority. Libya would join the process as an observer in 1999.

25. See, for instance, Ludvig Soderling, "Is the Middle East and North Africa Region Achieving Its Trade Potential?" Working Paper 05/90 (Washington: IMF, 2005); Michael Emerson and Gergana Noutcheva, "From Barcelona Process to Neighborhood Policy: Assessment and Open Issues," Working Document 220 (Brussels: Center for European Policy Studies [CEPS], March 2005); Hagemejer and Cieslik, "Assessing the Impact"; CEPS, "Economic Integration in the Euro-Mediterranean Region: Final Report" (Brussels, September 2009).

26. For details about the Deauville Partnership, see the G-8 Ministerial Declaration and Communiqués of May and September 2011, and the IFI (International Financial Institution) Coordination Platform of September 10, 2011. See www.imf.org/external/pubs/ft/survey/so/2011/CAR091011A.htm. See also World Bank, *From Political to Economic Awakening in the Arab World: The Path of Economic Integration*. A Report on Trade and Foreign Direct Investment for the Deauville Partnership, in Cooperation with the Marseille Center for Mediterranean Integration and Islamic Development Bank (Washington, 2012).

PART II

CONSEQUENCES AND POLICY OPTIONS

JONATHAN LAURENCE

7

Midwife or Spectator?
U.S. Policies toward North Africa in the
Twenty-First Century

American policymakers, academics, and pundits did not wait long to begin deconstructing the decade of events leading to 2011's revolutions in Tunisia, Egypt and Libya, and to reflect upon the collective failure to predict the imminence of regional political instability.[1] Unlike other recent "intelligence failures"—say, the discovery of nuclear proliferation or terrorist networks—the absence of prediction did not mean observers were taken by surprise. Many of the same North Africa experts and responsible officials during the George W. Bush and Barack Obama presidencies were convinced the Egyptian and Tunisian regimes' days were numbered because political and economic reform had not kept up with major social changes, from new demographic trends to the politicization of religion.

The American foreign policy establishment's collective dilemma was to know that the internal status quo was unsustainable while nonetheless sustaining it through a combination of inertia and fear of the unknown consequences of regime change.[2] The blunt talk of kleptocratic and autocratic tendencies that could be read in leaked diplomatic memorandums in 2010 exposed some of the pragmatic cynicism that lay behind American support for those regimes.

The exact formula of preconditions that induce political revolution is unknowable, but social changes in the last decade of North African life made political reform inevitable. The difficulties encountered with the project of Iraqi democracy did not dampen American enthusiasm for spreading democracy in the region. This placed the United States on the side of demonstrators during the spasm of political action by the Kefaya ("Enough") movement from 2003 to 2005, which helped set Egyptian politics down a path of confrontation. It was Kefaya's demonstrations that contributed to a "domino effect" that led to political prisoners and "sham democracy."[3]

Among the civil society organizations to emerge in opposition to the regimes, Islamist political factions stand out for their articulation of the impact of social changes. Their early influence in the postrevolutionary constituent assemblies and parliaments of North Africa is not happenstance. Under the *ancien régime*, mosques were often the only political and social outlet available in the context of otherwise repressive regimes, which led in effect to the Islamization of dissent.[4] The lack of good governance, democratic politics, and free elections helped make Islam the most common avenue for expressing dissent. In the absence of truly free political parties, freedom of association, and freedom of expression, mosques became the only place where the disenfranchised masses could gather and engage in political "participation." While official politics remained the realm of the wealthy and corrupt elite, religion was the realm of the silent majority.

That recent history helps explain the sweep of Islamist parties in the first postrevolution election results from Tunisia (41 percent), Morocco (27 percent), and Egypt (a combined 70 percent, including the hard-line Salafist al-Nour Party). The Tunisian al-Nadha Party received 14.5 percent of the vote back in 1989, and the Moroccan Justice and Development Party won nearly 13 percent of parliamentary seats in 2002. Political Islamists—of more or less moderate stripes—formed a parallel social network through places of worship and were in far better communion with a changing society than an out-of-touch ruling elite.

President Barack Obama's presidency has been punctuated by the regime changes that his predecessor hoped to hasten. Convinced that the prerevolutionary political stability could not last, the administration of George W. Bush tried to force the hand of several Arab and North African governments with a clear message: democratize or risk extinction. The current administration consistently approached the same brink with similar expectations but a different strategy for reaching the outcome. From the "New Beginnings" address in Cairo right through the brief speech welcoming post-Qaddafi Libya in October 2011, the Obama administration has consistently avoided the inflammatory rhetoric of a democratization "agenda" and focused instead on helping establish the *conditions* for democracy. Whereas Bush acted within a predictable rule-bound regional environment—albeit in the twilight of an authoritarian era—Obama has been dealt his hand from a deck of wild cards.

Seeking to lead by example, the previous administration created incentives to reform and provided autocracies a graphic illustration of what democracy might look like in the Middle East. Since taking office in 2009, however, Obama officials have shifted American policy away from a strategy of regime pressure and debates over foreign aid conditionality toward a greater emphasis on indigenous nongovernmental organizations (NGOs) and economic growth in North Africa. If democracy cannot take hold in the absence of a strong bourgeoisie, as Barrington Moore's adage has it, then the administration has joined European allies in an urgent quest to help grow and fortify a democratically minded middle class.

The gap between Bush and Obama administration policies toward North Africa may ultimately be seen as less about different objectives than different emphases and, above all, the wildly different context of political opportunity presented by the popular uprisings of 2011. Policies supporting the voluntary and for-profit sectors existed under the previous American administration, but they were destined to languish as long as the old regimes in Egypt, Tunisia, or Libya remained in place. Civil society could not flourish without greater freedoms and democratic elections, just as economic development strategies driven by investment and loans could not thrive within conditions of crony capitalism.

President Obama, however, has overseen a foreign policy transition to match the political transitions in the region. After being held captive to the three Rs that kept autocratic regimes in power—"rent, rhetoric, and repression"—American officials are joining their European allies in promoting the three Ms that will fuel growth and democracy: "money, market access, and mobility."[5] Motivated by the hope that more transparent and accountable systems will lead to greater stability, the Obama administration has consistently placed its wager on the people of North Africa—and their economies—rather than focus its energies more prominently on the often frustrating task of regime guidance, as under the previous administration.

This has entailed not only a continued commitment to accompany regimes on their paths of liberalization but also a larger focus on civil society actors and the cultivation of middle classes through investment and entrepreneurship. As Ruth Hanau Santini wrote, "Washington sees the success of the transition as dependent on significant economic growth based on innovation and accountable and efficient institutions."[6] The U.S. administration is building a set of democracy-promotion tools that rely on civil society and economic growth rather than cajoling regimes into reform-mindedness.

A further challenge for this administration has been to remain relevant in view of emergent regional powers and issues far removed from democracy promotion strategies. Turkish prime minister Recep Tayyip Erdogan's visit to Cairo in mid-September 2011 drew attention to the "Turkish model," and his applause lines were easier to discern compared to the respectful but subdued reception for President Obama's "New Beginnings," which studiously avoided "models." Erdogan, who donned the mantle of Palestinian nationalism and voiced criticism of Israel, beat Obama exactly where American presidents are vulnerable and constrained. The U.S.-Israeli relationship is precisely the issue about which Arab public opinion has been most critical of Obama—despite several recent American attempts to appear tough with the Israeli government while continuing to assure a domestic public of his loyalty to the alliance with Israel. This has likely contributed to the current American administration's resolve to focus on civil society, investment, and business loans, which are all areas where its expertise can help build lasting partnerships with the Maghreb.

When President Obama declined to personalize the Libyan intervention and opted for a NATO umbrella over American participation, he allowed French president Nicolas Sarkozy and U.K. prime minister David Cameron to brand the effort themselves—and to reap a greater share of the glory generated by Qaddafi's fall. Cameron and Sarkozy made triumphant visits to "free Tripoli" while Obama hailed a liberated Libya from the Rose Garden. On the other hand, the United States has been the commanding force behind air power—from Libya to Yemen and Pakistan—and maintained a robust presence in multilateral institutions, especially NATO. In the words of one German observer, "The Obama Administration has thus shown how to successfully fight terrorism: by avoiding overreactions, putting emphasis on a strong intelligence service and resorting to military violence in controlled doses only when it cannot be avoided."[7] The United States has also been the voice on the line with Egyptian leaders during moments of crisis in Egyptian-Israeli relations in 2011, from the Israeli counterinsurgency incursion to the siege of the Israeli embassy.

The focus on security issues and hard power, however, belies a broader and deeper decade-long American effort to encourage the gradual democratic opening of North African societies. As the spread of democracy allows more space for peaceful dissent, the Obama administration is taking stock of ongoing democratization efforts and placing its own stamp on them.

Democratization and Foreign Assistance

As the Obama administration crafted its response to the Arab Awakening, it was legitimate to ask what impact could be attributed to existing American democracy promotion and foreign aid programs in the region. Could the events in the winter and spring of 2011 be read, generously, as a vindication of the complex and multilayered bureaucratic structure of U.S. foreign assistance—and of the previous U.S. administration's strong push for democratization in particular?[8] The diverse budgetary lines established in support of that goal ranged from the Middle East Partnership Initiative and other State Department programs to the Millennium Development Corporation, USAID, the National Endowment for Democracy, and public-private partnerships.[9] American taxpayers have poured billions into military and development aid, but it is less well known that hundreds of millions of dollars also went into the nurturing of civil society and political participation.[10] This meant that the government had contacts in Tunis and Cairo who were not limited to secularist interlocutors.

In the first two years of Bush's democratization push, however, some of the early U.S. financial aid to Arab societies funded government programs and paid for government training, giving life support to the very system he hoped to change. Tamara Wittes, in a book published shortly before she joined the Obama administration as deputy assistant secretary for Near Eastern affairs, argued that the national interest was no longer served by supporting autocrats for stability's sake. Along with others, she saw the stirrings of growing popular demands for economic and political reform. With regard to "the development of liberal democracies" in the Arab world's major states, she asked at the time, would the United States help "midwife the birth of a democratic Arab future" or would "the United States be a mere spectator?"[11]

In fact, the Bush administration initially sent strong signals regarding American expectations for democratic reform. Beginning with Bush's 2002 State of the Union address, and the decision that August to not approve additional aid to Egypt, followed by Secretary of State Colin Powell's announcement of the Middle East Partnership Initiative (MEPI) at the end of that year, the administration sought to ratchet up pressure on regimes in the region. MEPI brought grant making into the State Department in a more significant way and has assumed some aspects of the role that the U.S. Agency for International Development had been fulfilling, but here in combination with diplomatic objectives.

In this respect it distinguished itself through its direct funding of indigenous Arab NGOs.[12] In MEPI's first few years, thousands of participants from North Africa and the Middle East undertook projects with American support. This approach aimed to develop "long-term alliances with the people of the Middle East rather than with specific ruling regimes."[13] In his November 2003 speech at the twentieth anniversary of the National Endowment for Democracy, President Bush criticized the notion that democracy was impossible in the Middle East. Secretary of State Condoleezza Rice's June 2005 visit to Egypt was bold for what she dared say in public: she called for the rule of law, the end of emergency rule, an independent judiciary, and freedom from fear of violence for democratic activists. Moreover, Congress in 2008 considered conditioning roughly 8 percent of U.S. military aid to Egypt on improvement in judicial reform, better police training, and elimination of smuggling tunnels on the Gaza border. Secretary of State Condoleezza Rice and Secretary of Defense Robert Gates weighed in heavily against these plans, and the clause was basically neutered— but not before it thoroughly enraged the Egyptian government.

The grueling years of state building in Iraq and Afghanistan may have actually diminished the Bush administration's sure-footedness by the end of its second term. Despite the aggressive rhetoric, the Bush administration did not follow its threatening language with commensurate actions. Wittes argued that the U.S. administration at the time "failed to speak up for those who challenge the system," such as Saad Eddine Ibrahim and Ayman Nour (and that in Tunisia it neglected to call out Zine el Abidine Ben Ali on press freedom violations in 2005).[14] The administration never did something as bold as taking a $100 million tranche from military aid and placing it into its democracy promotion budget. As Glenn Kessler wrote, "Near the end of Bush's term, the Egyptians felt so confident of their position that Rice was told she couldn't visit Egypt until she waived congressional restrictions on $100 million in military aid, which she did."[15] Secretary Rice's earlier outspokenness was a faded memory just eighteen months later, when she visited again in January 2007 on behalf of an administration sobered by insurgencies in Iraq and Afghanistan and electoral outcomes favoring Islamist parties in Gaza and Lebanon.

President Hosni Mubarak cooled bilateral relations after the Bush administration spoke of conditioning military aid on judicial and political reforms (that is, "unless you change, things will change"), and he subsequently declined to visit the United States. Although Mubarak resented the interference, the neoconservatives formerly of the West Wing viewed this as a small price to pay. Mubarak kept cashing the checks and did not touch his policies toward Suez or Israel, and he later received his comeuppance. Other observers might insist that the uprisings took place *despite* U.S. efforts. Then there are those who argue that any conclusion of U.S. influence is highly improbable given the contrast between America's state-centric approach and the bottom-up nature of the Tunisian and Egyptian revolts. Critics of U.S. (and European) policy say there was too much focus on politics and not enough on society. In a recent opinion piece, Anthony Cordesman counsels a whole-country approach: "Stop focusing on democracy, human rights and the rule of law" and give more sustained support for governance and local economies.[16]

Continuity or Change in U.S. Policy toward Egypt?

Faced with a set of North African regimes in flux, President Obama's foreign policy has been portrayed, at turns, as a catalyst for change or as a canny improvisation that has been able to do less with more. Did the North African uprisings of 2011 take the American administration by surprise, or were the popular revolts the long-awaited fruit of patient nurturing? Has the U.S. government fumbled the opportunity to positively influence events in their first year, or did American leadership and U.S.-sponsored institutions enable the jasmine revolutions and Libyan overthrow? The administration could be accused of *tout et son contraire*: crossed wires between the White House and the State Department on Egypt policy, surprised by the events in Tunisia, and practicing passivity in Libya until the French and British governments cajoled the United States into a military contribution. One American official said that the CIA knew Egypt was in an "untenable" situation, but "we didn't know what the triggering mechanism would be."[17] Another spoke of outright surprise: "We've had endless strategy sessions for the past two years on Mideast peace, on containing Iran. And how many of them factored in the possibility that Egypt moves from stability to turmoil? None."[18]

In support of the notion that U.S. policy helped catalyze change, there is the legacy of the Middle East Partnership Initiative, which has been embraced and amplified by the Obama administration. In 2008 Wittes called conditionality "the most controversial issue in promoting a reform policy" and argued in favor of more aid.[19] But above all, she found that U.S. foreign aid programs call out for greater "autonomy": direct more of U.S. funds to nongovernmental actors who focus on democracy and governance.[20] By 2011 half of the MEPI projects were direct partnerships with indigenous NGOs as opposed to large projects run by organizations inside the beltway. MEPI's budget grew from $29 million of reallocated funds in 2002 to $86 million in 2010. More than half of this amount ($52.9 million) was earmarked for MEPI's democracy and governance efforts, with $27.2 million tagged for civil society organizations.[21] In 2010 Obama's federal budget doubled requested funding for democracy and governance to $1.54 billion (though 86 percent of that was destined for Afghanistan, Pakistan, and Iraq) and requested an increase of 70 percent for MEPI.

On the other hand, some have suggested that Obama was downplaying democracy promotion in the interest of rallying North African regimes behind his efforts to advance a peace agreement. While the Obama administration was settling into place, the Egyptian government was still smarting from what it perceived as strong-arming and disrespectful treatment from the Bush administration, especially regarding the pace of political reform. Thus, when President Obama arrived with his June 2009 Cairo speech, the Mubarak regime's rancor outweighed any tangible pro-democracy dividends from the Bush administration's more aggressive tactics. American pressure regarding Ayman Nour and Saad Eddine Ibrahim was resented (although Ibrahim was acquitted in 2003 and Ayman Nour was released one month after President Obama's inauguration in 2009). Writing in the Washington Post, Glenn Kessler argued that "in public statements, references to democracy and reform were muted," and human rights issues were downplayed.[22] He quoted Secretary of State Hillary Clinton as saying that "we issue these [human rights] reports on every country," in an interview with Egyptian journalists in March 2009. "We consider Egypt to be a friend." It was reported in news media accounts that the State Department advised Secretary Clinton, during her first visit to Cairo, to avoid bringing up the issue of judicial persecution against pro-democracy activists and opposition figures. In the days before Obama's "New Beginnings" address, Ayman Nour wrote in the New York Times of his and his colleagues' "alarm" at "signals that the Obama's administration's support for democracy may have waned. This year, the United States has significantly reduced financing for democracy support in Egypt."[23]

In fact, rather than emphasize democracy promotion up front, the most tangible follow-on initiative was a focus on entrepreneurship in the Muslim-majority world instead. Obama thus shifted public focus away from regime behavior in order to allow other aspects of the relationship to flourish, for instance, through U.S. government–initiated civil society–private sector support in North Africa. This consisted of the Global Entrepreneurship Program, followed by the Presidential Summit on Entrepreneurship in the Muslim world, hosted by President Obama in April 2010 in Washington and including participants from all North African countries.[24] The summit had the declared goal of "highlighting the importance of social and economic entrepreneurship, and strengthening mutually-beneficial relationships with entrepreneurs in Muslim-majority countries and Muslim communities around the world."[25] The project has involved a number of follow-up conferences, including the U.S.-Maghreb Entrepreneurship Conference in support of private sector development held in Algeria in November 2010, and a follow-up entrepreneurship conference in Istanbul, Turkey, in October 2011.[26] The White House also sent National Security Council director Pradeep Ramamurthy to Algeria and Tunisia in July 2010, where he told local audiences that the United States sought to strengthen entrepreneurship between the United States and the Maghreb as a way of deepening the relationship between the Muslim communities in the United States and entrepreneurs in Muslim-majority countries. The Obama administration has helped create eight funds to promote science and technology in North Africa and expanded professional exchanges by more than 30 percent. "We've begun to deliver on the Cairo speech," Ramamurthy said in Tunis. "It's not just about changing minds, but building tangible partnerships. We see a strategic long-term vision for this."[27]

Winning Hearts and Minds:
Promote Democracy or Address Palestinian-Israeli Conflict?

There was little early positive reinforcement, at least in terms of Arab public opinion, for Obama's pragmatic focus. Surveys and mainstream Arab and Islamic commentators have suggested that the resonance of President Obama's historic speech at Cairo University in 2009 had already begun to fade within one year. The 2010 twenty-two-country Pew poll as well as media reports and editorials from across the Arab Muslim world indicated that despite the president's well-received speech, average Arabs and Muslims were not impressed by the U.S. administration's record.[28] Citizens of Muslim countries continued to hold overwhelmingly negative views of the United States (for instance, in Turkey and Pakistan only 17 percent expressed a positive opinion). In Egypt the favorability rating dropped from 27 percent in 2009 to 17 percent in 2010, the lowest rating in any of the Pew Global Attitudes surveys conducted in that country since they were initiated in 2006.[29]

As data from the *2010 Arab Public Opinion Poll* show (table 7-1), the continued resonance of the Israeli-Palestinian conflict overshadowed even the

Table 7-1. *2010 Arab Public Opinion Poll, 2009 and 2010*[a]
Percent

Topics	2010	2009
Views of President Barack Obama of the United States		
Positive	16	51
Neutral	16	28
Negative	62	23
Attitudes toward Obama administration policy in the Middle East		
Hopeful	16	51
Neither hopeful nor discouraged	20	28
Discouraged	63	15
Most disappointed with Obama administration regarding		
Palestine–Israel	61	n.a
Iraq	27	n.a
Attitudes towards Islam	5	n.a
Afghanistan	4	n.a
Human rights	1	n.a
Spreading democracy	1	n.a
Economic assistance	1	n.a

Attitude toward the United States	*2010*	*2009*	*2008*
Very favorable	2	3	4
Somewhat favorable	10	15	11
Somewhat unfavorable	38	31	19
Very unfavorable	47	46	64

Source: ShibleyTelhami, "2010 Arab Public Opinion Survey," conducted June–July 2010 (www.brookings.edu/~/media/Files/rc/reports/2010/0805_arab_opinion_poll_telhami/0805_arabic_opinion_poll_telhami.pdf [April 2012]).

a. Countries surveyed: Egypt, Jordan, Lebanon, Morocco, Saudi Arabia, and the United Arab Emirates.

n.a. = Not available.

most momentous attempts to reframe or reset relations.[30] This survey revealed that 61 percent of the respondents in Egypt, Morocco, Lebanon, Jordan, United Arab Emirates, and Saudi Arabia were most disappointed with Obama's Palestine-Israel policies; a 50 percent drop in support for Obama was recorded in Egypt. President Obama's response to the Gaza flotilla confrontation and his inability to move the Israeli and Palestinian parties forward were cited in numerous media reports from the region as a sign of Obama's diminishing commitment to his assertions in the Cairo speech, especially regarding the "suffering" and "deprivations" of the Palestinian people. One Egyptian commentator has argued that while President Obama said all the right things in Cairo, the Egyptian public thinks Washington has not delivered.[31] In a forceful article entitled "How Obama Lost Muslim Hearts and Minds," another academic wrote, "Unless Obama takes risks in the Middle East, he might end up leaving a legacy of broken promises and shattered expectations in the region."[32] In an op-ed column in the *Los Angeles Times*, a former Egyptian ambassador to the United States wrote that the "New Beginning" speech was highly successful, but to sustain the positive reaction generated by the speech, "concrete progress on a number of complex regional issues is imperative."[33] The first-year anniversary of the speech generated similar comments on Al Jazeera and in other electronic and print media.

In what must have been a stinging irony for the Obama administration, this came precisely after the period when the Obama administration's attempt at shuttle diplomacy in Israel and Palestine was most active, with the appointment of George Mitchell as special envoy for the Middle East in January 2009, followed by Mitchell's and Clinton's visits to the area that spring.

Meanwhile, with regard to democracy promotion, it would not be until September 2010 that a White House public statement explicitly referred to political reform in Egypt.[34] In December, just a month before the key January 25 demonstration in Tahrir Square, a high-level State Department official wrote in the *Washington Post* that "Egypt has an opportunity to fulfill the commitments its government has made to the Egyptian people as it prepares for next year's presidential election, if it takes steps to implement several changes to which it has committed"—including "a free, fair and transparent electoral process in 2011," as well as "the end of the long-standing state of emergency, under which the country has been operating since 1981," protections of "the universal rights of the Egyptian people," and media freedoms.[35]

Those who argue that the United States stayed ahead of events would point out that President Obama had in fact ordered contingency studies of succession scenarios soon after assuming office, and that he was the first in the situation room to know Mubarak would go.[36] In his reportedly frank conversation with the Egyptian president on January 28, Obama respectfully urged his elder to read the writing on the wall.[37] Relations between the Pentagon and the Egyptian and Tunisian militaries—whose senior officials remained in close contact throughout the unrest—may have been a key element in speeding their respective transitions.[38] In this light, decades of foreign military funding, training, and support of civil society—mere tens of billions compared to Iraq's trillions—offered a significant return. President Obama's dispassionate handling of "democracy promotion" illuminates an important distinction with respect to his predecessor. The president's calls to avoid violence in Tunis and Cairo—without saying much else publicly—suggest a more patient view of the route taken by freedom's march.

How did the United States measure up in the moment of Egyptian opportunity? Springborg argues

> The U.S. embraced [the revolution and Mubarak's] removal from power
> . . . because this seemed the best strategy to protect its security interests.
> Confident that its long-standing role as tutor to the Egyptian military,
> including provision of equipment, training, and logistical and mainte-
> nance support, would preserve the bilateral relationship and that the
> military would be a stronger political pillar once the failing and unpop-
> ular President Mubarak was jettisoned, Washington had little difficulty
> presenting its support for change as sincere. But its sincerity was limited
> to professions of need for change, not necessarily for democratization."[39]

U.S. Attitudes toward the Participation of Islamist Parties

Concerning the role of Islamist parties in Egyptian political life, Obama's Cairo speech committed the United States to respecting all democratically elected governments that guarantee human rights and equality and reject violence. Wittes argued that "expanding political freedoms is the best way to level the playing field." Although this could favor Islamist forces at the outset, it will also allow for the more pragmatically minded among them to emerge. "In a freer environment it will be easier to distinguish" among their competing factions, Wittes writes.[40] The more entrenched Islamists become as the dominant polit-ical alternative to the status quo, the more the language of Islamism becomes the [only] language of protest politics and other voices become marginalized."[41]

When asked point blank at the end of September 2011, "Will you be ready or prepared to sit in with a government with members of the Muslim Broth-erhood as members?" Secretary of State Clinton replied,

> We will be willing to and open to working with a government that has
> representatives who are committed to non-violence, who are commit-
> ted to human rights, who are committed to the democracy that I think
> was hoped for in Tahrir Square, which means that Christians will be

respected, women will be respected, people of different views within Islam will be respected. We have said we will work with those who have a real commitment to what an Egyptian democracy should look like. . . . So we hope that anyone who runs for election, and certainly anyone who's elected and joins the parliament, joins the government, will be committed to making Egypt work and be open to all Egyptians no matter who you might be.[42]

"Given the changing political landscape in Egypt," Clinton argued, the United States would benefit from engaging with and supporting all parties that are "peaceful, and committed to nonviolence, that intend to compete for the parliament and the presidency."[43] Back in January 2011, then White House press secretary Robert Gibbs said that Egyptian government reform had to "include a whole host of important non-secular actors that give Egypt a strong chance to continue to be [a] stable and reliable partner." Since the 2011 uprising, the Obama administration has acknowledged a potential role for the Muslim Brotherhood in the future of Egyptian politics. Secretary Clinton further confirmed that the administration would "[continue] the approach of limited contacts with the Muslim Brotherhood that have existed on and off for about five or six years." (However, according to an October 2011 article in the *Los Angeles Times*, "The U.S. ambassador in Cairo, Anne Patterson, has said she is not 'comfortable' enough with the idea to talk with Brotherhood figures herself."[44])

The administration also encouraged Tunisia and Libya to remain inclusive, pluralist, and respectful of human rights, with President Barack Obama saying that the Tunisian election of a constituent assembly in October 2011—which saw the Islamist al-Nadha Party emerge as a pluralist victor—was "an important step forward." "We look forward to working with the TNC and an empowered transitional government as they prepare for the country's first free and fair elections," President Obama said in the statement. "The Libyan authorities should also continue living up to their commitments to respect human rights."[45]

U.S. Policy Responses to the Arab Awakening

The U.S. administration's reformulation of American foreign policy following the Arab Spring is a continuation of President Obama's emphasis on entrepreneurship, civil society, and the building of a strong middle class. Central and Eastern European countries undergoing transitions two decades earlier were comparably better off economically *and* had institutional frameworks to help anchor their democratic development. In Obama's May 2011 address on Arab transitions, he made explicit reference to the European Union membership that served as "an incentive for reform" in post-1989 Central and Eastern Europe. However, no structures like the EU or NATO are waiting to guide Tunisian, Egyptian, and Libyan choices. Despite efforts to create a Union for the Mediterranean in 2008, that institution came just late enough to be firmly anchored in the paradigm of the "pre-Jasmine" era.

The administration's initial response to the Arab Awakening has been an effort to put in place the building blocks for new economic structures (see box 7-1). "We think it's important to focus on trade, not just aid; on investment, not just assistance," Obama said in spring 2011. "The vision of a modern and prosperous economy [should] create a powerful force for reform in the Middle East and North Africa." [46] Speaking to the houses of the British parliament later in 2011, Obama again evoked the link between economic development and political outcomes, speaking of the need to "deepen ties of trade and commerce" in order to "help them demonstrate that freedom brings prosperity."[47]

Part of the American legacy, it is hoped, will be to enable a fruitful period of autonomy for civil society and business in North Africa. In light of this goal, investment in creating the conditions for democracy may turn out to be a more stable long-term solution than the approaches of the past have been. The administration has been lobbying congressional leaders to commit greater resources to the new strategic opportunities, with unprecedented priority being given to both the voluntary and for-profit sectors. In addition to debt relief and debt swap arrangements aimed at allowing more investment in job creation and entrepreneurship, the Middle East Partnership Initiative, now ten years in existence, is a mature and active mainstay of American diplomacy in the region. Furthermore, USAID Cairo launched a $65 million program for "democratic development" (elections, civic activism, and human rights) in March 2011.[48]

The model of transatlantic cooperation that framed the transition of Central and Eastern European countries is a precedent that this administration would like to emulate, albeit within contemporary budgetary constraints. The Obama administration has therefore pursued concrete cooperation with European and other partners at the G-20 and G-8 Summit in Deauville, which led to pledges of up to $38 billion for North African countries.[49] (Another main lender is the European Investment Bank, providing $6 billion in loans through 2013, and the International Monetary Fund and World Bank are also

---

Box 7-1. *Economic Steps Announced by President Obama in May 2011 Speech*

1. Ask the "World Bank and International Monetary Fund to present a plan" to G-8 summit to "stabilize and modernize the economies of Tunisia and Egypt"; support the governments that will be elected. Urged other countries to help Egypt and Tunisia meet near-term financial needs.

2. "Relieve a democratic Egypt of up to $1 billion in debt," and work with Egyptian partners to invest these resources to foster growth and entrepreneurship. "Help Egypt regain access to markets by guaranteeing $1 billion in borrowing" that is needed to finance infrastructure and job creation. Help newly democratic governments recover stolen assets.

3. Work with Congress to "create Enterprise Funds to invest in Tunisia and Egypt." Modeled on funding that supported the transitions in Eastern Europe after the fall of the Berlin Wall. The Overseas Private Investment Corporation will "launch $2 billion facility to support private investment across the region." Work with the allies to "refocus the European Bank for Reconstruction and Development so that it provides the same support for democratic transitions and economic modernization in the Middle East and North Africa."

4. "Launch a comprehensive Trade and Investment Partnership Initiative in the Middle East and North Africa." Work with the EU to facilitate more trade within the region, build on existing agreements to promote integration with U.S. and European markets, and "open the door for those countries who adopt high standards of reform and trade liberalization to construct a regional trade arrangement." Combat corruption, bureaucracy, patronage; help governments meet international obligations.

Source: White House, "Remarks by the President on the Middle East and North Africa," State Department, Washington, May 19, 2011 (www.whitehouse.gov/the-press-office/2011/05/19/remarks-president-middle-east-and-north-africa [April 2012]).

---

encouraging the pursuit of public-private partnerships in Tunisia and Egypt, though some observers have questioned these economies' readiness, especially in the banking sector.[50])

American and European officials have also scrambled to expand the competence of the one post–cold war era institution that can easily be extended to North African countries: the European Bank for Reconstruction and Development (EBRD). In April 2011 U.S. secretary of the treasury Timothy Geithner pushed to promote democracy in the region by making more loans to businesses. Four months later, the EBRD began granting loans to public authorities and private firms in Egypt, Morocco, Tunisia, and Jordan. The

EBRD commitment will rise to 2.5 billion euros annually, to "foster the development of the private sector" and promote foreign direct investment. In order to improve the investment climate, the projects will range from privatizations and job creation efforts to efficiency improvements in energy and water usage, and from banking reform to private-public partnerships, such as private sector investment in infrastructure and services.[51] As an assistant treasury secretary and member of the EBRD's board of governors argued in a speech to the bank's sixty-one member states, in North Africa just as in Eastern Europe before it, "authoritarian political systems limited the freedoms of the citizens of these countries, and in both instances the economic systems were dominated by cronyism and state control that limited the regions' economic potential.[52]

Further echoing the would-be parallels between the two regional transitions, Secretary of State Hillary Clinton named William Taylor as the new ambassador to lead the new Middle East Transitions Office.[53] This office is a direct successor to the 1991 Freedom Support Act Office, which coordinated diplomacy after the USSR's collapse. The office will begin by leading State Department coordination on policy toward Egypt, Tunisia, and Libya.[54]

Conclusion

Democratic and Republican administrations have long sought to mitigate the impression that at its worst, bilateral counterterrorism cooperation serves to cynically prop up useful dictators. The Libyan intervention in 2011 gave the United States an opportunity to clarify its stance. Will Arab public opinion reveal that the American drones that delivered Colonel Qaddafi's convoy to the forces of the Libyan National Transitional Council make up for the U.S.-made tear gas used on the crowds in Tahrir Square? One of the administration's most delicate tasks has been to balance the expression of American national interest in a way consistent with revolutionaries' total ownership of their new regimes. As Bruce Riedel, a former CIA agent, said in admiration about Obama's Libyan intervention, "No ground footprint, no U.S. casualties and no responsibility for the day after."[55]

But the changes set in motion are in their early stages, and new balancing challenges await the administration. Only months had passed since Ben Ali's and Mubarak's departures from power when President Obama said in May 2011 that it would be "years before these revolutions reach their conclusion."[56]

Any consideration of U.S. influence on regional developments must take into account the liberalization of economic flows. The value of free trade agreements on paper is tied to what private citizens are allowed to make of them. In the past, a security agenda triumphed over the economic one. Now, to help the middle-class poor and the underemployed, the U.S. administration must do all it can to avoid reinforcing oligarchies and oligopolies that characterized *fin-de-regime* Egypt and Tunisia. Moore's aphorism still echoes: "No bourgeoisie, no democracy." U.S. influence in the region in the days ahead will depend on a calm accompaniment from afar, combining "hard power"—the billions in security guarantees and military hardware that the United States can give, sell, or withhold—and "soft power"—the millions in support of local economic development and civil society networks in support of a strong middle class.

Notes

1. See, for example, Kenneth Pollack and others, *The Arab Awakening: America and the Transformation of the Middle East* (Brookings, 2011); Council on Foreign Relations, *The New Arab Revolt: What Happened, What It Means, and What Comes Next* (New York, 2011).

2. Elliot Abrams, "Outlook: Egypt Protests Show George W. Bush Was Right about Freedom in the Arab World," *Washington Post*, February 1, 2011 (http://live.washington post.com/outlook-02-01-11.html [March 2012]).

3. Joy Samad, "Egypt on the Brink: From Nasser to Mubarak/On the State of Egypt: What Caused the Revolution," *British Journal of Middle Eastern Studies* 38, no. 3 (2011): 445–49; Tarek Osman, *Egypt on the Brink: From Nasser to Mubarak* (Yale University Press, 2010).

4. Omer Taspinar and Jonathan Laurence, "Will Europe Shrink from the Arab Spring?" *World Politics Review*, December 2011 (www.worldpoliticsreview.com/articles/10997/will-europe-shrink-from-the-arab-spring [December 2011]).

5. On the three Rs, see Tamara C. Wittes, *Freedom's Unsteady March* (Brookings, 2008). On the three Ms, see European Commission and the High Representative of the Union for Foreign Affairs and Security Policy, "A Partnership for Democracy and Shared Prosperity with the Southern Mediterranean," March 8, 2011 (http://eeas.europa.eu/euromed/docs/com2011_200_en.pdf [March 2012]). According to the High Representative, Catherine Ashton, the three Ms are "Money—resources that can go into the region to help support the transition to democracy, the support for civil society and of course the economic needs of countries. For example the loss of tourism in Egypt and Tunisia. Secondly market access—the importance of making sure that we give advantages in trade and the people can take advantage of that by being able to

export and import properly. And thirdly mobility—the ability of people to move around, for business people to be able to conduct business more effectively." See "Remarks by EU HR Ashton on Arrival to Extraordinary European Council on Southern Neighbourhood and Libya" (www.eu-un.europa.eu/articles/fr/article_10792_fr. htm [March 2012]).

6. Ruth H. Santini, *The Transatlantic Relationship after the Arab Spring* (Brookings, June 2011).

7. Guido Steinberg, "Hydra of Global Terror," *Qantara.de,* September 16, 2011 (http://en.qantara.de/Hydra-of-Global-Terror/17296c17801i1p464/index.html [March 2012]).

8. Including, notably, by former officials Charles M. King and Elliot Abrams.

9. The State Department's broad strategic objectives are indicative: governing justly and democratically (GJD), peace and security, investing in people, economic growth, and humanitarian assistance. GJD is further broken down into four categories: "Rule of Law and Human Rights: Assists constitutional and legal reform, judicial independence and reform, the administration of and access to justice, protection of human rights, prevention of crime, and community-based efforts to improve security. Good Governance: Strengthens executive, legislative, and local government capabilities and improves transparency and accountability for government institutions; also strengthens anti-corruption programs. Political Competition and Consensus Building: Promotes free, fair, and transparent multiparty elections, and promotes representative and accountable political parties committed to democracy. Civil Society: Strengthens independent media, nongovernmental organizations (particularly advocacy functions), think tanks, and labor unions." See Stephen McInerney, *The Federal Budget and Appropriations for Fiscal Year 2011. Democracy, Governance, and Human Rights in the Middle East* (Washington: Project on Middle East Democracy, April 2010) (www. pomed.org/wordpress/wp-content/uploads/2010/04/fy11-budget-analysis-final.pdf [March 2012]).

10. Through the following programs: the Middle East Partnership Initiative (MEPI); the Bureau for Democracy, Human Rights, and Labor (DRL) at the Department of State; the USAID Office of Democracy and Governance within the Bureau for Democracy, Conflict, and Humanitarian Assistance (DCHA); and the recently initiated Near East Regional Democracy (NERD) program. There has also been funding for institutions outside of the government like the National Endowment for Democracy (NED) and for multilateral institutions such as the UN Democracy Fund (UNDEF), the G8's BMENA "Foundation for the Future" (supporting NGOs), "Fund for the Future" (job creation), and Human Rights and Democracy Fund (HRDF). See McInerney, *Federal Budget and Appropriations;* Jeremy Sharp, "The Broader Middle East and North Africa Initiative: An Overview," Report RS02253 (Congressional Research Service, Library of Congress, February 2005) (http://fpc.state.gov/ documents/organization/43293.pdf).

11. Tamara C. Wittes, "The Promise of Arab Liberalism," *Policy Review,* no. 125 (June–July 2004).

12. Jeremy Sharp, "U.S. Foreign Assistance to the Middle East: Historical Background, Recent Trends, and the FY2011 Request," RL32269 (Congressional Research Service, Library of Congress, June 15, 2010) (www.fas.org/sgp/crs/mideast/RL32260. pdf [March 2012]).

13. Wittes, *Freedom's Unsteady March* (2008), p. 89.

14. Ibid., p. 94.

15. Glenn Kessler, "Obama and Mubarak and Democracy—An Accounting," *Washington Post*, January 29, 2011 (http://voices.washingtonpost.com/fact-checker/2011/01/obama_and_mubarak_and_democrac.html [March 2012]).

16. Anthony Cordesman, "Be Careful What You Wish for in Arab World," *Financial Times*, January 27, 2011 (www.ft.com/intl/cms/s/0/87bd5f98-2a52-11e0-b906-00144feab49a.html#axzz1oeKp5AUh [March 2012]).

17. Helen Cooper and Mark Lander, "White House and Egypt Discuss Plan for Mubarak's Exit," *New York Times*, February 3, 2011 (www.nytimes.com/2011/02/04/world/middleeast/04diplomacy.html?pagewanted=all [March 2012]).

18. David E. Sanger, "As Mubarak Digs in, U.S. Policy in Egypt is Complicated," *New York Times*, February 5, 2011 (www.nytimes.com/2011/02/06/world/middleeast/06policy.html?pagewanted=all [March 2012]).

19. Wittes, *Freedom's Unsteady March*, p. 116.

20. Ibid., p. 117.

21. McInerney, *Federal Budget and Appropriations*.

22. Kessler, "Obama and Mubarak."

23. Ayman Nour, "Rigged to Lose," *New York Times*, June 2, 2009 (www.nytimes.com/2009/06/03/opinion/03AymanNour.html?_r=1&scp=69&sq=%22ayman+nour%22&st=nyt [March 2012]).

24. See U.S. Department of State, "Global Entrepreneurship Program (GEP)," April 26, 2010 (www.state.gov/r/pa/scp/fs/2010/140960.htm [March 2012]).

25. White House, Office of the Press Secretary, "A New Beginning: Presidential Summit on Entrepreneurship," April 26, 2010 (www.whitehouse.gov/the-press-office/a-new-beginning-presidential-summit-entrepreneurship [March, 2012]).

26. See U.S.–Algeria Business Council, "USABC Calendar of Events" (www.us-algeria.org/events.html [March 2012]).

27. Quote from http://tunisia.usembassy.gov/policy/news2/business-and-finance-post-activities/following-up-on-the-entrepreneurship-summit/transcript-of-mr.-ramamurthy-press-interview (February 24, 2011; URL no longer active).

28. Pew Research Forum, "Obama More Popular Abroad than at Home," Pew Global Attitudes Project, June 17, 2010 (http://pewresearch.org/pubs/1630/Obama-popular-abroad-global-american-image-benefit-22-nationglobal-survey [March 2012]); Yassin Musharbash, "Obama's Cairo Speech, A Year Later," *Salon.com*, June 7, 2010 (www.salon.com/news/feature/2010/06/07/Cairo_speech_year_open2010 [March 2012]); Marwan Bishara, "Is Al Qaeda Winning?" *Aljazeera.net*, January 14, 2010 (http://blogs.aljazeera.net/imperium/2010/01/14/al-qaeda-winning [March

2012]); Alaa Bayoumi, "The Undoing of Obama's Cairo Speech," *Aljazeera.net*, January 14, 2010 (http://english.aljazeera.net/news/middleeast/2010/03/20103138156966488. html [March 2012]).

29. Pew Research Forum, "Obama More Popular."

30. Shibley Telhami, "2010 Arab Public Opinion Poll: Results of Arab Opinion Survey Conducted June 29–July 20," August 2010 (www.brookings.edu/reports/2010/0805_arab_opinion_poll_telhami.aspx [March 2012]).

31. Musharbash, "Obama's Cairo Speech, a Year Later."

32. Fawaz Gerges, "How Obama Lost Muslim Hearts and Minds," June 19, 2010 (http://arabnews.com/opinion/article69017.ece [April 2012]).

33. Nabil Fahmy, "The Cairo Obama, One Year Later," *Los Angeles Times*, June 7, 2010 (http://articles.latimes.com/2010/jun/07/opinion/la-oe-fahmy-20100607 [March 2012]).

34. White House, "Readout of President Obama's Meeting with President Mubarak of Egypt," September 1, 2010 (www.whitehouse.gov/the-press-office/2010/09/01/readout-president-obamas-meeting-with-president-mubarak-egypt [March 2012]).

35. Michael H. Posner, "Another Chance for Egypt to Commit to Transparency," *Washington Post*, December 18, 2010 (www.state.gov/j/drl/rls/rm/2010/153125.htm [March 2012]).

36. David D. Kirkpatrick and David E. Sanger, "A Tunisian-Egyptian Link that Shook Arab History," *New York Times*, February 13, 2011 (www.nytimes.com/2011/02/14/world/middleeast/14egypt-tunisia-protests.html?pagewanted=all [March 2012]).

37. Reportedly, his parting words were: "I respect my elders. And you have been in politics for a very long time, Mr. President. But there are moments in history when just because things were the same way in the past doesn't mean they will be that way in the future." See Kirkpatrick and Sanger, "A Tunisian-Egyptian Link that Shook Arab History."

38. "Tunisia: 'America Took Control of the Situation,'" *France24.com*, January 20, 2011 (www.france24.com/en/20110120-tunisia-america-took-control-of-the-situation-canard-enchaine-mich%C3%A8le-aliot-marie-eco-activists-spies-food-shortages [March 2012]).

39. Robert Springborg, "Whither the Arab Spring? 1989 or 1848?" *International Spectator* 46, no. 3 (2011): 5–12, p. 9.

40. Wittes, *Freedom's Unsteady March*, p. 145.

41. Ibid., p. 75.

42. Hillary Rodham Clinton, "Interview with Sharif Amer of Al-Hayat TV," U.S Department of State, September 29, 2011 (www.state.gov/secretary/rm/2011/09/174882.htm [March 2012]).

43. Except as otherwise indicated, all quotes in this paragraph come from Paul Richter and David Zucchino, "U.S. Will Build Contacts with Muslim Brotherhood," *Los Angeles Times*, July 1, 2011 (http://articles.latimes.com/2011/jul/01/world/la-fg-us-brotherhood-20110701 [March 2012]).

44. Doyle McManus, "Mosque and State," *Los Angeles Times*, October 23, 2011 (http://articles.latimes.com/2011/oct/23/opinion/la-oe-mcmanus-column-islamists-20111023 [March 2012]).

45. Lucy Madison, "Obama Congratulates Libya on Liberation," *CBS News*, October 23, 2011 (www.cbsnews.com/8301-503544_162-20124389-503544/obama-congratulates-libya-on-liberation/ [Apr. 2012]).

46. White House, "Remarks by the President on the Middle East and North Africa," State Department, May 19, 2011 (http://photos.state.gov/libraries/guyana/5/press release/Remarks-by-the-President-on-the-Middle-East-and-North-Africa.pdf [March 2012]).

47. "Full transcript of Barack Obama's speech to UK Parliament at Westminster Hall," *NewStatesman.com*, May 25, 2011 (www.newstatesman.com/2011/05/nations-rights-world-united [March 2012]).

48. Robert Springborg, "U.S. Responses to Arab Upheavals," roundtable discussion at the Transatlantic Security Symposium 2011, Rome, October 2011 (www.iai.it/pdf/DocIAI/iai1114.pdf [March 2012]).

49. Rachel Ziemba, "The News from Marseilles: Pledges for the Arab Spring," *EconoMonitor.com*, September 12, 2011 (http://qa.economonitor.com/analysts/2011/09/12/the-news-from-marseilles-pledges-for-the-arab-spring/ [March 2012]).

50. Akram Belkaid, "Auf sich allein gestellt," *Die Tageszeitung*, October 11, 2011 (www.taz.de/1/archiv/digitaz/artikel/?ressort=me&dig=2011%2F10%2F11%2Fa0094&cHash=fab6ff2419 [March 2012]).

51. See Andrew Torchia, "EBRD to Start North Africa Lending by Mid-2012," *Reuters Africa*, October 11, 2011 (http://af.reuters.com/article/investingNews/idAF JOE79A06620111011?feedType=RSS&feedName=investingNews&sp=true [March 2012]); "EBRD Shareholders Back Expansion in North Africa, Middle East," *Wall Street Journal*, October 5, 2011; EBRD-ADB-ADF, "Memorandum of Understanding between EBRD and the African Development Bank and the African Development Fund," September 10, 2011 (www.afdb.org/fileadmin/uploads/afdb/Documents/Legal-Documents/SIGNED%20MEMORANDUM%20OF%20UNDERSTANDING %20BETWEEN%20EBRD%20AND%20ADB%20AND%20ADF.pdf [March 2012]).

52. Jack Ewing, "Development Coalition Looks to Aid North Africa," *New York Times*, May 19, 2011 (www.nytimes.com/2011/05/20/business/global/20ebrd.html [March 2012]).

53. United States Institute of Peace, "U.S. Institute of Peace Expert Named State Department Special Coordinator for Middle East Transitions," September 15, 2011 (www.usip.org/newsroom/news/us-institute-peace-expert-named-state-departments-special-coordinator-middle-east-tran [March 2012]).

54. Josh Rogin, "State Department Opens Middle East Transitions Office," *Foreign Policy Online*, September 12, 2011 (http://thecable.foreignpolicy.com/posts/2011/09/12/state_department_opens_middle_east_transitions_office [March 2012]).

55. Peter Nicholas and David Lauter, "Kadafi Is Another Notch on Obama's Lethal-Force Belt," *Los Angeles Times*, October 20, 2011 (http://articles.latimes.com/2011/oct/20/world/la-fg-obama-kadafi-20111021 [March 2012]).

56. Richard Wolf, "Obama Makes Case for Reshaping Mideast," May 26, 2011 (www.usatoday.com/news/world/2011-05-25-obama-speech-great-britain_n.htm [May 2012]).

ALAN WOLFE

8

The Power of False Analogies: Misunderstanding Political Islam in a Post-Totalitarian World

"We have seen their kind before," President George W. Bush said of those who attacked the United States on September 11, 2001. "They're the heirs of all the murderous ideologies of the 20th century. By sacrificing human life to serve their radical visions, by abandoning every value except the will to power, they follow in the path of fascism, Nazism and totalitarianism. And they will follow that path all the way to where it ends in history's unmarked grave of discarded lies."

For Bush the stakes posed by the terrorist attack were much higher than those posed by one nation's invasion of another or by the grim realities of ethnic cleansing. "This is not . . . just America's fight," the president declared. "And what is at stake is not just America's freedom. This is the world's fight. This is civilization's fight. This is the fight of all who believe in progress and pluralism, tolerance and freedom." With the stakes that high—indeed, with the stakes as high as they could possibly be—the war would have to be fought with every tool available to the United States. "We will direct every resource at our command—every means of diplomacy, every tool of intelligence, every instrument of law enforcement, every financial influence, and every necessary weapon of war—to the destruction and to the defeat of the global terror network."[1]

In speaking this way, Bush borrowed the language of the past to talk about the challenges posed by the future. His basic assumption was that the success

---

of al Qaeda, and by extension any militant Islamic movement, returned the West to the era in which totalitarian states, by seeking to gobble up their neighbors, posed a threat that could only be met by resolute force. It is clear that Bush was strongly influenced by a group of intellectuals and policymakers who viewed militant Islam as a new form of fascism: Muslim states, in their view, were all too often governed by Nazi-like strongmen who suppressed dissent at home and sought to expand their control abroad. Despite the criticism the term "Islamofascism" has received for conflating a political ideology with a religion, Christopher Hitchens, for one, defended it on the grounds that "both movements are based on a cult of murderous violence that exalts death and destruction and despises the life of the mind."[2] Islamic terrorists, according to this entire way of thinking, talk locally but think globally. When we combat political evil today we are therefore engaged in a replay of the struggle against the radical evils of yesterday.

In this chapter I argue that those who conceive the problem of Islamic militancy in this way rely on a fundamental misunderstanding of the politics of the Arab and Muslim world. September 11, for all the destruction it wrought, proved not to be the wave of the future with respect to Islam. The Arab Spring, by contrast, *will* prove to be a significant turning point. And what it ought to remind us is that analogies to the era of totalitarianism, unhelpful to begin with, are especially inappropriate when trying to understand the sweeping changes currently taking place in North Africa and the Middle East. My argument consists of two steps. First, I show that the totalitarianism of the 1930s and 1940s emerged under unique conditions unlikely to ever appear again. Second, I briefly consider the events of the Arab Spring in order to demonstrate that neither the autocratic rulers who were overturned nor the popular movements that overturned them have much in common with the events that took place in Europe more than a half century ago.

What Made Hitler Possible

The concept of totalitarianism that became so popular in the years after World War II was based on the historical experience of three countries: Italy, where the term had been invented, and then Nazi Germany and the Soviet Union. The theorists of the concept, including Hannah Arendt, Carl Friedrich, and Zbigniew Brzezinski, held that a combination of pernicious ideological thinking, dictatorial accumulation of state power, ruthless methods of propaganda and terror, charisma and the adulation of leadership, and aggressive foreign policy intentions had created an entirely new political reality. The books elaborating this concept became contemporary classics. But not only did their authors lack access to documents that have since become available, they were too close to the horrors just passed to have sufficient perspective on their ultimate meaning. As a result, they failed to anticipate the collapse of the Soviet Union and could not foresee how thoroughly postwar Germany—indeed all of postwar Europe—would turn its back on the twentieth century's history of violence.

A new generation of historians has emerged challenging the assumptions of the totalitarian model. The basic conclusion of these historians can be summarized as follows: far from being the wave of the future, as the totalitarian regimes and their defenders frequently asserted, both Nazi Germany and Stalinist Russia were created at a time when a number of highly unusual conditions converged to shape the specific form both states took. This finding could not be more relevant to the way we think about militant Islam today. If the conditions that brought about totalitarianism cannot be replicated, straining to avoid the appeasement of "evildoers" could not be more self-defeating. No one can doubt that the conditions prevalent in the Arab and Muslim world today are unstable and that it is impossible to predict what might happen in Egypt and Syria, let alone in the ever-present conflict between Israel and its Arab neighbors. Still, even if we cannot know what will happen, we can be fairly sure what will not. The return of totalitarianism is not on the world's agenda.

Totalitarianism, first of all, was a direct result of World War I. "The first World War made Hitler possible," writes Ian Kershaw, Hitler's most accomplished biographer, and the same could be said for Lenin or Mussolini.[3] None of the leaders that took their nations to war in 1914 realized just how long and bloody that conflict would be, and it was the peculiar political genius of the totalitarian dictators to explore the resulting resentments for their own ideological ends once the war finally came to an end. Totalitarianism was a massive reaction against the spirit of liberal optimism that had dominated much of the late nineteenth century. Populations that had seen irrationality on so massive a scale in the trenches could not be surprised by politicians preaching fear and creating campaigns of mass hysteria in peacetime. Totalitarianism required extensive psychological preparation, and the futility of World War I provided it.

Militarily speaking, World War I was like no other war before it. In previous European wars one hoped, not always successfully to be sure, for a quick defeat of the enemy after which conditions would return to normal. World War I, by contrast, radicalized the whole idea of warfare. This war, the historian Alan Kramer writes, was geared "toward systematic, total exploitation of enemy civilians and the resources of the conquered territory. From cultural destruction, in the sense of deliberate targeting of cultural objects, the war moved to a 'culture of destruction'—the acceptance of the destruction, consumption, and exploitation of whatever it took to wage war (including the lives of one's own soldiers as well as the enemy's)."[4] The totalitarian state's coercive capacity, from this perspective, was not created out of thin air; it was built upon a state that had already come into existence to fight as ruthlessly as possible. "The most spectacular and terrifying instance of industrial killing in this country was the Nazi attempted genocide of the Jews," another historian, Omer Bartov, concludes. "Neither the idea, nor its implementation, however, can be understood without reference to the Great War, the first truly industrial military confrontation in history."[5]

As in Germany, so in Russia. "The First World War brought communism into being," as the late Martin Malia put it in *The Soviet Tragedy*. Not all that popular, possessing an ideology wildly inappropriate for actual Russian conditions, excessively conspiratorial and sectarian, Lenin and the Bolsheviks never could have assumed power in any kind of open competition. But World War I and its aftermath created conditions perfect for their methods. "Normal politics were suspended, the economy was nationalized and militarized, culture was turned to propaganda, and private life was eclipsed by public purpose," Malia went on. "No nation's social order could survive such intrusion unaltered, and that of fragile, rickety Russia least of all. Her economy, her society, and her political system were radically transformed from what they had been in 1914."[6] It was, moreover, not just at its start that the shadow of World War I loomed over the Soviet system. Knowing full well that communism's triumph was made possible only by Russia's defeat in one world war, Stalin was determined to prevent another catastrophic military defeat in the coming one, and he continued the Soviet Union's militarization and industrialization unabated.

For something like totalitarianism to happen again, something like World War I would have to happen again. It is certainly possible that the world could experience another truly global war: conflicts between nations spilling over into violence are unlikely ever to disappear. But the pernicious effects on political life evident in so many countries in the aftermath of World War I were not due to the violence of the conflict per se, nor even to the defeats suffered by Germany and Russia. It was the very senselessness of the war, the unexpected number of casualties, the inability to make visible progress on the front that did so much to produce the apocalyptic style of politics in which totalitarian leaders thrived. *That* kind of war is impossible to image happening again, if for no other reason than the existence of nuclear weapons. Obviously nuclear weapons create the potential for horrendous political evil; the prospect of their use in the Middle East or over disputes between India and Pakistan is too frightening to contemplate. Yet because of their sheer destructive power, nuclear weapons make protracted trench warfare, and its particularly irrational legacies, obsolete. Either the possession of nuclear weapons will deter such a war from being fought in the first place, or it will, hopefully never, produce a war whose huge number of casualties will be predicted because they will be so expected.

If the war that started totalitarianism is unlikely ever to be repeated, so is the war that ended it. World War I is remembered for its irrationality. World War II will always be recalled for the sheer scale of the destruction it caused. The Jews, of course, were the primary victim of Hitler's murderous obsessions. But World War II also produced its own share of death and destruction everywhere. If anyone doubted the cost in human lives necessary to bring the era of totalitarianism to a close in the 1930s, they knew by the 1940s just how extensive those costs could become. This is not to suggest that the costs were too high. But it does serve as a reminder of the havoc that totalitarianism could wreak.

It is surely worth emphasizing, therefore, that in Europe, where so much of the carnage of World War II was felt, the desire to go to war has been all but extinguished. In the years since totalitarianism's passing, Western European societies gave up their imperial ambitions, formed first a commercial and then a political union, demilitarized themselves, aided and supported democratic movements in the Eastern bloc, survived domestic terrorism without completely abrogating liberal democratic procedures, and made clear their skepticism toward America's reliance on doctrines of preventive warfare in Iraq. "In the first half of the century," writes Stanford University historian James Sheehan in *Where Have All the Soldiers Gone?* "European states . . . were made by and for war. . . . In the century's second half, European states were made by and for peace."[7] To the American neoconservative writer Robert Kagan, Europe's skepticism toward militarism represents the victory of naive Venus over tough-minded Mars; no better proof of the attraction of appeasement exists than this general European failure to recognize the need for a strong national defense. But another interpretation of Europe's aversion to militarism is more persuasive. Given the historical experience of totalitarianism, it makes far more sense to view the postwar European experience as evidence of just how much Europeans have learned from their totalitarian past—and how determined they are to avoid repeating the conditions that gave rise to it. It is difficult to know which to admire most: postwar Europe's success with democracy or, with the admittedly significant exception of the Balkans, its experience of peace.

The economic circumstances that led to the era of totalitarianism were almost as unique as the military ones. One of them was the rapid hyperinflation that gripped the Weimar Republic in 1923, the same year in which Hitler conducted his Munich putsch; prices at the peak of the inflation doubled every forty-eight hours. Economically speaking, hyperinflation all but destroyed the German middle class. If one believes, as many political sociologists do, that a strong middle class is a prerequisite for a well-functioning democracy, hyperinflation's immediate political consequence was to fuel the rise of extremist political parties of both the right and left. But the psychological and cultural effects of hyperinflation may have been greater than either its economic or political effects. Just as World War I's futility contributed to the sense that the world lacked any sense of order, hyperinflation undermined bourgeois ideas of prudence, long-term investment, and merit. "People just didn't understand what was happening," wrote the publisher Leopold Ullstein at the time. "All the economic theory that had been taught didn't provide for the phenomenon. There was a feeling of utter dependence on anonymous powers—almost as a primitive people believed in magic—that somebody must be in the know, and that this small group of somebodies must be a conspiracy."[8] In modern industrial societies, when currency loses meaning, everything loses meaning. Even though hyperinflation was eventually brought under control in Weimar Germany, its contribution to the rise of fascism cannot be underestimated.

Even more devastating than hyperinflation was the U. S. stock market crash in 1929 and the subsequent worldwide Great Depression. In the years after the crash, unemployment in Germany expanded dramatically; roughly one-third of all Germans were without work in 1932, and the percentages were even higher in the major industrial areas. The political effects registered almost immediately. "As Germany plunged deeper into the Depression," writes the British historian Richard Evans, "growing numbers of middle-class citizens began to see in the youthful dynamism of the Nazi Party a possible way out of the situation."[9] The political effects may not have been good, but Hitler did have answers to the economic catastrophe. He blamed Jewish capitalists for its persistence, pursued autarkic economic politics that promised to end Germany's dependence on foreign investors, and sponsored rapid remilitarization of the country in ways that would create jobs and stimulate further growth. The crisis atmosphere spawned by a badly functioning economy fostered a crisis atmosphere in politics; without the chaos represented by idle workers, food and product shortages, and unused industrial capacity, it is hard to imagine the Nazis even getting an electoral foothold, let alone rising to the highest levels of power and retaining that power as long as they did.

Hyperinflation and depression, in short, when added to the pot already brewing in the aftermath of World War I, increased people's receptivity to the idea that strong-armed ruthlessness offered the only path to stability. "The Great Slump almost inevitably increased social and political tensions everywhere," Volker Berghahn, a German historian, points out in *Europe in the Era of Two World Wars*. "Violence that had become part of daily life during World War I and the years thereafter returned, and with it reappeared men who had a vision of the future that was different from the civilian one of the mid-1920s. . . . The most radical elements came to believe that the struggle could easily be won by the ruthless annihilation of the internal enemy."[10] There is no direct line from the worldwide Great Depression to the extermination camps, but there is an indirect one. Extremist politics requires crisis conditions, and the economic collapse of the early 1930s provided more than its share.

Why Totalitarianism Will Never Happen Again

In the context of today's world, any return to the combination of hyperinflation and depression that gave totalitarianism its breathing room is about as unimaginable as any war on the scale of World War II. Hyperinflation can still happen; Chile, Yugoslavia, and Zimbabwe have all experienced it in recent years. But not only is it rare, its chance of recurring in heavily industrialized countries is close to nonexistent. The closest the United States has ever come to hyperinflation in recent years was the 18 percent rise in prices under Jimmy Carter, but in the long history of hyperinflation, this was less than a blip. America's bout with excessive inflation did have its political consequences: Ronald Reagan was elected in 1980 in large part because of it. Although the entire episode was accompanied by talk of the Latin Americanization of the American economy, the United States, like all advanced capitalist democracies, had in place fiscal and monetary tools unavailable to political leaders in the

1920s. Before long the inflation of the 1970s was brought under control without any damage to the structure of democratic politics.

These days policymakers worry more about deflation than hyperinflation. While tools exist to prevent prices from rising too rapidly, there are no especially helpful tools available to government when prices decline too fast; once interest rates are lowered to zero in the hopes of stimulating aggregate demand, they cannot be lowered any further. Deflation could therefore have dangerous effects on democratic forms of government if it persists too long. But the most serious case of deflation in recent years, Japan's, lasted for decades, and despite the fact that liberal democracy did not have deep historical roots in that country, its deflation did not result in anything like a turn toward totalitarianism. Because of what happened during Weimar, we have a pretty clear understanding of how hyperinflation can create the conditions for political extremism. No one knows whether prolonged periods of deflation, should they spread from country to country, would have anything like similar political consequences. But even if deflation were to reinforce economic stagnation and political gridlock, as it did in Japan, it would be highly unlikely to contribute to the same sense that the world is spinning hopelessly out of control that happens when prices increase hour by hour. Hyperinflation leads to a politics of fervid enthusiasm. Deflation is more likely to produce a politics of sullen despair.

Toward the end of 2008, the United States and other countries around the world began to experience one of the worst recessions of the post–World War II era. Comparisons to the era of the Great Depression were not long in forthcoming. One can certainly imagine a situation in which a prolonged and severe recession could result in threats to democratic stability: the crisis in the eurozone already seems to be giving rise to right-wing parties. Because of globalization, national governments have less control over their economies than they did during the heyday of Keynesian economic policymaking, as the European situation also demonstrates. Globalization could also fuel massive anger at the foreign capitalists and financiers held to be responsible for the crisis. Countries could become engaged in a protectionist competition with each other. Hostility toward immigrants, blamed by xenophobic politicians for stealing jobs away from loyal and patriotic workers, could intensify. Were all these developments to combine and reinforce each other, the contemporary world's free trade system would be severely challenged—and with it, extremist policies and politicians would find themselves attracting greater support.

Remarkably, however, nothing quite resembling this scenario happened in the wake of the Great Recession. The reason may well lie in the ways both economics and politics have changed since the late 1920s and early 1930s. The initial U. S. response to the deteriorating economic conditions of the earlier era was protectionist; in more recent times, despite the domestic unpopularity of free trade, as well as the severity of the recent recession, politicians from both parties in the United States remain committed to an open world economy. In large part this may be due to the lack of any credible alternatives; for all the passion of the demonstrations led by antiglobalization forces, no one has developed a credible model for promoting growth along autarkic political lines in a capitalist world as interconnected as today's has become. Nor are more radical solutions all that attractive, for, as the economic historian Harold James points out, "The obvious types of reaction against globalization—fascism, Stalinism, and their economic manifestations in managed trade and the planned economy—are forever discredited."[11] In Europe as well, austerity programs may, in the short run, exacerbate the crisis, at least according to economists who believe that the immediate need, given the low risk of inflation, is far greater stimulus. Still, even in Europe the most pessimistic thinkers don't envision something like an ongoing and deep recession; although economic conditions in 2011 are as severe as any time since the 1930s, they are not a repeat of the 1930s. There is no reason to believe that anything like the radically authoritarian right-wing forms of political expression produced by the events of an earlier era is on the contemporary political agenda anywhere in the advanced capitalist world.

There is still another reason to doubt the return of totalitarianism: one totalitarian system existing all by itself is something of an impossibility. Because they all came to power in the aftermath of World War I and faced similar challenges in the drastic economic conditions of the 1920s and 1930s, totalitarian leaders watched each other carefully and applied the lessons of the other regimes to themselves. "The Bolshevik Revolution and the first phases of Soviet practice radically changed the political situation in Italy and Germany, not least in affecting what could now be imagined, what seemed to have become possible," writes the historian David D. Roberts. "Lenin influenced Mussolini, Mussolini and Stalin both influenced Hitler, and the advent of Nazism changed the situation for the Stalin regime in the Soviet Union. Indeed, there is plenty of evidence of mutual admiration and influence, rivalry and fear, all constituting a kind of web connecting the three regimes."[12] Though ideological opposites, these totalitarian regimes were operationally similar. Each system required terror because the other system had terror. Prop-aganda had to be organized and systematic in one because it was organized and systematic in the other. Totalitarianism required an enemy, and when the enemy was itself totalitarian, the existence of one regime made possible the continued existence of the others. Little or nothing about totalitarianism was predetermined, but the unique political atmosphere of the 1920s, 1930s, and 1940s, by strengthening totalitarianism in one place, strengthened it in all.

The fact that totalitarianism existed on the extreme right as well as the extreme left during the 1930s and 1940s made democracies such as Great Britain, France, and the United States feel doubly threatened; no matter which way they turned, there was a vicious dictator facing them. Yet because the totalitarian regimes were so interdependent, the collapse of one unexpect-edly prepared the ground for the collapse of all the others. The defeat of the Nazi regime required the military might of the Soviet Union, and when World War II ended, it seemed as if the Stalinist regime had been strengthened by its victory. Quite the opposite proved to be the case. Without Hitler's dictatorship, Stalin's was doomed; the Soviet Union went out of official existence in 1991, but it had already lost much of its totalitarian character even before Stalin's death in 1953 and had lost it completely by the time of the Twenty-Second Party Congress of 1962. With no totalitarian enemies to sustain it, the Soviet system turned in on itself, producing more than its share of corruption, assaults on civil liberty, and meddling in the affairs of other countries, but little or none of the massive killing and sheer everyday terror of the Stalinist period. Although American foreign policymakers continued to emphasize the Soviet threat during the last two decades of the Soviet Union's existence, persuaded that once a society had become a totalitarian dictatorship it would always remain one, the leaders of those last few years, now all but forgotten, were in no position either to threaten the West or to contain the longings of their own people for a fresh start.

Totalitarianism came into existence when the countries attracted to it were undergoing rapid militarization and industrialization without many of the features of modernity already in place. Germany and Italy were among the last nations in Europe to become unified nation-states, and the borders of the Soviet Union were never fixed. In both Italy and the Soviet Union, some lived traditional lives not unlike the peasants of the feudal period while others embraced futurism in art and politics and worshipped the avant-garde. None of these countries had had much experience with liberal democracy, and in one of them, Germany, the brief and unhappy life of the Weimar Republic only contributed to liberal democracy's destruction. Totalitarianism, in other words, offered the lure of quick journey into the modern world. The rate of industrialization and militarization would be so fast as to put liberal democracy to shame.

Totalitarianism's inability to survive the conditions that brought it into existence has had the consequence of undermining its attractiveness to societies that are seeking the same goal of rapid modernization today. The most interesting case in this regard is China. Chinese leaders are determined to turn their country into a major industrial power and to exercise all the political influence that comes with that status. They have, in addition, no real interest in democracy; public opinion is carefully monitored, demonstrations against the regime are rarely permitted, the Internet is controlled, and nothing like free elections takes place. It is therefore quite striking that contemporary China, while certainly not democratic, cannot be described with any accuracy as totalitarian either. "Under conditions that elsewhere have led to democratic transition," writes the political scientist Andrew Nathan about the years since the death of Mao, "China has made instead a transition from totalitarianism to a classic authoritarian regime, and one that appears to be stable."[13]

To promote economic growth, its leaders have opened its economy to some degree to the world economy. China's army has become more professionalized and less politicized. Party and state are increasingly differentiated. Less overtly communist in its ideological coloration and leadership styles, China is less threatening to the United States; by assuming out-of-control American debt, the Chinese are in fact supporting Americans in their lifestyle rather than threatening the West militarily. As a result, far from viewing the Chinese as an aggressive power that the United States ought never to appease, American politicians routinely overlook Chinese violations of human rights in order to keep the Chinese market open for American products. China's recent history suggests that neither liberal democracy nor totalitarianism is the only path to modernity. In the world as it currently exists, there are other alternatives clearly on the authoritarian side, and the Chinese, as well as other societies from Qatar to Peru, are finding ways of relying upon them.

The evils of totalitarianism, in conclusion, were unique to a particular time and place. Policymakers and intellectuals inclined to see the specter of totalitarianism in the world today ought to think a bit more about the historical comparisons they throw around so loosely. There exists enough political evil in the contemporary world to turn anyone's stomach, and people truly as rotten to their core as Hitler and Stalin do kill innocent others in the name of a cause. Many of them will use state power, if they can obtain hold of it, to oppress their own citizens, often in the cruelest of ways. If opportunities present themselves, some of them will seek to satisfy their ambitions to gain additional territory or interfere in the affairs of other states through whatever military force they can accumulate. But none of this bears even the slightest resemblance to what took place in Munich in 1938. No leader on the world stage today could ever create a political system as cruel and as expansionist as those that were fashioned by Hitler, Stalin, and their henchmen; the military, economic, political, or cultural conditions of the contemporary world would not permit it. We live in a post-totalitarian world, and policymakers, rather than relying on dubious historical analogies, should learn to deal with it as it is.

The Lessons of the Arab Spring

It is highly unlikely that anything like totalitarianism will ever return, but this nonetheless continues to be routinely ignored by a number of Western intellectuals and policymakers, especially when dealing with the Arab and Muslim world. "He is doing as another evil man did before him," proclaimed Mitt Romney in 2007 during his first round as a Republican presidential candidate, "conditioning minds to acquiesce to the elimination of a nation."[14] Such comments put Romney in good company. The man to whom he was referring, Iranian president Mahmoud Ahmedinejad, had been compared to Hitler by Italian prime minister Silvio Berlusconi, German chancellor Angela Merkel, pundits Charles Krauthammer and Bernard Lewis, a slew of Israeli political leaders, Newt Gingrich, the U.S. State Department, and conservative Christian preacher John Hagee. One man was the unquestioned head of a major military power who actually carried out his plans to try to exterminate the Jews, while the other is an increasingly unpopular figurehead in a relatively weak regime who rhetorically denies Israel's right to exist. But this did not prevent Hitler-Ahmedinejad comparisons from popping up all over the place. Analogies to the totalitarian era, it would seem, will not go away.

But go away they should. Totalitarianism requires a particular kind of dictatorship, and while the dictators of our era are bad enough, they are not reincarnations of Hitler. Therefore it could not be more significant that even autocrats such as these are beginning to disappear. Certainly 2011 was not a good year for them. From Egypt to Libya, and perhaps extending eventually to Syria, leaders who had clamped down on their own people have found themselves removed from power by the very subjects they once held in such contempt. Thus do strongmen become weak-kneed. They cower, and the rest of the world rightly cheers.

There are of course lessons to be learned from all this. Surely one of them is that these men, odious as they may be, are anything but reincarnations of Hitler. The decidedly inglorious, if not pathetic, way that once powerful leaders such as Mubarak or Qaddafi met their end should remind us that it is one thing to run corrupt and oppressive regimes and another entirely to deploy an astonishingly powerful military apparatus in the service of world conquest and the elimination of an entire people. The hawkishly inclined want us to believe that the United States cannot have an enemy unless he is deemed to be a carbon copy of the bad guy against whom the good war was fought. But while ordinary Germans never rose up to topple the dictator who ruled them, ordinary Tunisians and Egyptians did. Far from being tightly run societies organized from the top down with no possibility of dissent, Arab states proved themselves to be full of democratically inclined protestors intent on removing their leaders from power. We cannot know what will come next. But what has occurred already shows again that in trying to understand the Arab and Muslim world today how little we can be guided by the events that dominated Europe in the 1930s and 1940s.

One other analogy with the totalitarian period has surfaced during the events of the Arab Spring, and it too should be rejected as unhelpful. We may wish to believe that the current revolt against autocracy is merely a replay of that which eventually toppled the communist regimes in the Soviet Union and Eastern Europe, but the latter were legacies of the totalitarian period. I can understand why some who are transfixed by the Arab Spring may be seduced by this vision of how communist regimes met their fate. Yet those who cheer on the protestors share with those who exaggerate the power of their oppressors the same conviction that the world of yesterday offers instruction for the realities of today. Totalitarianism, from this point of view, is still alive—it is not so much that it threatens us as it once did but more that it seems to offer lessons in how to resist it.

This interpretation, alas, may prove as false as the one that sees new Hitlers appearing everywhere. Because totalitarianism was so evil, it seemed to follow that resistance to it, unable to mobilize much support on its own, required outside help to achieve its success. That way of thinking does not apply to the events of the Arab Spring. To be sure, those who believe in democracy in the

West ought to welcome the new forces unleashed by these popular uprisings. But they must also resist the temptation to suffocate them with their help. Not only are today's tyrants less capable than past totalitarian dictators of engaging in massive violence, the victims of their rule are likely to see outside intervention as neocolonialist rather than humanitarian. Of course, the people in the streets of Cairo or Tripoli can use assistance. But precisely because those people are in the street—and therefore not pining away in Siberian gulags or being killed in extermination camps—they have more control over their fate than the victims of totalitarianism ever did.

How we think about evil ultimately shapes how we respond to it. From John Foster Dulles's denunciations of communism to the war on terror launched by George W. Bush, American leaders have shown a fatal attraction to the idea that America's enemies are the incarnation of Satan. Contemporary political and economic conditions may make it impossible for totalitarianism to reappear, but this will not stop those determined to project U.S. power abroad from seeing threats from Islamic militancy everywhere, even in the popular movements associated with the Arab Spring, and comparing such militancy to fascism or communism (or both). The idea that new and potentially all-consuming ideological movements threaten us at every turn provides too many facile answers as to how we ought to organize our national security posture, even if those answers prove to be unhelpful, if not dangerous. Already one hears frequent statements in the West that the final result of these movements will be the coming to power of militantly Islamic movements who will threaten the rest of the world, and especially Israel, in new and frightening ways.

For this reason, I believe we ought to be encouraged not only by Barack Obama's success in killing Osama bin Laden and helping with the removal of Qaddafi, but by the restraint of his rhetoric in doing so. On the one hand, Obama never backed down from the task of punishing the former for his horrendous acts and giving assistance to those determined to overthrow the latter. On the other hand, he also resisted the temptation to portray the events of 2011 as a struggle between the forces of good who deserve our full support and the forces of evil who warrant our complete condemnation. Obama seems to recognize that the world we are entering bears little resemblance to the one we have left. That may be the single greatest accomplishment of his presidency.

It has been decades since Hitler (and Stalin) threatened the West. The world we live in today, while certainly containing its share of evil leaders and movements, is not nearly as threatening to global peace and security as the world in which they flourished. Yet as important as it is to conclude by saying how much better things are, it is also important to insist that, for better or worse, things are different. Threats exist. Threats will always exist. But at least as far as the Arab and Muslim worlds are concerned, if the Arab Spring teaches us anything, it is that responses based on another time and place are not going to help us either understand what those situations represent or help us in responding to them.

Notes

1. Transcript of President Bush's address to a joint session of Congress, September 20, 2001 (http://archives.cnn.com/2001/US/09/20/gen.bush.transcript/).

2. Christopher Hitchens, "Defending Islamofascism," *Slate.com* (www.slate.com/id/2176389/).

3. Ian Kershaw, *Hitler: A Biography* (New York: Norton, 2008), p. 47.

4. Alan Kramer, *Dynamic of Destruction: Culture and Mass Killing in World War I* (Oxford University Press, 2007), p. 68.

5. Omer Bartov, *Murder in Our Midst: The Holocaust, Industrial Killing, and Representation* (Oxford University Press, 1996), p. 4.

6. Martin Malia, *The Soviet Tragedy: A History of Socialism in Russia, 1917–1991* (New York: Simon and Schuster, 1995), p. 273.

7. James J. Sheehan, *Where Have All the Soldiers Gone? The Transformation of Modern Europe* (Boston: Houghton Mifflin, 2008), p. 221.

8. Cited in George J. W. Goodman (Adam Smith), *Paper Money* (New York: Summit Books, 1981), p. 60.

9. Richard J. Evans, *The Coming of the Third Reich* (New York: Penguin Press, 2004), p. 246.

10. Volker R. Berghahn, *Europe in the Era of Two World Wars: From Militarism to Genocide and Civil Society, 1900–1950* (Princeton University Press, 2006), p. 69.

11. Harold James, *The End of Globalization: Lessons from the Great Depression* (Harvard University Press, 2001), p. 223.

12. David D. Roberts, *The Totalitarian Experiment in Twentieth-Century Europe: Understanding the Poverty of Great Politics* (New York and London: Routledge, 2006), p. 21.

13. Andrew J. Nathan, "Authoritarian Resilience," *Journal of Democracy* 14 (2003): 16.

14. Mitt Romney, "Remarks at Yeshiva University," Yeshiva University, New York City, April 26, 2007 (www.presidency.ucsb.edu/ws/index.php?pid=77268#axzz1gjPSY3ka).

ROBERTO ALIBONI

9

Societal Change and Political Responses in Euro-Mediterranean Relations

The European Union has long developed important and comprehensive relations with North Africa in the framework of the various initiatives it has launched and undertaken in the Mediterranean. In the context of EU external relations, the policy toward the Mediterranean, that is the Euro-Mediterranean policy, has a prominent role. As part of the EU neighborhood, North Africa is not only an important commercial and economic partner but also a relevant strategic factor.

At the same time, in the past fifteen years, the societies in North African countries, along with those in the Levant, have undergone deep changes. Because of immigration, these changes are affecting European societies as well. What is their impact on the important EU–North Africa political relationship just mentioned? How do old and new EU policy responses fit with these changes in North African societies?

Previous chapters in this book have analyzed key aspects of North African societal change. This chapter takes into consideration EU political initiatives and responses toward North Africa and the Mediterranean in the Euro-Mediterranean framework, with a view to evaluating their interaction with social change stemming from North Africa.

A brief outline of the European-EU responses and initiatives toward the Mediterranean and North Africa is useful at this point. In the 1990s, in their initial stage, EU policies were pursued with an optimistic perspective: the EU believed that international and developmental cooperation with southeastern Mediterranean governments would allow for changes in the regimes' authoritarian nature and bring about reforms and democratization in the region.

Then the evolution and reinforcement of Islamism, the use of terrorism by Islamist groups, and the poor understanding of the differences among Islamist trends led Europe to believe that the obstacles to democratization lay less in the authoritarian nature of incumbent regimes than in Islamism.[1] This convinced Europe, in a shift from optimism to pessimism, to lend growing support to the authoritarian regimes, although not without hesitations and reservations. The latter were dropped following 9/11, which turned support for democracy into sheer rhetoric and strengthened, in contrast, support for existing authoritarian regimes in a context of growing interstate security-oriented cooperation. At the beginning of 2011, the widespread crisis of authoritarian Arab regimes (the so-called Arab Spring)—which arose in the Mediterranean area and among partners of the EU's Mediterranean policies—suddenly shed vivid light on the contradiction between the EU and its members states' democratic rhetoric left over from the previous optimism and the support actually provided to authoritarian, yet allied, North African regimes. This contradiction represents the failure of the EU Euro-Mediterranean policy. This failure has been accompanied by political and institutional weakening of the EU due to increasing renationalization trends, which together make Europe's perceptions of change in relations with North Africa, the Mediterranean, and the whole Arab World rather uncertain and problematic, with strong implications for policymaking.

In keeping with this outline, the first section explores the EU-Mediterranean policy's optimistic stage, which focused on democracy support and its interaction with social, cultural, and human factors and societal change. The second section considers the emergence of pessimism in EU-Mediterranean policy due to the impact of Islamism and cultural factors, which shifted the emphasis from promoting democracy to promoting stability. The third section examines how this policy shifted toward unreserved pessimism and delves into the consequences of 9/11 for immigration issues as part of Euro-Mediterranean politics and relations. The concluding section considers the effects of past and current policies and perceptions on Europe's ability to generate a useful response to the realities and opportunities of the Arab Spring.

Democracy and Societal Change in Euro-Mediterranean Relations

This section considers the EU's policy objectives of democratization and political reform in its Mediterranean neighborhood, particularly in the field of social, cultural, and human relations. It describes the policies pursued by the EU in this respect and the roles of the actors involved and concludes with some comments on the interaction and mutual impacts between EU policy, civil societies, and societal change in North African societies.

Objectives of EU Policies toward the Mediterranean

The broad objective of EU foreign policy is the expansion of democracy, which is pursued by transposing abroad its member states' experience and values of democratization, development, and integration. This overall approach underpins not only the EU's foreign policy but also its security policies, as the expansion of democracy to neighboring areas and the world is seen as a path to security. The nexus between democracy and security is the cornerstone of the EU Common Foreign and Security Policy (CFSP). With regard to the Mediterranean, both the EU foreign policy's objectives of political reform and the nexus between reform and security in the neighborhood were clearly set out in the 2003 European Security Strategy: "Our task is to promote a ring of well governed countries to the East of the European Union and on the borders of the Mediterranean with whom we can enjoy close and cooperative relations."[2]

This approach, while loosely stemming from the concept of the EU as a "civilian power," was suggested by some analysts during the cold war period but was articulated more specifically at the end of the cold war, when the EU had to revise its approach to its Central and Eastern European neighbors. It chose to include these countries to prevent their instability from jeopardizing the EU's political and economic "acquis," and the conditions set out for them to join the EU—the 1993 Copenhagen principles—were also those that constituted the rationale of the EU's CFSP: "Membership requires . . . stability of institutions guaranteeing democracy, the rule of law, human rights, respect for and protection of minorities, the existence of a functioning market economy." Enlargement has been, above all, a policy aimed at promoting democracy.

This policy is clearly reflected in the EU's Mediterranean policies as well: the 1995 Euro-Mediterranean Partnership (EMP, the most organic Euro-Mediterranean policy framework of those initiated by the EU), the ongoing European Neighborhood Policy (ENP, which in 2004 chiefly replaced the EMP bilateral dimension), and, at least in principle, the 2008 Union for the Mediterranean (UfM, which having fully replaced the EMP still has not begun operations). In fact, all EU Mediterranean policies stress democracy as a priority that all partners are supposed to share and be willing to achieve. As with Central and Eastern Europe, EU policy toward the Mediterranean is fundamentally geared toward political reform and democracy with the aim of strengthening European security.

With promotion of political reform and democracy at the helm of the EU's Mediterranean policy, the policies of economic development and social, cultural, and human cooperation implemented within its framework are also meant to contribute to achieving this goal. The modernization, welfare, and the societal change the latter are expected to generate are regarded as inherent agents of democratic political change as well. Thus the third "pillar" of the Barcelona Declaration promotes "partnership in social, cultural and human affairs: developing human resources, promoting understanding between cultures and exchanges between civil societies."[3] The third pillar contemplates common action to ensure dialogue and respect between cultures and religions, develop the role of the mass media, support the development of human resources, facilitate human exchanges, improve health and well-being, stimulate social development, foster civil society and exchanges between young people, and regulate migration and take care of migrants.

Aside from common action to foster cooperation with partners in the social, cultural, and human dimensions, the Barcelona Declaration's third pillar also contemplates common action to suppress social scourges, namely illegal immigration, terrorism, drug trafficking, and international crime and corruption, which are equally connected to societal change. This aspect of the third pillar— rather marginal in the first, optimistic stage of Euro-Mediterranean cooperation— subsequently acquired primary importance as a consequence of the strategic change wrought by 9/11 and the parallel institutional evolution in the EU, during which a fourth pillar on Justice and Home Affairs was introduced. A full-fledged policy bringing together justice, security, and freedom consequently evolved within the EU as well as part of its external relations, and this was incorporated into the framework of Euro-Mediterranean relations.

Set out in 1995, the third pillar agenda of Euro-Mediterranean cooperation has remained substantially the same, albeit with several remarkable additions, such as the inclusion of the "gender" concept in the last work program approved by the 2005 Euro-Mediterranean Summit. Today, with the EMP dismantled and the EU financial instrument reformed (from Mesures d'Accompagnement [Accompanying Measures] to the European Neighborhood and Partnership Instrument), existing programs for Euro-Mediterranean cooperation in the social, cultural, and human dimension are implemented essentially within the framework of the regional ENP policies or are mainstreamed within the bilateral ENP action programs.

In sum, Euro-Mediterranean cooperation is generally directed at achieving domestic political reform in the southeastern Mediterranean countries. In this context societal, cultural, and human changes are supported (and their negative outcomes suppressed) as factors of political change.

Role of Civil Society in Euro-Mediterranean Policy

To support social, cultural, and human factors as channels for political reform, the EU employs both top-down and bottom-up approaches. Given the official nature of the EMP and its successors, the top-down approach leverages intergovernmental relations, which have priority in this context. The European Commission and national governments promote ministerial conferences having social and cultural agendas. These conferences generally adopt nonbinding action frameworks that individual governments then develop to different degrees in their respective countries. For example, the first EuroMed Ministerial Conference on Strengthening the Role of Women in Society was held in Istanbul on November 14–15, 2006, and a second one was held in Marrakesh on November 11–12, 2009. In addition, the ENP action plans embed numerous measures and agendas regarding social, cultural, and human affairs.

However, direct support to civil society, that is, the bottom-up approach, is of particular significance, as clearly stated in the Barcelona Declaration: "[The EMP partners] recognize the essential contribution civil society can make in the process of development of the Euro-Mediterranean partnership and as an essential factor for greater understanding and closeness between peoples."[4]

The importance the EU assigns to civil society stems from the connection it sees between the latter and its democracy promotion agenda. In fact, in Western nations a vibrant civil society is perceived as an essential condition for democracy to flourish.

This link between civil society and democracy was significantly tested in the experience of the Conference for Security and Cooperation in Europe, in particular with regard to its "human dimension."[5] The end of communism and the emergence of democracy in Central and Eastern European countries have been ascribed to a significant extent to the rise of civil societies in those countries and the support they received from the West (as in the case of Solidarność). With the end of the cold war, the West's security focus shifted to the "arc of crisis" stretching from Morocco to Central Asia and, more generally, to Europe's southern approaches, and the need to promote political reform shifted to these southern areas as well.[6] Thus the EU transposed the nexus between civil society and democracy to the Mediterranean.

The conclusions about the link between civil society actors (CSAs) and democracy drawn by political leaders, practitioners, and public opinion were supported by the key research performed by Augustus Norton and his colleagues and published in two well-known volumes on civil society in the Middle East and North Africa. The policy brief is ultimately that in order to promote democracy in these regions, their civil societies have to be strengthened.[7] As aptly noted by Annette Jünemann, the strategy of democratization broadly espoused in Europe is "based on the assumption that there is a causality between civil society [and] democratization."[8]

Which civil society is the EU supporting? While a small part of EU funding is extended directly to non-EU CSAs and nongovernmental organizations (NGOs) based in the partner countries, most funding is assigned to support networks of both EU and non-EU NGOs, that is, cooperative undertakings between northern and southern CSAs. Direct support to non-EU NGOs is provided primarily through the EIDHR (European Instrument for Democracy and Human Rights). Funding to joint EU and non-EU networks is provided via a program of "decentralized cooperation" managed today by the ENP (and in some cases even by EIDHR).[9] (A list of these programs and related details is shown in appendixes A and B.)

Networking and the bottom-up model it introduces are innovative approaches.[10] The EU considers Euro-Mediterranean cooperation by means of networks much more effective than intergovernmental relations when it comes to transmitting values and driving societal and political change. It is also worth noting that European CSAs and NGOs perceive their role as channels to democracy as far more relevant to democracy promotion than the role of official European actors. The NGOs consider themselves "normative and value-laden" actors, thus destined to exert a decisive influence on political as well as societal change in the EU partner countries and provide a larger and more genuine contribution to political reform than the EU or national governments.[11]

Societal Change and EU Mediterranean Policy

Thus far the objectives and frameworks for EU policy toward the Mediterranean have been considered. Now the focus shifts to the interaction between this policy and societal change in North Africa.

How have North African and Arab Mediterranean civil societies reacted to the EU policy of decentralized cooperation and networking? What has been the outcome of the EMP's bottom-up policy described above? In truth, the outcome has been uneven and, in any case, rather modest.

The Arab governments have limited the participation of nationally based NGOs in EU programs as much as possible and most of all have prevented their NGOs from receiving funds from the EU. Many sectors of society and culture (nationalists and Islamists of various brands) rejected the offer of cooperation, which they regarded as gross political interference, or remained indifferent to it. Islamist thinkers have rejected the very Western notion of a politically conscious and active civil society (*al-mujtama al-madani*), arguing for an alternative concept of citizen or civic society (*al-mujtama al-ahli*) that builds on families, clans, and religious institutions.[12] Only a limited number of North African NGOs have been willing to identify themselves as normative and value-laden actors, in keeping with their European counterparts' thinking.

On the other hand, for all the importance given to the bottom-up approach in EU Euro-Mediterranean discourse, in reality, the resources given to NGOs and their networks are aimed less at allowing them to take independent action than at advancing official and governmental policies. Think of the Anna Lindh Foundation, whose agenda is under the control of a board that includes representatives of all the Euro-Mediterranean governments!

The weakness in the bottom-up approach is one of the reasons why the EU has failed to understand the societal level changes occurring on the southern shore of the Mediterranean and to account for the real needs of the southern societies when trying to push governments to introduce reforms. In fact, in the last twenty years, North African civil societies have experienced significant societal change deriving from the acceleration in globalization—including enhanced relations with the EU—and the accompanying economic change.[13] Civil society in North Africa is in flux today, shifting between weakness and strength, old and new, tradition and innovation, but there is no doubt that it is growing and strengthening. Where will this changing civil society go from here?

The significant societal change that has affected North Africa and the Levant in the past two decades has proven to be only partially oriented toward Western values and solutions, and in no way was influenced by the EU. There is a pressing concern in given cultural frameworks to pursue change autonomously, rather than to take part in the kind of universalistic convergence the West is preaching and expecting.

The first part of this volume, which deals with North African society, attests that actual change is evolving in directions that are not necessarily congruent with EU objectives, models, and proposals. For instance, there have been important but unexpected developments regarding women in North Africa, such as the emergence of an Islam-based feminism.[14] By the same token, information technologies, while contributing to cosmopolitan and Westernizing trends, have also contributed to the emergence of a globalized Islam, as there is no obligatory relationship between the means to multiply information and the information's content.[15] Then there is the factor of religion, which has evolved, particularly in North Africa, not only toward conservative and radical trends but also toward reform-oriented, moderate Islamism as well as a more individualistic practice of Islam.[16] While the West is quick to notice change when it converges with its own views, it seems to ignore divergent or autonomous transformations.

In sum, not only is the EU notion of civil societies in North Africa inadequate, but it is unable to capture the particular civil society dynamics stirred up by societal change there. Faced with the EU initiatives, some elements of North African civil societies are either rejecting or espousing them, but a much larger contingent is crafting its own alternative responses, ideas, and opportunities. Civil society players in the region are not opposing democracy but rather are looking to establish their own democratic profile.

If this is the situation, it is evident that EU actors—the EU delegations in the southern Mediterranean capitals as well as the EU NGOs networking with their Mediterranean counterparts—because of their own rigid "normative and value-laden" agendas, have difficulty receiving that message. More than that, they risk misunderstanding or not understanding at all the ongoing societal change and consequently missing the opportunities for dialogue that exist and are important.

This rigidity is so entrenched that it also affects or hampers relations with the Arab NGOs that share the EU's philosophy, adopt a universalistic approach, and are responsive to European and Western initiatives. Even in this case, the basically Eurocentric style of EU-Western cooperation—whether at the official or civil society level—generates unilateral approaches by EU actors and perceptions of interference and prevarication among the southern Mediterranean NGOs that agree to cooperate with Western programs.[17]

Remarks

In the first, optimistic stage of its policy toward the Mediterranean, the EU agenda to foster democratic reform in North Africa and the Levant focused on a unilateral and Eurocentric concept of democracy, at both the top-down and bottom-up levels. This concept was "normative and value laden." Such an approach was attractive for only a small segment of North African civil society and prevented the EU from understanding the political dynamics stemming from societal change there. These dynamics were generating a need for democratic change but were also asserting evolving cultural and societal differences from Western paradigms of democracy and society. Under these circumstances the Euro-Mediterranean initiative proved too rigid and unarticulated, unprepared to identify other kinds of convergence and to accommodate differences. As a result, despite optimism and enthusiasm—or perhaps because of that— this initiative failed to provide a fitting policy response to both the governments and societies of the southern Mediterranean.

Europe's Response to Islamism

The relationship between European policies in the Mediterranean and Islamism has been problematic. EU governments and European opinion have viewed the Islamist agenda as inherently anti-Western and undemocratic. This has led European regional policy to uphold the stability of authoritarian Arab regimes, even when Islamists have won democratic elections. Islamism, however, is also subject to the ongoing societal change affecting the Arab-Muslim world. While societal change has profoundly modified earlier Islamist perspectives, this evolution has been largely ignored in Europe. This has contributed to the inconclusiveness of EU Mediterranean policy, and today, in the context of the Arab Spring, it risks hindering EU policy toward the Mediterranean (as it did earlier) and preventing Europeans from grasping a good opportunity to get out of their Islamist dilemma.

Europe and Islamism

The "optimistic" stage of the EU Mediterranean policy in the 1990s and its objective of democratization were based on the expectation that Arab regimes would have proceeded with gradual reform. Arab governments proved very reluctant, however, to adopt reforms in the political realm, alleging that this would open the door to Islamists, terrorism, and fundamentalist political regimes. At the end of the day, no reforms were ever adopted.

In 2000, when the EMP collapsed, many in Europe blamed this on authoritarian Arab regimes and their unwillingness to reform. However, like the Arab governments, the Western chancelleries thought that what was preventing reforms from being undertaken was Islamism. This attitude was encapsulated by U.S. undersecretary of state Edward Djerejian, who commented back in December 1991 on the elections in Algeria (in which the Islamist party dominated the first round), "One man, one vote, one time," meaning that a religious regime, once in power, would never hand government back to a secular opposition. In Europe at the time, the Algerian elections and the civil war that followed opened a thorny debate. On the one side were those concerned about the risk of an Iran-like Islamic republic in the Mediterranean. On the other side were those who were disturbed by the EU-European governments' indifference to—and at times even support for—a coup d'état that seemingly stripped the FIS (Front Islamique du Salut) of a legitimate electoral victory and opened the way for a military regime as well as an array of human rights abuses.

When the Barcelona Declaration was signed in 1995, the European governments did not eliminate the possibility of Islamists being included in the political process as a consequence of reforms. However, they had no serious ideas on how this could be done or if it were really feasible. To be honest, European governments did not totally accept the equation made by the Arab regimes between Islamists and terrorists, and in many cases they extended political refugee status to various Islamist opposition figures. But to be on the safe side, their (unspoken) response was that democratization should preferably be attained by making regimes more liberal rather than by letting Islamists in. Over time, Islamism evolved, and EU governments broadly took note of that. Nonetheless, their response remained unchanged. So the EU and its governments did not manage to address the ambiguity. Perhaps, more than being conservative, they proved to be somewhat slothful.

After 9/11, however, while not dismissing democratization rhetoric, the EU member states moved closer to their Arab partners' conflation of Islamism with terrorism and assumed a rather securitized stance. As usual, there were important differences among EU member states, but in general the EU governments began to mute their advocacy for reform in the southern Mediterranean. They attenuated pressure in the EMP framework by introducing co-ownership (a principle that became the backbone of the ENP), which allows for reforms only within limits acceptable to and accepted by individual partner countries, as well as by turning a negative conditionality into a kind of positive one.[18] The EU countries' new security approach strengthened over time and turned into diffuse and significant interstate security cooperation, that is, cooperation between national security services and police forces, backed up by European common actions implemented by Brussels in the framework of the EU's fourth pillar.

In 2006 the victory of an Islamist organization, Hamas, in the Palestinian elections (preceded in 2005 by the electoral inroads of the Muslim Brotherhood in the Egyptian parliamentary elections) immediately resulted in a replication of the Algeria sequence, although in a significantly more explicit and unambiguous way: the Western countries boycotted the winners and, along with Fatah, prevented them from assuming power. Admittedly, in 2006 Western ideas about Islamists and terrorists were more sophisticated than in 1991–92. Yet, as a rule, government decisions were hardly made on the basis of nuanced academic analyses. As in 1991, when the election of FIS members implied the risk of an Islamic republic being established in the Mediterranean, so in 2006, the election of Hamas put at risk the Camp David Peace Accord, its follow-ups, and Israel's security. Therefore, despite academic analyses of Hamas that provided a nuanced profile, the organization was put on the list of terrorists in both the United States and the EU.[19]

All in all, in the course of the past fifteen years, the EU governments have shifted from perplexity to full distrust with respect to Islamists, and from distrust to trust and cooperation with respect to authoritarian Arab governments, now seen as bastions against Islamists and terrorism. There can be no doubt that European governments—be they on the left, as in Spain, or center-right, as in Italy and France—are supported by a majority of conservative opinions with regard to Islamist parties. This conservative vision is rooted in a one-dimensional perception of Islamists as believers unable and unwilling to articulate a political perspective inspired by, but nevertheless separate from, their religion. The idea that Islamist movements can be similar to the Christian democratic movements in Europe is either ignored or dismissed as an indefinite possibility in a distant future. In the government and mass culture of Europe, as well as in the media, the political, cultural, or social developments in the Middle East are practically unknown, and so the perception of Islamism is limited to the stereotype of a transnational believer fanatically committed to restoring the dominion of the *ummah* by any means, terrorism being no exception.

However, even before the start of the new millennium, a large body of academic opinion set out evidence and analyses attesting to the fact that there are numerous Islamist parties and movements that reject violence and accept democracy. Sociologists and political analysts showed the emergence of a secular political space of sorts, which is national rather than transnational in character and aims at toppling incumbent authoritarian regimes to install democracy rather than the kingdom of God.[20] However, this body of research in no way altered the official position of reluctance and distrust toward Islamism, in particular after the Hamas victory in the Palestinian elections. European governments kept supporting the authoritarian Arab states—especially with regard to the Mediterranean area, where they have an ad hoc policy—until January 2011 when people, without referring to Islam (or to the United States or Israel), toppled the Tunisian and Egyptian tyrannies, ironically doing in a few days the job that Europe was at first unable and then unwilling to do in fifteen years. Taken aback, EU governments forgot that their rhetoric of democratization was officially in force and imprudently tried to save the regimes. Only later did they realize that and had to take a step backward, one whose significance remains to be seen.

Social Change and Islamism in North Africa

Despite the fundamentally negative attitude of the EU and European governments toward Islamism, pressure from academic debates and the democratic rhetoric of Euro-Mediterranean policies have compelled them to accept, at least in principle, the need for an official engagement with emerging democratic Islamist trends. So, during the first decade of the 2000s, engagement with Islamists became a pervasive theme and generated a vast literature. This debate has produced no concrete results, though. Engagement with Islamist NGOs as well as political parties and movements has been much talked about, yet it has consistently failed to materialize.[21] If one talks with officials and diplomats, the explanation is typically that Islamists are neither interested in dialogue nor attracted by European cooperation initiatives; but the real explanation is that instructions from governments are extremely conditional and based on ensuring security and political interests rather than exchanges. The problem for EU governments is less the genuine nature of Islamists' democratic thinking or actions than their divergence from Western political and security interests. Consequently, Islamists, as very aptly put by Kristina Kausch and Richard Youngs, "judge the range of EU initiatives—insofar as they are even aware of them—to be about containing rather than engaging Islamism."[22]

Even after the Arab Spring, Islamism remains a nonstarter for most of the conservative European constituencies—not to mention the xenophobic, racist, and Islamophobic parties standing to the right of conservatives—and for the governments that represent them. Why such obstinate reluctance and distrust? One can argue that aside from the strenuous strategic opposition just mentioned, most Europeans, even if better informed today than they were ten or twenty years ago, still ignore or misunderstand the substance and reality of Islamism's evolution.

In Western and European views, the notion of Islamists—like that of democracy considered in the previous section—remains unrelated to societal change. Just as EU democracy promoters cannot see the democratic substance of societal change in the Arab countries because that change is less in keeping with Western than with Islamic cultural models and concerns, likewise EU governments fail to see the democratic substance of Islamist trends because they continue to see Islamism as a political activity inherent to religion. Instead, societal change in the Arab world has brought about a more pronounced distinction between political and religious activities, which may actually make today's Muslims much like today's Christians, as well as Islamist parties like Christian democratic parties.

The great change in this arena has been analyzed and registered by academic sociological studies, in particular, by proponents of the post-Islamist school of thought.[23] According to this school, in the past twenty years, with the idea of the Islamic state based on *sharia* having proved unfeasible or mistaken, the majority of Muslims have opted for achieving their political interests and objectives in the framework of national states and through democratic means—that is, in a sphere that is separate or separable from religion. The new Islamist parties are quite different from those at the end of the 1980s and the beginning of the 1990s. As Olivier Roy argues in chapter 2 of this volume, the new Islamists, while not secular, are operating in "a more democratic, open, and realistic political space."

As Roy further notes, this distinction between spheres also reflects a more comprehensive trend whereby established religions and churches turn increasingly into "faith communities" (for example, neo-Sufism), in which religion recedes from a public to a more individual and personal sphere.[24] This process of separation and differentiation does not affect culture, though, and reinforces identity. Societal change produces its own responses, and Islamist trends express and evolve in their own way, regardless of Western paradigms.

Europeans' difficulty in understanding this process can be gauged by how they read developments in Turkey since the Adalet ve Kalkınma Partisi (AKP, Justice and Development Party) acceded to power. Europeans have few difficulties in considering the Turkish AKP a democratic, albeit Islamist, party as they assume that it has been shaped in a secular and pro-Western context. However, the real reason the AKP has a democratic character is that in the course of the 1990s, it dropped its weak traditional religious dimension and turned into a modern Islamist party, strongly supported by neo-Sufism. No doubt, the process may have been facilitated by the secular context in which the AKP happened to arise (and by the Ottoman heritage). However, the process is the same as the evolution of Islamism in the broader Mediterranean, and as soon as the Muslim Turkish cultural reidentification progresses a little more in the next few years, this similarity will be more visible. Sunni Turks and Sunni Arabs are on the same path, and the circumstances that have allowed a democratic Islamism to rise very quickly in Turkey will sooner or later emerge in Arab countries as well. This political and cultural convergence is very strong. In fact, it is also emerging in the field of foreign policy, as—with the Arab Spring—Turkey's strategic convergence with the West is turning into a strategic convergence with the Arabs, at least where transitions to democracy will actually prevail.

Remarks

The societal change unfolding in the Arab countries of North Africa, in the Mediterranean, and, more broadly speaking, in the Middle East is generating a distinction between religion and political action in which the respective activities of these two realms acquire more autonomy from one another. Political activities take place in a secular space, increasingly separate from religion, and seek the implementation of democratic regimes rather than Islamic republics. In this democratic political perspective, though, these cultures and societies provide different responses from those that Western democracies are expecting.

This evolution has been and continues to be ignored by EU governments and the EU's Euro-Mediterranean policy. This is why the authoritarian regimes could tell the EU in the 1990s that Islamism was the reason they were unable to proceed with reform and, subsequently, convince the EU that Islamists were a common enemy that the EU and the regimes had to fight together. In this way, the EU, which started out with the idea of promoting democracy, failed to identify the right partners and ended by supporting undemocratic rather than democratic factors. In 2011, after the Arab Spring toppled or put into question existing authoritarian regimes, the EU's misinterpretation of Islamism risks once again, despite the deafening and perhaps futile Western rhetoric concerning democratization, hindering or even preventing the difficult move of North Africa and the Middle East toward establishing democratic regimes in the region.

EU and Immigration

In this section, I examine immigration as the third failure in Euro-Mediterranean policy. A Eurocentric democracy promotion agenda and distrust of Islamism are interfering with the EU's ability to grasp how societal change in the southern Mediterranean countries is relevant to the earlier European agenda of reforms. Distrust of Islamism is expressed in the common view that Muslim immigration is a dangerous intrusion into the cultural and social fabric of Europe and a proxy for religious fundamentalism, radical political Islam, and terrorism. The ongoing securitization of immigration reflects the last stage of a shift in EU Mediterranean policy from the earlier 1990s democratic optimism to post-9/11 pessimism, from idealism—as misconceived as it might have been—to neo-realism. The latter mindset will hinder strategic renewal of the EU vision for the southern Mediterranean and relations with this region in the aftermath of the Arab Spring.

Terrorism and Immigration: Two Sides of the Muslim Coin

The machinery of the Euro-Mediterranean Partnership ran out of steam in 2000. Four years of inconclusive talks about defining a common reform-oriented platform and the beginning of the second *intifada* in Palestine made clear that the EMP's political ambitions had come to an end. As stated earlier, the long-standing and lingering European perception of the nexus between Islamism and terrorism grew stronger with 9/11, and European concerns focused on countering Islamist-based terrorism. In this context EU policy decidedly shifted support to Arab authoritarian regimes and to cooperating with them to counter Islamists and enhance EU security.

The attacks in Madrid, London, and Rabat gave Europe confirmation that its new approach was right. European countries, while not waging a war against terrorism and with more pragmatism than the United States, initiated a systematic response based on policing and intelligence, new institutions in the Justice and Home Affairs framework, and enhanced border control. In the first decade of the 2000s, as pointed out in the introduction, pessimism prevailed over optimism: Europe sidelined the reformist and forward approach of the 1990s, which fundamentally relied on collective efforts in the EU, and set in motion a securitized approach leveraging containment and defense, mostly run by national governments.

In this approach, the fight against terrorism dovetails with the fight against illegal immigration. Immigration, especially illegal immigration, is regarded as a potential channel for terrorism, not only because terrorists can enter the territory under the guise of immigrants, but above all because those who have immigrated—recent arrivals as well as the generations coming from past immigration—could be exposed to radical Islam emanating from North Africa and the Levant. Thus immigration, seen as a proxy of terrorism, is securitized, too.

Furthermore, immigration, whether legal or illegal, generates cultural and social anxiety among European people and feeds undemocratic political trends, xenophobia and racism, millenarianism, and apocalyptic fears, as well as Christian fundamentalism. So immigration turns into a security issue not only because of its "proximity" to terrorism but also, and especially, because it is regarded by large sectors of conservative European constituencies as a danger for European social and cultural integrity. Immigrants come from many quarters; however, anxiety concentrates on Muslim immigrants because of the nexus with terrorism and Islamism and because Islamism, Islam, and Muslims in general are more culturally assertive and have a stronger, structured identity than other immigrant groups.[25]

At the end of the day, according to European perceptions, terrorism and immigration are two sides of the same Islamic or Muslim coin, and what substantially raises anxiety and leads to securitization is the potential emergence of a European Islam. Against this threat, in the first ten years of the 2000s, Euro-Mediterranean policies built on a strategy that could be defined as "forward containment," targeting Islamism and even Islam as the matrix for terrorism and immigration spillovers. This strategy is based primarily on support for local authoritarian regimes to enable them to stop or limit spillovers at the source. "Externalization" in various forms is the policy whereby the EU implements its forward containment strategy in Euro-Mediterranean relations, especially with regard to immigration.

EU Immigration Policies and Strategies

Freedom of movement in the EU space is defined and regulated by the implementation of an area of "freedom, security and justice" whose external dimension includes regulations also for non-EU citizens wishing to enter the area and circulate in it, as set out in the "Global [comprehensive] Approach to Migration" that the EU is gradually implementing.[26] The policy aims to ensure control over entrance and circulation and puts in place conditions to encourage immigration to be circular in its nature, that is, conditions that favor the return of immigrants to their country of origin. Immigration is subject to visas, and visas will be liberalized to the extent that sending countries comply with the conditions set by the EU. These conditions are essentially intended to make sure that sending countries—with EU technical and financial assistance—prevent illegal emigration, stop migrants who cross their territory while heading for Europe, and are ready to readmit into their territories both their own citizens and people who have transited. If countries comply with these conditions, visas will be delivered more quickly and easily, although within the specific limits and conditions laid down by the individual EU member states.

This mechanism is destined to be embedded, on a country-by-country basis, into the framework of "Mobility Partnerships"—of which only three exist so far (with Cape Verde, Georgia, and Moldova—none with a Muslim Mediterranean country). Bilateralism prevails. As a result, readmissions are preferably negotiated by the sending countries within the framework of their bilateral relations because they have more opportunities and flexibility in this way to link readmission to other objectives they wish to attain, such as more financial aid and so forth. On the other hand, the EU receiving countries can exert a stricter and more discretionary control over immigration at the bilateral and national level. On the whole, the European approach is restrictive and aligned on the lowest common denominator to the most restrictive national policies. Immigration is in the hands of national governments, which consider it a key security question they want to control directly and substantively.

Alongside the Mobility Partnership frameworks to come, the EU member states have set up and are now reinforcing an EU agency (Frontex) to concretely control borders in addition to the already strict ground and sea control exerted by national states. In sum, embedded or not in Mobility Partnership schemes, readmission, externalization of police tasks vis-à-vis immigration from farther afield, and border controls are the policies Europe is implementing to ensure complete control over immigration into its territory and, if possible, the return of migrants after a short- or long-term stay—in a word, an updated version of the former German policy of immigrants as *Gastarbeiter* (guest workers).

Societal Change in the EU States

The EU "Global Approach to Migration" is a mechanism that makes access possible on the condition that it is strictly controlled. It is a skeleton framework or a lowest common denominator that all members share and whose implementation they can modulate according to their own requirements. Given this broad EU framework, it is up to the states to choose a long-term strategy to make sense of migration. In fact, most states understand that beyond the "Gastarbeiter" approach and the *"bon usage"* they can make of circularity, a rather large number of immigrants are already citizens, and a sizeable number of current immigrants will remain. What to do with them? In general, the response is either assimilation or multiculturalism. Are these the best long-term strategies to adopt?

Chapters 1, 2, and 10 in this volume stress that, for reasons relating to societal change in North Africa and the Mediterranean, the past and current immigrants that the EU has to deal with today are more conspicuous for their individual than their collective profile. In chapter 2, Roy suggests that religion is disconnecting from culture and becoming more of an individual act. Fargues in chapter 1 describes the demographic and economic circumstances that are sending a wave of "single" immigrants toward Europe, that is, individuals coming from a demographic transition and whose family burden (children or aging relatives) is minimal. While this single status is bound to be superseded at some point in time, changes in religiosity are more structural and also associated with and reinforced by the effects of deterritorialization.[27] Both kinds of social change seem to make the standard European multiculturalist and assimilationist strategies obsolete. In fact, both presuppose the existence of a tie between religion and culture that is outflanked by either assimilation, which makes religion recede to a totally private sphere, or by multiculturalism, which turns religions into communities of faith similar to the Ottoman "millet," that is, minority communities.[28]

Remarks

What the EU states need to do is deal with cultural differences through a liberal perspective, delinking differences from their supposedly religious roots. In a liberal and dynamic society exposed to global change, cultural differences will confront and adjust to one another in the private sphere without taking on public relevance. Once again, European and EU responses are inadequate, short-sighted, and almost totally blind to the societal change occurring in the southern Mediterranean and its political implications. I have argued that what limits and distorts immigration policies is the nonsecularized Islam—a theologically fundamentalist Islam—that Europeans perceive behind a society that is, in actuality, changing and diversifying. As is the case with misunderstandings about democracy and moderate Islamism, European policies toward immigration are also skewed and paralyzed by either ignorance of or hesitation to acknowledge societal change in North Africa and the broader Arab world.

Findings and Conclusions:
Prospects after the Crisis of the Old Arab Order

The question this chapter has tried to address is how EU initiatives and North African societal change interact. More crucially, it has inquired whether the EU is accounting for societal change in drafting and carrying out its Euro-Mediterranean policies.

To answer this question, three issues have been analyzed:

—*democracy*, that is, the way in which the EU has tried to encourage reforms and democracy in North African partner countries through social, cultural, and human relations, in particular by promoting networking among both EU and non-EU civil society organizations;

—*Islamism*, that is, the EU perception and appreciation of the democratic potential of Islam-inspired political actors, in particular with regard to their accession to power; and

—*migration*, that is, the impact of Islamism and Islam on European societies as a consequence of immigration.

What follows is a general overview of the findings.

First, apparently most Europeans retain a strongly undifferentiated perception of Islam, in which religion, culture, and governance are not really separated from one another. In other words, Muslim people and countries are perceived as not secularized at all and, for this reason, as holding attitudes fundamentally incompatible with Western values, which make relations difficult to manage. As a result, despite statements to the contrary and a large and lasting intellectual debate, most Europeans hardly believe that Islam-inspired political parties and groupings can seriously pursue their agendas in a democratic way. More often than not, they believe that those agendas are inherently undemocratic, as it is impossible for them to imagine democratic governments and societies that are not of a secular nature. By the same token, Europeans believe that Muslims—those living in their native countries but especially those living in Europe—find it difficult to separate their religious identity from their culture, leading to a fault line that could endanger the European social and political fabric.

This European perspective contains two fallacies. The first regards the concept of democracy. EU Mediterranean policy, in tune with the large majority of European opinion, adheres to a concept of democracy that is generally tailored to Western values, be they moral, cultural, or historical. This Eurocentric approach causes Europeans, more often than not, to mistake the values and customs in Arab societies for would-be models of Arab democracy. For example, the official reintroduction of polygamy in postrevolutionary Libya is bound to be regarded mostly as an undemocratic measure, whereas whether Libya is going to emerge as a democracy or not depends on other factors.

The second fallacy is that culture and religion in today's Islam are inextricably interwoven, which is simply not the case. In the past twenty years, the fundamentalist movement, which has tried to assert and strengthen precisely that tie between religion and culture, failed to impose its view. Societal change has created a secular space of sorts, in which individual Muslims—at home and in Europe—respond in keeping more with their culture and individuality than with religion. If questioned today on issues in referendums or at the polls, their answers would accord with their personal and cultural preferences rather than with the dictates of religion. That does not mean that they would disavow religion, but that they would strike a new personal balance between religion and culture.

These findings suggest that with regard to democracy, Islamism, and migration, the EU does not base it Euro-Mediterranean policies on the societal realities in the Arab world today. While the motives for the failure of EU strategies toward the Mediterranean have been analyzed from the political and economic points of view, what this chapter has tried to stress is the mismatch between North Africa's societal evolution and realities and the objectives and rationales of EU Mediterranean policy. In particular:

—There is, first of all, a strong contradiction in EU policy, which asks for political reforms that, paradoxically, it deems the people unable to deliver. This is why EU policies, despite rhetorical references to democracy building, have in fact evolved to support authoritarian regimes. From another perspective, a rigid Eurocentric concept of democracy—defined in the literature as "normative and value laden"—has prevented the EU from identifying democratic forces and their achievements in North Africa and, thus, from supporting them, in keeping with its own goals.

—Second, Islamist parties and groups have occasionally been acknowledged but never seriously engaged. The Tunisian and Egyptian revolutions have been enthusiastically hailed, but as soon as it became clear that they would bring the Islamists to power, this enthusiasm has given way to deep concerns and soul searching, and to an even greater gap between rhetoric and real objectives—a double standard the West seems unable to shed.

—Third, while the EU Commission keeps announcing allegedly more liberal immigration policies, in reality, in the individual EU member states, Muslim immigrants continue to be contained and singled out by conservative and restrictive national policies. Again, EU governments take for granted the identification between Muslim culture and religion, which is actually waning and changing. In this manner, they are still fighting an enemy that no longer exists.

The uprisings in Tunisia and Egypt have exposed the EU Mediterranean policy's contradiction between rhetorical support for democracy in the Arab countries versus actual support for autocratic regimes as supposed providers of stability and security. They have also revealed the EU and its member states' inability to interpret the state of play and ongoing change in Arab societies. The Western media, public opinion, and governments have interpreted the uprisings as moves toward democracy in the Western sense. No doubt, in Tunisia and Egypt—partly in Yemen as well—the first move came from people and groups open to Western ideas. The use of the Internet and the role played by social networks contributed to a belief among Western political analysts and scholars that here was a new wave of democratization like that observed in Central and Eastern Europe after the events in 1989. Subsequently some authors began to make more apt comparisons to 1848, as a longer-term, less predictable, and more tortuous outcome than that of 1989.[29] By summer 2011 it was clear that the vanguards of Tahrir Square and Avenue Bourguiba had acted as midwives to history and that what history is generating is a political struggle in which Western-style democracy plays only a very minor role. The struggle is between the Islamist masses exposed to the kind of societal change that has been described in this volume and an array of conservative Islamist groups, ranging from the Muslim Brothers to the Salafists and other fundamentalist groups.

If the real dilemma is between moderate and conservative Islamists, there should be no doubt about whom the West and Europe should support. On this point, however, they are hesitating, because they know that whether democratic or undemocratic, the Islamists who win the elections will not necessarily align with Western interests in the region, in particular on Israel and the Palestinians. From this perspective, the contradiction between security as democracy versus democracy as stability cannot be easily dismissed. So the majorities in Europe (from governments to public opinion) are still reading Islamism as an undifferentiated and negative reality. Rather than viewing moderate Islamists as partners, they are unsure whether to try to ensure soft changes from the previous to the future regimes or to support the weak and confused Western-style liberals. Either choice would be a great mistake.

European uneasiness over North Africa and the Mediterranean is reflected in the changes to Euro-Mediterranean policies in the last few years and the weakness of the policy responses to Arab Spring developments. In 2008 France's proposal to set up an intergovernmental Mediterranean Union separate from the EU and excluding non-Mediterranean member states was turned into an EU initiative, which established the Union for the Mediterranean (UfM).[30] The UfM was supposed to demonstrate the superiority of an intergovernmental undertaking with respect to the EU Commission–run Euro-Mediterranean Partnership. However, in December 2008 the UfM came up against the Israeli invasion of Gaza, a classic Mediterranean political stumbling block. The Gaza crisis attested to the political impotence of the UfM (which had absolutely no influence during the crisis) and proved a deadly blow to it. Today, despite efforts by several EU member states to prop it up, the UfM is practically nonexistent. The outcome of replacing the EMP with the UfM is that the political and multilateral dimension of Euro-Mediterranean relations has disappeared. Furthermore, seen today through the prism of the Arab revolts against tyrannies, the character of the UfM meetings—in which the same tyrants were pompously and amicably received by the European leaders and the co-presidency was held by Mubarak—suggested that something was definitely wrong.

Immediately after the outbreak of the first revolts, in March 2011, the EU Commission presented a set of improvements and additions to existing policy frameworks in the guise of a new policy of "Partnership for Democracy and Shared Prosperity." Later on, in May, the Commission presented a renewed version of the ENP, which as of today is the leading EU policy framework for dealing with the Mediterranean. None of these measures introduces significant innovations. They are helpful yet are not up to the ongoing changes. Mention also must be made here of the weak role played by the EU High Representative for CFSP and the unconvincing results from the new European External Action Service during the crisis (both undoubtedly primarily rooted in the weakness of the member states). All in all, there is once again a gap between rhetoric and deeds: the EU has tried to present its responses to the crisis as innovative. In reality, these responses have simply improved existing instruments but have not even hinted at any strategic revision.[31]

To sum up, this chapter has argued that a deceptive political perspective is affecting the EU's Euro-Mediterranean policies, which are caught between optimism and pessimism, support for democracy and support for autocratic regimes, with the aim of ensuring European security. This situation is not new nor—as I have just argued—has it been changed by the EU's responses to the developments of the Arab Spring.

What must be retained from this analysis is the reflection on how deeply EU policies misread societal and related political change in North Africa and the Mediterranean at large. As I have underscored, the EU tends to see an inherently undemocratic and violent bias in Islam and Islamism, hardly recognizing that societal change has made many Islamists develop a democratic and nonviolent perspective. I conclude by referring to Wolfers's well-known paradigm: the EU policy toward the Mediterranean, while presenting itself at the outset as pursuing "milieu goals" in relations between Europe and North Africa, has increasingly emerged over time as a policy pursuing "possession goals." [32] In the Wolferian conceptual paradigm, this corresponds to pursuing the strictly unilateral interests of the EU (and its member states), more often than not at odds with alleged cooperation and democratization aims. The Arab Spring still offers the opportunity to turn a page, but so far it has not been grasped.

Appendix A. European Neighborhood and Partnership Instrument (ENPI)–EuroMed Regional Projects: Aims and Partners

Audiovisual and Media

Euromed Audiovisual III

Contributes to intercultural dialogue and cultural diversity helping build up cinematographic and audiovisual capacity in the Mediterranean partner countries. Algeria, Egypt, Israel, Jordan, Lebanon, Morocco, Occupied Palestinian Territories, Syria, and Tunisia.

Civil Society and Local Authorities

Civil Society Regional Program

Strengthens southern Mediterranean civil society so that it can trigger a more democratic debate at the national level and in the framework of the Euro-Mediterranean Partnership and of the Union for the Mediterranean. Algeria, Egypt, Israel, Jordan, Lebanon, Morocco, Occupied Palestinian Territories, Syria, and Tunisia.

CIUDAD (Cooperation in Urban Development and Dialogue)—
Sustainable urban development

Aims to help local governments in the ENPI region address urban development problems in a sustainable manner, promoting cooperation between local actors and their EU counterparts. South: Algeria, Egypt, Israel, Jordan, Lebanon, Morocco, Occupied Palestinian Territories, Syria, and Tunisia. East: Armenia, Azerbaijan, Belarus, Georgia, Moldova, Russia, and Ukraine.

Civil Protection

Program for Prevention, Preparedness, and Response to Natural and Manmade Disasters (PPRD South). Algeria, Egypt, Israel, Jordan, Lebanon, Morocco, Occupied Palestinian Territories, Syria, Tunisia, Albania, Bosnia-Herzegovina, Croatia, Montenegro, and Turkey; Libya and Mauritania are observer countries.

Civil Society Facility

Component 1: Strengthening capacity of civil society, through exchanges of good practices and training, to promote national reform and increase public accountability, to enable partners to become stronger actors in driving reform at the national level and in implementating ENP objectives.

Component 2: Strengthening nonstate actors through support to regional and country projects, by supplementing the funding available through thematic programs and instruments.

Component 3: Promoting an inclusive approach to reforms by increasing the involvement of nonstate actors in national policy dialogue and in the implementation of bilateral programs.

Culture

Anna Lindh Foundation for the Dialogue between Cultures

Brings people and organizations of the region closer together and promotes dialogue through opportunities to work together on projects. Algeria, Egypt, Israel, Jordan, Lebanon, Morocco, Occupied Palestinian Territories, Syria, Tunisia, as well as all twenty-seven EU member states and remaining members of the Union for the Mediterranean, making a total of forty-three countries.

Euromed Heritage IV

Contributes to the exchange of experiences on cultural heritage, creates networks, and promotes cooperation. Algeria, Egypt, Israel, Jordan, Lebanon, Morocco, Occupied Palestinian Territories, Syria, and Tunisia.

Education and Training

Erasmus Mundus

Promotes cooperation between higher education institutions through encouraging partnerships, mobility, and exchanges of students, researchers, and academic staff. East: Armenia, Azerbaijan, Belarus, Georgia, Moldova, Russia, and Ukraine; South: Algeria, Egypt, Israel, Jordan, Lebanon, Morocco, Occupied Palestinian Territories, Syria, and Tunisia.

Tempus IV—For higher education

Supports the modernization of higher education, creates opportunities for cooperation among actors in the field, and enhances understanding. East: Armenia, Azerbaijan, Belarus, Georgia, Moldova, Russia, and Ukraine; South: Algeria, Egypt, Israel, Jordan, Lebanon, Morocco, Occupied Palestinian Territories, Syria, and Tunisia.

Gender Issues

Enhancing Equality between Men and Women in the Euromed Region

Supports gender equality and the full implementation of the Convention on the Elimination of All Forms of Discrimination against Women, increases knowledge on gender-based violence, and backs the follow-up to the Istanbul Ministerial Conference on Gender. Algeria, Egypt, Israel, Jordan, Lebanon, Morocco, Occupied Palestinian Territories, Syria, and Tunisia.

Information Society

EUMEDRegNet (Euro-Mediterranean Regional Networks)— Information society cooperation

Supports the development and reform of the "information society" in the ENPI South countries and fosters cooperation with the EU. Algeria, Egypt,

Israel, Jordan, Lebanon, Morocco, Occupied Palestinian Territories, Syria, and Tunisia.

Migration

Euro-Med Migration III

Contributes to the development of a Euro-Mediterranean area of cooperation on migration and assists partner countries in their efforts to find solutions to various migration-related issues. Algeria, Egypt, Israel, Jordan, Lebanon, Morocco, Occupied Palestinian Territories, Syria, and Tunisia.

Political Dialogue

Middle East Peace Projects (Partnership for Peace)

Supports local and international civil society initiatives that promote peace, tolerance, and nonviolence in the Middle East. Israel, Jordan, and Occupied Palestinian Territories.

Youth

EuroMed Youth IV

Supports and strengthens the participation and contribution of youth organizations and youth from the Euro-Mediterranean region to the development of society and democracy, and promotes dialogue and understanding. Algeria, Egypt, Israel, Jordan, Lebanon, Morocco, Occupied Palestinian Territories, Syria, and Tunisia.

Source: ENPI Info Center (www.enpi-info.eu).

Appendix B. ENPI–EuroMed Regional Projects: Budget and Time Frame

Units as indicated

Project	Theme	Budget (millions of euros)	Time frame
Euromed Audiovisual III	Audiovisual and media	11	2009–12
Civil Society Regional Program	Civil society and local authorities	1.5	2010–12
CIUDAD—Sustainable urban development	Civil society and local authorities	14	2009–13
Civil Protection (PPRD South)	Civil society and local authorities	5 (ENPI–IPA)[a]	2009–12
Civil Society Facility	Civil society and local authorities	26.4 per year	2011–13
Anna Lindh Foundation for the Dialogue between Cultures	Culture	7 (+ 6 from states)	2012–14
Euromed Heritage IV	Culture	17	2008–12
Erasmus Mundus II	Education and training	29	2009–10
Erasmus Mundus III	training	66	2011–15
Tempus IV—for higher education	Education and training	60 in 2009 54.2 in 2010 51.5 in 2011	2008–13
Enhancing Equality between Men and Women in the Euromed Region	Gender issues	4.5	2008–11
EUMEDRegNet—information society cooperation	Information society	5	2008–12
Euro-Med Migration III	Migration	5	2012–14
Middle East Peace Projects (Partnership for Peace)	Political dialogue	Annual budget: 5–10	Ongoing
EuroMed Youth IV	Youth	5	2010–13

Source: ENPI Info Center (www.enpi-info.eu).
a. IPA, Instrument of Pre-Accession Assistance. For other acronyms, see appendix A.

Notes

1. In this text, I use the terms Islamist and Islamism to refer to a political actor or movement inspired by Islam. See Laura Guazzone, "Islamism and Islamists in the Contemporary Arab World," in *The Islamist Dilemma: The Political Role of Islamist Movements in the Contemporary Arab World,* edited by Laura Guazzone (Reading, U.K.: Ithaca Press, 1995), pp. 3–38 (in particular, pp. 4–5).

2. European Security Strategy, *A Secure Europe in a Better World: European Security Strategy* (Brussels, December 12, 2003) (www.consilium.europa.eu/uedocs/cmsUp load/78367.pdf [March 2012]).

3. Euro-Mediterranean Conference, *Barcelona Declaration*, November 27–28, 1995 (http://trade.ec.europa.eu/doclib/docs/2005/july/tradoc_124236.pdf [March 2012]).

4. Ibid.

5. On the transposition of the "human dimension" of the Conference on Security and Cooperation to the Conference on Security and Cooperation in the Mediterranean project (proposed by Spain and Italy in 1990 but then not implemented), see Laura Guazzone, "La cooperazione socio-culturale nella regione euro-mediterranea: Presupposti e realizzazioni", in *L'Italia tra Europa e Mediterraneo: Il bivio che non c'è più,* edited by Fulvio Attinà and others (Bologna: Il Mulino, 1998), pp. 143–58.

6. See George Joffe, "Europe Security and the New Arc of Crisis: Paper 1," in *New Dimensions in International Security, Part 1,* Adelphi Papers 265 (Washington: International Institute for Strategic Studies, 1992), pp. 53–68; Curt Gasteyger, "Europe Security and the New Arc of Crisis: Paper 2," Adelphi Papers 264 (Washington: International Institute for Strategic Studies, 1992), pp. 69–81.

7. Augustus R. Norton (ed.), *Civil Society in the Middle East,* vol. 2 (Leiden: E.J. Brill, 1995). See also Jillian Schwedler, *Towards Civil Society in the Middle East?* (Boulder and London: Lynne Rienner, 1995).

8. Annette Jünemann, "The EuroMed Civil Forum: 'Critical Watchdog' and Inter-cultural Mediator," in *A New Euro-Mediterranean Cultural Identity,* edited by Stefania Panebianco (London and Portland: Frank Cass, 2003), pp. 84–107. She quotes John P. Entelis, "Civil Society and the Authoritarian Temptation in Algerian Politics: Islamic Democracy versus the Centralized State," in *Civil Society in the Middle East,* edited by Augustus R. Norton, vol. 1 (Leiden: E.J. Brill, 1995), pp. 45–86.

9. Decentralized cooperation, that is, cooperation among nongovernmental and nonofficial actors, was implemented by the EU even before the Barcelona Process, in relations with Central and Eastern European countries and to some extent in the "New Mediterranean Policy" (a policy activated between the end of the 1990s and the establishment of the EMP). See Fabrizio Pagani, "La cooperazione decentrata come strumento del Partenariato euro-mediterraneo," in *L'Italia tra Europa e Mediterraneo: Il bivio che non c'è più,* edited by Fulvio Attina (Bologna: Il Mulino, 1998), pp.159–75.

Regarding the role of the EIDHR, see European Commission–External Relations, *EIDHR: Strategy Paper 2011–2013,* April 21, 2010 (http://ec.europa.eu/europeaid/ what/human-rights/documents/eidhr_strategy_paper_2011_2013_com_decision_21 _april_2011_text_published_on_internet_en.pdf [March 2012]). This paper plans actions and allocates funds to objectives and areas. It allocates a total of 165.4 million euros to civil society (the share of the Middle East being around 30 percent).

10. Stefania Panebianco, "The EMP's Innovative Dimension of a Cultural Dialogue: Prospects and Challenges," in *The Barcelona Process and Euro-Mediterranean Issues from Stuttgart to Marseille*, edited by Fulvio Attinà and Stelios Stavridis (Milan: Giuffré, 2001), pp. 99–120.

11. Jünemann, "EuroMed Civil Forum," quoting R. Mabro, "Civil Society in the History of Ideas and in European History," in *The Role of NGOs in the Development of Civil Society: Europe and the Arab Countries* (Amman and Vienna: Arab Thought Forum–Bruno Kreisky Forum, 1999), pp. 29–48.

12. See Jünemann, "EuroMed Civil Forum," and Ibrahim Ferhat, "Die Arabische Debatte über Zivilgesellschaft," in *Probleme der Zivilgesellschaft im Vorderen Orient*, edited by Ibrahim Ferhad and Heidi Wedel (Opladen: Leske und Budrich, 1995), pp. 23–48.

13. See chapter 3 in this volume.

14. *Ibid.*

15. See chapter 4 in this volume. See also Sergio Noya Noseda, "Islam in Internet o Internet Islamico?" *Italiamondoarabo* 14, no. 2 (2004): 118–25.

16. See chapter 2 in this volume.

17. Mustapha Kamel al Sayyid and Henry J. Steiner (eds.), *International Aspects of the Arab Human Rights Movement. An Interdisciplinary Discussion Held in Cairo in March 1998* (Harvard Law School Program, 2000) (www.law.harvard.edu/programs/hrp/documents/InternationalAspectsofArabHumanRightsMovement.pdf [March 2012]).

18. Between 1995 and 2000, EU aid and other forms of support to Mediterranean partners could be withdrawn or diminished if they failed to comply with expected reforms (negative conditionality); after 2000, partners, now expected to comply with "owned" reforms only, are extended supplementary aid and other support if they comply (positive conditionality). In other words, the policy shifted from penalties to rewards.

19. Paola Caridi, *Hamas: From Resistance to Government?* (Jerusalem: Palestinian Academic Society for the Study of International Affairs, February 2010); Amr Elshobaki and others, "Domestic Change and Conflict in the Mediterranean: The Cases of Hamas and Hezbollah," Paper 65 (Lisbon: Euro-Mediterranean Study Commission [EuroMeSCo], January 2008) (www.euromesco.net/images/65eng.pdf [March 2012]).

20. See Muriel Asseburg, ed., "Moderate Islamists as Reform Actors, Conditions and Programmatic Change," SWP Research Paper 4 (Berlin: Stiftung Wissenschaft und Politik, April 2007); Nathan J. Brown, Amr Hamzawy, and Marina Ottaway, "Islamist Movements and the Democratic process in the Arab World: Exploring the Gray Zones," Carnegie Paper 67 (Washington: Carnegie Endowment for International Peace, March 2006) (www.carnegieendowment.org/files/CP67.Brown.FINAL.pdf [March 2012]).

21. Kristina Kausch, "Plus Ça Change: Europe's Engagement with Moderate Islamists," Working Paper 75 (Madrid: Fundación para las Relaciones Internacionales y el Diálogo Exterior [FRIDE], January 2009).

22. See Kristina Kausch and Richard Youngs, "The End of the 'Euro-Mediterranean Vision,'" *International Affairs* 85, no. 5 (2009): 963–75; Michael Emerson and Richard Youngs (eds.), *Political Islam and European Foreign Policy. Perspectives from Muslim Democrats of the Mediterranean* (Brussels: Center for European Policy Studies [CEPS], 2007); Nona Mikhelidze and Nathalie Tocci, "How Can Europe Engage with Islamist Movements?" in *Islamist Radicalisation: The Challenge for Euro-Mediterranean Relations*, edited by Michael Emerson, Kristina Kausch, and Richard Youngs (Brussels: CEPS, and Madrid: FRIDE, June 2009), p. 151–69.

23. See Olivier Roy, *The Failure of Political Islam* (Harvard University Press, 1995); Gilles Kepel, *Jihad, expansion et déclin de l'islamisme* (Paris: Gallimard, 2000); Khosrokhavar Farhad and Olivier Roy, *Irán, de la revolución a la reforma* (Barcelona: Bellaterra, 2000). For the philosophical background of post-Islamism see, above all, the works by Abdolkarim Soroush.

24. See chapter 10.

25. See Felice Dassetto, "Islam et Europe: Au défi d'une rencontre de civilisations," in *Europe et Mondes Musulmans. Un Dialogue Complexe*, edited by Amine Aït-Chaalal and others (Brussels: GRIP–Editions Complexes, 2004), pp. 143–64.

26. See European Commission, "The Global Approach to Migration and Mobility," COM (2011) 743 final, November 18, 2011 (www.emnbelgium.be/sites/default/files/attachments/com_communication_global_approach_mobility_and_migration.pdf [May 2012]).

27. See Olivier Roy, *L'Islam mondialisé* (Paris: Editions du Seuil, 2002).

28. See chapter 10.

29. See Shlomo Avineri, "1989? Not Really; 1848? Perhaps," *Bitterlemons-International.org*, edition 25, August 11, 2011 (ww.bitterlemons-international.org/inside.php ?id=1426 [April 2012]); Robert Springborg, "Whither the Arab Spring? 1989 or 1848?" *International Spectator* 46, no. 5 (2011): 5–12.

30. Roberto Aliboni and Fouad M. Ammor, "Under the Shadow of 'Barcelona': From the EMP to the Union for the Mediterranean," Paper 77 (Lisbon: EuroMeSCo, January 2009); Rosa Balfour, "The Transformation of the Union for the Mediterranean," *Mediterranean Politics* 14, no. 1 (March 2009): 99–105; Senén Florensa, "Union for the Mediterranean: Challenges and Ambitions," in *Med2010, IEMed Mediterranean Yearbook* (Barcelona: European Institute of the Mediterranean, 2011), pp. 58–67.

31. Timo Behr, "Europe and the Arab World: Towards a Principled Partnership," Center for Applied Policy Research-*CAP Perspectives*, no. 2 (March 2011); Nathalie Tocci and Jean-Pierre Cassarino, "Rethinking the EU's Mediterranean Policies Post-1/11," Working Paper 11/06 (Rome: Istituto Affari Internazionali, March 2011); Christian-Peter Hanelt and Helmut Möller, "How the European Union Can Support Change in North Africa," Spotlight Europe 2011/01 (Gütersloh: Bertelsmann Stiftung, February 2011).

32. Arnold Wolfers, *Discord and Collaboration: Essays on International Politics* (Johns Hopkins University Press, 1962).

OLIVIER ROY

10

The West and the Islamist Challenge: Toward a Common Religious Market?

A key issue in relations between the West and the Middle East is religion, either defined as a faith or reduced to a culture. There is nevertheless a dissymmetry in the conception of the role played by religion in politics, both in the West and between the West and the Arab world. In Europe, despite a steady offensive from the Catholic Church to put Christianity at the core of the European identity, secularization is seen as the trademark of Europe: even the populist movements that insist on Europe's Christian identity define it precisely as an identity, not a faith (no populist leader in Europe is known for attending church services and praying in public). In the United States, conversely, whatever the constitutional principle of separation of church and state, religion plays an important role in American politics. The stress the Christian right puts on the second coming of Christ has a clear impact on turning U.S. support for Israel from a strategic alliance into some sort of theological pact, while the "ban the sharia" movement contributes to presenting Islam as a strategic threat, dismissing the Arab Spring as a mere illusion.

In the meantime, in the Arab Middle East, the recent electoral victories of the Islamist parties (in Tunisia, Egypt, and Morocco) and the prospect of similar victories elsewhere in the region in the near future have once again (more than thirty years after the Islamic revolution in Iran) raised the issue of the growing role of Islam in public life, not to mention in international relations. (For instance, will the Egyptian Muslim Brothers adopt a pragmatic or dogmatic approach to the issue of Israel?) While the recent stress on religious identity on all three sides (the United States, Europe, and the Arab Middle East) highlights the historical divide between Islam and Christendom, the populist or religious movements everywhere have a common agenda that stresses conservative family values and rejects a secularization they feel has gone too far. This agenda alarms liberal secularists who, from Israel to the American Bible belt to Tunis, feel on the defensive. If we want to put the role of religion in transatlantic relations into perspective, we have to go explore it in greater depth.

Clash or Dialogue of Civilizations: the Same Misplaced Premises

Interestingly enough, the debate on religion is based on a consensus: the Huntingtonian concept of the "clash of civilizations" is usually the common starting point, even when it is turned into a more politically correct "dialogue of civilizations." The common paradigm asserts that there are two different territorialized civilizations (Islam and the "West," where the latter is supposedly "Christian", secular, or both), defined by two different cultures that are either the secularized byproduct of the two different religions or are embedded in them. According to this perception, even if the secularization process may have reduced the scope of "religion as faith" within the West, the ensuing secularized space nevertheless remains profoundly Christian because, in this case, religion has simply turned into a culture.

These civilizations are territorialized, and the displacements of populations on both sides are understood in terms of colonialism (the French in Algeria), migrations, or diasporas, which means that a population that migrates is supposed to remain definitively linked with its place of origin and to bring its own culture to the new host country. History is revisited along this parallel axis: after centuries of forward marches and retreats (Islamic conquests, Crusades, Reconquista, the two sieges of Vienna by the Ottomans), a sudden dissymmetry in industrial development and rationalization of the state opened the door for Western colonial encroachments on the Middle East, initiating an era of Western "superiority" that the wave of nationalism and Islamism emerging in the mid-nineteenth century has not been able to reverse. Thus hotly debated contemporary issues, such as the Muslim labor migrations to the West or the post-9/11 wave of radical Islamic terrorism, are seen as part and parcel of a fifteen-centuries-long struggle and divide. The contemporary debate on multiculturalism occurs in the context of a very long history.

In reality, however, there is an initial obvious flaw in this apparent symmetry between two competing civilizations: if the Middle East is defined as

Muslim or Islamic, in terms of both religion and culture (automatically putting the Middle Eastern Christians in the category of a foreign supported minority), the definition of the West is more complex or more ambivalent: is the most dominant trademark of the West Christianity as a religion or secularism? Of course this would require an in-depth debate on what secularism is: is it the absence of religion from the public space (such as the *laïcité* in France) or just a "cold" religion turned into a dominant culture, which does not presuppose faith nor religious practices. A more sophisticated analysis, found for instance in Marcel Gauchet's writings, considers Christianity as the "religion of the coming out of religion," implying that secularism in its different forms is a product of a configuration (sacralization of the state) unique to Christianity.[1] The implicit conclusion would be to consider secularism a product of Christianity while Islam has been unable to produce anything comparable. Making Christianity a prerequisite for a true process of secularization means that Islam cannot be secularized without a previous theological reformation. Hence the issue of setting up a "good" Islam—reformed, liberal, feminist, and, why not, gay friendly—is often presented as a prerequisite for democratization. The supposed sequence would be development of a liberal Islam leading to secularization of the public sphere, thus making possible the establishment of a true democracy. In this sense, the Arab Spring seems to have sprung out of nowhere, which explains why so many Western observers are quite happy to see it replaced by an Arab "winter," which fits better with the culturalist clichés about Islam.

This explanation, however, seems to be both too theoretical and too close to the platitudes of the clash of civilizations since it ignores the concrete practices and political alignments of the religious actors, both in the West and in the Middle East. As far as Europe is concerned, even if canon law and philosophical debates may have provided some intellectual tools to conceptualize secularization, the strong opposition (and persistent lamentations) of the Catholic Church to different forms of secularization shows that the relationship is more conflictual and does not conform with a view of the West as a homogeneous cultural and religious entity. The Church did oppose both secular control over religion (French Gallicanism and Austrian Josephism) and the modern separation of church and state (the Syllabus of Errors written by Pope Pius IX of 1864 rejected this concept). Yet such homogeneity is automatically assigned to the Middle East, as if Islam had a definite and permanent definition of what politics should be. But, as we shall see, the actual attitude of Muslim societies toward the process of democratization is not based on a theological quest about "what does the Koran say?" but on a recasting of religious norms and values in a de facto secularized public sphere, even if the dominant narrative is still religious. In a word, even if the process of autonomization of politics and religion has been different, such a process is what we are witnessing in the Arab Middle East today.

The problem is that the premises of the clash of civilizations are shared not only by many intellectuals and experts but also by Western public opinion and policymakers, who all stress the need for a theological reform of Islam deemed unavoidable and yet, for some, also impossible. For instance, the policies devised by Western governments to deal with Mediterranean Muslim countries are also based on these premises (even if there is a debate on their efficiency): the use of the terms multiculturalism as well as integration or assimilation presupposes that there are two distinct cultures that can either coexist or struggle; the promotion of democratization and good governance in the Middle East, through training programs and nongovernmental organizations, means that democracy is exported as if it were a specific Western product alien to traditional Eastern cultures; even the protection of the Middle Eastern Christians is expressed in terms of "solidarity" with them, as if Christianity were a trademark of the West. In parallel, the bulk of the Middle East Muslim *ulamas* (religious scholars), as well as the governments, treat Muslim migrants in the West as if they were part of a diaspora: Morocco, Algeria, and Turkey try to keep a hold on Islamic institutions in the West and sponsor religious training. The Al-Azhar University in Cairo considers itself, and is often considered by others, the expression of a mainstream Islam that can establish norms for any European Muslim. The dialogue of civilization process, set up to counter the "clash of civilizations," enforces in fact the idea that the Mediterranean is divided between a Western Christian side and an Eastern Muslim entity. I contend here that the premises of this perception are being challenged by the changes in religiosity affecting both religions, in the context of globalization, but that neither Western nor Eastern policy and opinion makers have grasped the extent of the change. There is a definitive gap between perception and the reality of social changes.

The Wrong Debate in Europe: Multiculturalism versus Assimilation

"Multiculturalism" and "assimilation" presuppose that the close connection between territory, religion, and culture is still at work and that this has been and still is a great challenge for Western countries. While the debate on immigration in the United States focuses on the immigration of Catholic Latinos, in Europe the debate on Islam is largely shaped by the process of massive immigration that started in the 1960s and led to the permanent settlement of a huge Muslim population in Western Europe. Immigration and fear of Islamic radicalism are thus intimately linked in Europe. This debate on "Islam in Europe" has had a spillover effect on European policy toward the Middle East.

The tools that European states have forged to integrate Muslim migrants are based on the premise of the encounter between two "civilizations." These tools have taken the form of two models of policy, both officially aimed at ensuring the integration of the second generation of Muslim migrants: the mostly French "assimilationist" model and the Northern European "multiculturalist" model. Although apparently in total contradiction, they in fact share the same basic assumption that there is a permanent connection between religion and culture. In the assimilationist model, new citizens should join a new national secular political culture and thus give up their faith or limit it to the private sphere: to join a new culture is to accept a new definition of religion and embrace the secularism that has explicitly been constructed against religion (*laïcité*). In the multiculturalist model, religion is perceived as being permanently linked with a culture of origin, and thus both terms (religion and culture) are used almost as synonyms: "Muslim" tends to be used as a neoethnic term and not as a reference to an individual faith (hence the headlines on the "Muslim revolt" during the youth riots in the French suburbs in 2005). I argue that both models are in fact modern transcriptions of the old European Westphalian principle *cujus regio, ejus religio* ("whose region, his religion," that is, subjects are to accept the religion of their ruler).[2]

For the French model, assimilation is conditioned on a prerequisite: secularization. There can only be integration if religion is restricted to the private sphere. Laïcité is more or less the official "religion" or at least political ideology: instead of being cast in terms of neutrality (which is both the letter and the spirit of the 1905 law that ensured the separation of church and state), it is too often presented as a system of positive values that supersedes religious norms and beliefs. Assimilation here has something to do with the process of conversion, and the state has the right to check on conformity with the model. (See, for instance, the decision of the Conseil d'État to confirm the denial of citizenship to a *burqa*-wearing Moroccan woman.) Hence laïcité appears to be more a state ideology or at least a national political culture than just a set of rules of the game. It is implicitly cast as some sort of "official" religion. I do not want to make a too far-fetched comparison, but it somehow resembles the forced conversions imposed on the Muslims who became subjects after conquest (for example, in Spain after the fall of Granada in 1492).

Conversely, according to the multiculturalist model, the second generation of immigrants should be allowed, and even encouraged, to stick with their culture of origin—that of the country of origin. But the group is defined as a "minority," where religious and ethnic patterns are lumped together. Multiculturalism is not *métissage* (racial or cultural mixing) because it does not suppose a synthesis, a quest for a higher identity that could subsume the pristine identities beyond the purely legal definition of citizenship. What does come to mind here is the Ottoman model of the *millet* (religious community governed by its own religious laws): in this context, it is quite logical to hear proposals to integrate some part of the *sharia* into a personal status code that can be managed by religious courts of arbitration (as the Archbishop of Canterbury proposed in 2008). Moreover, to use a religious criterion to define a minority means that, symmetrically, the dominant group is also defined by its religion, even if it is a secularized form of that religion. This is still the *cujus regio, ejus religio* framework. Thus it is not by chance that Prime Minister Tony Blair waited until he had left Downing Street before announcing his conversion from Anglicanism—the Church of England—to Catholicism.

In this sense, the policy of the European states is a policy of reterritorialization, a refusal to acknowledge the contemporary forms of mobility (religious, ethnic, geographic, or even occupational). It territorializes the second generation of migrants, either by assimilation or by granting them minority status, and reterritorializes the populations of the southern shores of the Mediterranean to prevent them from moving northward.

This has been the common thread since the launching of the Barcelona Process in November 1995. To sum up, the policies set down in that process have included:

—preventing new migrations by developing the southern Mediterranean tier;

—integrating Muslims settled in Europe through a policy of some sort of affirmative action;

—defusing political radicalism by fostering peace between Israel and the Palestinians (which means that European Muslims are still perceived as constructing their political identity as foreign Middle Eastern actors); and

—preventing religious radicalization through a "dialogue with Islam."

And implementing these policies too often has meant negotiating with the authoritarian ruling regimes from the Middle East. This is tantamount to putting in place a policy of reciprocal capitulations: the Europeans are supposed to protect the Christian Middle Eastern minorities (they failed but feel guilty; see, for instance, the debate on the Armenian genocide), while Muslim states speak in the name of a supposedly Muslim diaspora in Europe (as some Arab countries tried to do during the Danish cartoons affair). The Ottoman *millet* paradigm is back or, more precisely, never ceased to be at the core of the definition of a peaceful trans-Mediterranean coexistence.

Thus the whole approach to Euro-Mediterranean relations is still based on geostrategic security considerations rather than acknowledgment of an in-depth tectonic change.

The Deculturation of Religions

What is the problem with these models? My point is not to advocate an idealist new model; the issue is that these paradigms just do not work. To understand the main trends that now operate within the Mediterranean context, different models are needed.

I will sum up the main reasons why the old paradigms do not work. First, religions are increasingly disconnected from the cultures in which they were embedded. Immigration and secularization have separated cultural and religious markers. Many Muslims nowadays feel that religious norms (for instance, *halal* food) could be applied in a Western cultural context (halal fast food). Wearing the veil is expressed more in terms of personal choice and freedom than as a wish to perpetuate a traditional culture. Fundamentalisms are both a consequence and a factor of deculturation: they shun and even fight the surrounding traditional cultures seen more as pagan than profane.

Second, to identify a religion with an ethnic culture is to ascribe to each believer a culture or an ethnic identity that he or she does not necessarily feel comfortable with. Conversely, it supposes that any member of an ethnic community belongs to a faith, while he or she may in fact reject or just ignore it. To identify religion with culture runs against true religious freedom, which also includes the right not to believe and the right to change religion. In Muslim countries the debate is exacerbated by the growing number of open conversions from Islam to Christianity, or "apostasy," which is punishable by death according to many traditional Muslim scholars. The debate on the meaning of religious freedom that has followed the Arab Spring is a clear indication of that trend: the traditional conception of freedom being tolerance for a minority group (the Copts in Egypt) is challenged by the definition of religious freedom as an individual human right.

Religions express themselves more and more as "faith communities" instead of as established churches or ethnonational groups, although traditional clerical establishments resist the trend. It is not by chance that traditional Middle Eastern Christian churches, embedded in centuries-old cultures, are slowly disappearing while Protestant evangelism is making a breakthrough in Muslim societies, both in North Africa and in immigrant communities. Symmetrically, Islamic fundamentalist movements in Europe (including radical ones) are attracting many converts. The culturally embedded religions are in crisis: the Catholic Church, the traditional forms of Islam, liberal Lutheran Protestantism, Christian orthodoxies, Eastern Christian churches—they are challenged by evangelism, Salafism, and neo-Sufism.

Third, to identify religion with culture also means identifying European Muslim citizens as a "Middle Eastern diaspora" and thus importing the Middle Eastern conflicts into the European space, precisely at a time when such importation is perceived as a source of potential tension. For instance, the supposed identification of second-generation Muslims with the Palestinians as a consequence of watching Al Jazeera in Arabic has been largely exaggerated.[3]

A final reason why the old paradigms do not work is demonstrated in the emergence of a post-Islamist generation during the 2011 events in the Middle East. For those involved in the uprisings, the great revolutionary movements of the 1970s and 1980s are ancient history, their parents' affair. This new generation is not interested in ideology. Their slogans were pragmatic and concrete: *"Erhal!"*—"Get out!" Unlike their predecessors in Algeria in the 1980s, they made no appeal to Islam; rather, they were rejecting corrupt dictatorships and calling for democracy. This is not to say that the demonstrators are secular, but they are operating in a secular political space, and they do not see Islam as an ideology capable of creating a better world. And the same goes for the other ideologies: the demonstrators were nationalists (look at all the flag waving) without advocating nationalism. Particularly striking is the abandonment of conspiracy theories: the United States and Israel (or France in Tunisia) were no longer identified as the cause of all the misery in the Arab world. The slogans of pan-Arabism have largely been absent, too, even if the copycat effect that brought Egyptians and Yemenis into the streets following the events in Tunis shows that the "Arab world" is a political reality.

This generation is pluralist, undoubtedly because it is also individualist. Sociological studies show that it is better educated than previous generations, better informed, often with access to modern means of communication that allow individuals to connect with one another without the mediation of political parties (which in any case are banned). These young people know that Islamist regimes have become dictatorships; neither Iran nor Saudi Arabia holds any fascination for them. Indeed, those who have been demonstrating in Egypt are the same sort of people who came onto the streets in Iran to oppose Ahmedinejad in 2009.

The blurring of the religious borders is also illustrated by the wave of cross-directional conversions: not only has there been a wave of conversions to Islam among young Europeans but also a wave of conversions to Christianity among Muslims, in Europe as well as in North Africa and the Middle East. These conversions are possible because, beyond the religious differences, there has been a growing convergence on "religiosity," that is, the way a believer experiences his or her faith. This quest is now individual, based on the search for personal "realization," and is done in a growing "common religious market" where the products are easily accessible (religious TV channels, Internet, travels) and increasingly shaped along the same marketing patterns. For instance, the new Islamic TV preachers, like the Egyptian Amr Khaled, borrow not only the techniques but also the values and psychology from the evangelist TV preachers.

Pressures on the Muslim communities in Western Europe and the endeavors of their members to find some sort of "compatibility" (not necessarily compromise) between their religious practices and the dominant paradigm of what a religion is or should be have led to what I call the "formatting" of Islam. The consequence of this formatting is to place Islam within the same paradigm as the other religions. What is the new "format" that Islam is now increasingly sharing with the other religions in the West? There are three dimensions to it:

—*Convergence of religiosities*: in other words, defining faith and the believer's relationship to his or her religion, often in terms of a spiritual quest. The market offers a wide range of products to fulfill one and the same demand. This demand thus tends to be standardized by the market, which reflects the consumers' image of what the products are supposed to be. Nowadays, religion is no longer defined by anthropologists or philosophers and less and less by the "professionals"—clerics or preachers—who are chasing after the convert-customer. Individual conversions often illustrate this itinerant, nomadic, even eclectic characteristic of the new believer.

—*Convergence of definition*: the notion of "religion" becomes a normative paradigm with no specific content. It is the designation of any system as a religion, without taking account of the content that makes it a religion. These days it is the courts that decide in the event of dispute, even though they claim not to deal with matters of theology. Even, and perhaps especially, in countries where there is a strict division between religion and power (France, the United States) that prohibits the state from defining what a religion is, it is still necessary to say what is entitled to the label of a religion, even if only to enable religious freedoms, entitlements, and practices (exemption from tax, chaplaincy, definition of places of worship, dietary exemptions, religious holidays). Democratization and human rights theory tend to standardize the definition of religion in order to treat everyone equally (with the consequence of putting ethnic and religious minorities on the same footing). Secularism thus creates religion since, in order to keep it at a distance, it must assign religion a place and therefore define it as a "pure religion."[4] Formatting aims to standardize the manifestation of religion in the public sphere and thus put "religious practice" under control, from the wearing of the headscarf by Muslim women to the erection of an *eruv* (a thread that turns a neighborhood into a private sphere for Shabbat) around an orthodox Jewish neighborhood to the right (or prohibition) to smoke hashish (a demand by the Rastafarians in the United States, which was rejected) or to drink wine (Christian mass in prohibitionist countries).

—*Convergence of religious institutions*: the figure of the "priest" or "minister" tends to define all religious practitioners or professionals. Thus ulamas become "theologians," and imams and rabbis become "parish" leaders. In the name of maintaining equality among believers, the law, the courts, and also the institutions tend to format all religions in the same way. For example, in extending the principle of chaplaincy to Islam, the army and the prison authorities reinforce the institutional alignment of Islam with Christianity. In this sense, we can speak of the "churchification" of religions by courts and states.

But there are other trends that affect Muslims, whether or not they live in the West. These include the process of "self-service" (taking from a given religion what fits one's needs and only that); of hybridization (borrowing from other religions practices, techniques, such as Zen meditation, and forms of spirituality, or even borowing from other domains, such as marketing); and juxtaposing very secular attitudes and practices (night clubs, heavy metal music) with the affirmation of being a true believer. In a word, everything linked with the process of individualization of faith contribute precisely to making the return to Islam (on the model of the born-again Christian) compatible with the process of democratization. Hence some very visible patterns, such as the younger generation's rejection of previous generations' cultural Islam (which might take the form of adherence to fundamentalist norms, as in Salafism), may paradoxically work in favor of the disconnection of religion from the public sphere. It is not theological reformation that leads to democratization, but the individualization of faith, whatever form it may take.

A Growing Gap in Perceptions, but a Growing Convergence in Practices

Unfortunately, Europe has not taken these changes into account; it still refers to an outdated perception of what Islam could mean as a "culture" instead of paying attention to the consequences of the disconnect between religion and culture. Instead of trying to pursue an elusive multiculturalism or to impose an assimilation based on the wrong perception of its "common values," Europe should stick to its principles:

—Deal with religions as "simply" religions, not as the expression of cultures or ethnic groups. Recognize faith as an individual and free choice and promote freedom of religion by treating all religions equally, but only as religions.

—Do not confuse ethnolinguistic minorities with faith communities. Both exist in the EU, but each kind of group should be dealt with according to different legal paradigms: freedom of religion is not the same thing as minority rights, although they could of course overlap. (This is why, for instance, I am not happy with the term "islamophobia.") A faith is a choice, whereas a racial or ethnic identity is, at least in the beginning, a given fact or an appellation bestowed from outside. The confusion between the two jeopardizes the way citizenship and personal freedom have been established as the basic principles of democratic political life.

One last point is that the paradigms I am criticizing do not reflect the new patterns of mobility and settlement around the Mediterranean. The bulk of migrations now come from beyond the Mediterranean. There is no longer a massive labor migration stemming from the Mediterranean countries. Fluxes are more fluid, circulation also goes in both directions: elderly Europeans are settling in Tunisia and Turkey for retirement, and the jet set has its fashionable quarters in Morocco. Many second-generation immigrant college graduates or entrepreneurs are looking for job opportunities or are investing in business and companies that focus on trans-Mediterranean joint ventures (real estate, travel agencies, import-export, medical activities, education, holiday resorts, and so on). The increasing number of people with dual citizenship facilitates these new patterns of circulation. The informal or grey economy also, by definition, plays on these transnational networks, which go far beyond family ties and "ethnic business."

Migrations from the Mediterranean areas (not the new migrations from China, Iraq, Afghanistan, or sub-Sahelian Africa) are more flexible, temporary, and reversible than before. In fact, we should speak more of labor mobility or even professional mobility than labor migration: some educated young Moroccans may have a French passport, take a job in London, then return to Morocco or go to Abu Dhabi to open a business. Instead, governments try to fix the population: visa restrictions force people to move less but also to stay once they are in the West, legally or illegally, whereas they could move more easily if they felt more secure about their administrative status. The social status of many second-generation immigrants has improved and is slowly changing matrimonial patterns. The old pattern—marrying a cousin from the *bled* (home village) in order to bring new family members into Europe—is not dead but is increasingly being replaced by individual choice among young graduates and entrepreneurs.

Despite this shift in labor patterns and expectations of mobility, students and relatives are treated too often as potential immigrants. The fact that a country like Turkey is hardly exporting manpower any more is not taken into consideration. The process of territorialization has been unable to stop illegal migration while thwarting many positive dynamics for mutual development. This endeavor to territorialize the populations is a legacy of the old model of territorial nation-states.

And yet the ongoing construction of a European political entity runs counter to the paradigm of the nation-state and is more in tune with contemporary forms of mobility. Often mocked and despised, the evolutionary and elusive European Union, where flexibility and bureaucracy make strange but already mature bedfellows, could deal perfectly with our Mediterranean complexity. Instead of aping the nation-state or dreaming of past empires, Europe could look positively upon its own incompletion as a better tool to manage fluxes, deterritorialization, and globalization. Europe has inaugurated a new relationship with territorialization: there are different groupings and boundaries (the twenty-seven member states of the EU, the Schengen Area, and the eurozone, for example) and a permanent virtual expansion because of its inability to define a real border.[5] As we have seen, this does not mean an open space—borders have too often been replaced by internal fences, walls, and ghettoes—but at least there is a juxtaposition of different spaces.

By the same token, whatever the ups and downs of the Arab Spring and a possible conservative Arab backlash, it is clear that the sudden stress on religion in the public sphere that will follow the electoral victories of the Islamist parties will not reconnect religious practices with traditional cultures. On the contrary, it will highlight the diversity of the very conceptions of how religious norms and references can be translated into the public sphere. There is a big gap (for instance, as far as women's status is concerned) between the strict implementation of sharia, as advocated by the Salafis, and the recasting of religious norms into more universal, conservative values—as promoted by the Turkish AKP (Justice and Development Party) or the Tunisian al-Nahda Party (from the restriction of alcohol consumption to moral censorship)—that are closer to Utah's public regulations than to Saudi sharia norms. Any institutionalization of democracy, even if the actors are not specifically "liberals," will turn religious freedom into a personal individual right. Thus tensions between national identities (emphasized by the rising populist movements in the Arab Middle East, Europe, and the United States) and the individual freedoms of citizens will rise. Even if a religion is dominant in statistical terms, even if it has shaped the national identity, the right to believe in any religion—or the right not to believe—is part and parcel of a modern democracy. It will be no surprise if, from Oklahoma to Upper Egypt, the debate on identity and freedom will revolve around religious issues.

Notes

1. Marcel Gauchet, *The Disenchantment of the World* (Princeton University Press, 1999).

2. Translation from www.merriam-webster.com/dictionary/cujus%20regio,%20ejus%20religio.

3. No youngster who participated in the 2005 riots in France waved a Palestinian flag, and when Al Jazeera decided to create a channel in English, it was precisely because few European Muslims are able to watch it in Arabic. (By the way, the English language channel is far more moderate precisely because it aims at a non–Middle Eastern audience.)

4. Olivier Roy, *Secularism Confronts Islam* (Columbia University Press, 2007).

5. The phrase "permanent virtual expansion" refers to a moving border, with new potential member states declaring themselves after each enlargement.

CESARE MERLINI

11

The Challenge of a Changing Arab Islam in Future Transatlantic Relations

Europe lost its global dominance during the twentieth century. The United States assumed the role of the number one world power, but with the transition into this century, it has been increasingly seen as surrendering that primacy—the extent and nature of the surrender being the subject of much current literature.[1] Does that mean that "the decline of the West," the scenario Oswald Spengler depicted almost a century ago, is finally coming true, after having been repeatedly dismissed or recalled ever since?[2] What is the West today?

There is of course a broader West which, besides Europe and the United States, includes Canada, a NATO member, and to various degrees countries that lie further afield, such as Australia and New Zealand. Vast peripheral areas such as Eastern Europe and Latin America—which share many features of a common history, culture, and society—can also be identified. Then there are border, or bridging, areas. The extraordinary post–World War II development of Japan, for instance, a nation of the Far East, has been closely associated with the West, from its tight alliance with the United States to its participation in the G-7. Turkey, also a non-Western country, has been a NATO member and a long-standing candidate for joining the EU. Today's Brazil, however, unlike yesterday's Japan, wants an independent role as a rising power alongside China and India. And Recep Tayyip Erdogan, the Turkish prime minister, now leads a government aspiring to a regional role and to becoming an emerging economy, defined in terms of its own culture and religion. In sum, the West's boundaries are uncertain. The question is: are they shrinking or broadening?

At the center of the West is still the United States, whose leadership has been recognized more or less enthusiastically for a sizable part of the last century. Its current decline in primacy, now also perceived by many Americans, has many facets, some of which border on the paradoxical. Most evident is its geo-economic decline as a consequence of the emergence of rival economic powers, made possible by worldwide free trade and investment within an international system that is largely a product of the West, above all, of U.S. predominance. *How America Fell behind in a World It Invented* is the subtitle of a recent book by two well-known commentators on the current status of the United States as compared to the past.[3] For now, however, the American economy remains well ahead of second-place China, which has a population four times as large.

But there is also talk of a geostrategic decline, despite the fact that the United States is by far the largest military power, surpassing all of the next seventeen in the global hierarchy combined and deploying some eleven aircraft carrier fleets on nearby as well as remote seas and oceans, with as many as 2.5 million military personnel having been sent to foreign bases over the last decade. Coincidentally, in keeping with this paradox, the discourse about America's decline in relative geopolitical terms became more widespread among historians and observers indulging in comparing the lonely position of the United States at the top of the global power pyramid—after its "victory" in the cold war—with that of the Roman or British empires.[4] More sober analyses were content with calling the United States a "reluctant sheriff" or defining it as "the indispensable nation."[5] The question is: to what extent do even such measured assessments still apply today?

In fact, when talking about the West, the most frequent, if implicit, reference is to the northern transatlantic space, made up of the United States and the European Union, the latter with its traditional ambivalence between a body of shared institutions and a cluster of the small to medium-size sovereign states that happen to belong to them. After cold war transatlantic solidarity—often idealized well beyond reality—and against many odds, the alliance survived the demise of its raison d'être. With the end of the Soviet empire, the European partners still enabled the most far-reaching process of spreading democracy ever, after having seconded the American leadership in bringing about a newly multipolar but highly interdependent and relatively less bellicose world. It is within this new world that a power shift from the West to Asia is taking place. Now, given such a power shift, are the dethroned Europe and the declining United States bound to separately become remnants of the past? Or do they still share enough strategic and economic interests to suggest that, by acting coherently and using complementary capabilities, they can exert sufficient influence on the course of events for quite some time to come?

The Europeans tend to question the legitimacy of U.S. leadership less now—suffice it to mention the case of Sarkozy's France—but its efficacy more—Merkel's Germany may be the most significant example here. On the other hand, they are no longer seen as important partners by a growing proportion of Americans. Even many liberal internationalists implicitly or explicitly consider Europe's contribution to the building of a new world order negligible and tend to focus on the rising powers, in view of the fact that the United States may need partners in the future even more than in the past, unless it goes isolationist.[6] Europe's inadequate military contribution to the onus of upholding international security is a major factor in such neglect, followed by the aforementioned institutional ambiguities of the "European identity" and the related return to national priorities in many EU member states—none of which is a global power if considered separately. Among conservative Republicans and pious Christians, the neglect turns into disdain for a *vieux continent* (old continent) prone to godless secularism, overgenerous welfare, and international appeasement, particularly in the rhetoric of an election year.[7] Only a small minority point to the fact that the European Union, even if loosely knitted, is still the world's largest international player in trade, investment, research, and foreign aid, well above China and India, in addition to being the region most in accord with the United States regarding the desirable future shape of the global system.[8]

Things have been further complicated by events following the 2008 financial—turned economic—crisis. From the collapse of subprime mortgages in the United States to the crisis of the euro, the two shores of the Atlantic have been made more aware of their mutual dependences and influences, including the negative ones. High and growing public indebtedness has become an unwelcome common feature—along with, by the way, the perception of inadequate political leadership. At the moment of this writing, it is hard to evaluate the depth and predict the duration of the economic downturn or its possible long-term global impact. In any case, a further descent of the West appears to be a reasonable forecast, with two consequences worth mentioning. First, the exposed weaknesses of economic liberalism could affect the stability of an international order based on interdependence and constructive international cooperation. A new emphasis on multipolarity could even suggest a return to an order based on balance of power, as in nineteenth-century

Europe.[9] Second, and independent of the world order, recent economic constraints may seriously impinge upon foreign policy options and the tools that both Americans and Europeans have applied in many regions, including the one dealt with in this book.

Moreover, Western polities and societies are affected by the changing global status of the states they belong to. Attention is drawn here to the rise of populist, xenophobic, and reactionary European parties or movements, opposed to their countries taking on a larger burden in terms of peacekeeping, human rights protection, fair development assistance, and, above all, receiving labor migrants, in spite of their need for them. This last problem is shared by the United States, but its most acute issue is the widening internal gap in income and wealth, to the detriment of the middle class and the American dream of fairness and equal opportunity, once a source of pride and promoted as a model for rising economies, such as Brazil. Common to both sides of the Atlantic, aside from debt, is also the waste that characterizes their way of living, particularly in the United States—hardly a model for emerging countries, much less poor ones.

These problems in the economic and political fabric of the Western nations risk affecting the strength of their societies, which are undergoing, like the others, various kinds of transformation. Two features may be of specific interest here. First, these transformations are common to Americans and Europeans to a larger extent than to most other societies. Second, these changes are generally at a more advanced stage than in the rest of the world, though often less rapid at present, as a consequence. Of the five areas of societal change discussed elsewhere in this book in relation to the Arab world, it may be of interest to underline that transatlantic commonalities seem to be more evident in the areas of gender relations and Internet penetration, even though the latter is higher in the United States (78 percent) than in the EU (61 percent).[10] Some discrepancies are visible instead with regard to migrations, both for the obvious cultural differences vis-à-vis the phenomenon (the United States is a nation of immigrants while Europe is new to the challenge) and for the different ethnic and religious mix of the newcomers. Possibly the area in which the difference has become most evident, at least in the past two decades, is religion, including the way faith is the object of proselytism. Nevertheless, the importance that American youth attach to faith in one's personal life appears to be less than among the older generations, a trend in keeping with attitudes on the other side of the Atlantic.[11] More generally, a recent poll has shown that the

American public is converging with the European public in that they no longer see their culture as superior to that of other nations to the extent they used to.[12]

Before turning to Arab Islam, I want to go back for a moment to the "surrender" of two centuries of Western global hegemony. Such a development should not hide the huge impact this "great culture," to use Spengler's terminology, has had on other civilizations, first thanks to Europe, then mainly to America. Even assuming that the world will inevitably "de-westernize" to some extent as a consequence of the West's decline and the rise of new powers and cultures—who likely will have their own ideas with regard to alternative global structures—the current international system will continue to feel a decisive Western imprint in the future.

Arab Islam as an Interlocutor with the West

Samuel Huntington identified nine civilizations, more or less the same as Spengler had done nine decades earlier. The West was one, of course; Latin America was another; Japan, another, and so on. Then he famously said that they are bound to clash the way nations clashed in the past. In a widespread Western narrative, especially among conservatives, Islam has been the clashing civilization par excellence. As in previous episodes in history, the existence of large and expanding multitudes contributes to the alarm. Muslims represent a growing component of the global population. According to the Pew Forum, their share is projected to reach 24.9 percent in 2020 and 26.4 percent in 2030, compared to 23.4 percent in 2010.[13] Beyond the demographic factor, Islam is an important and complex reality, and the challenges it provides for Western countries and societies are multiple and occasionally turn—or are perceived as turning—into threats.

Attention here is limited to that part of Islam that is Arab. This is not the largest portion: the five top Muslim populations are not found in any Arab country. Nor is this contingent currently among the most economically important: no Arab state is among the BRICS, the group of rising powers, and only one—pre–Arab Spring Egypt—was listed by Goldman Sachs among the Next Eleven, the potentially emerging economies that hope to follow China, India, and Brazil one day.[14] No Arab state is among the G-8, and only one, oil-rich Saudi Arabia, is among the G-20, the supposedly new board room of "Interdependence Inc." Despite recurrent demands for an "Arab bomb," the few initial and vulnerable attempts to build a nuclear device, like the one Pakistan has and Iran is apparently seeking to build, were stopped by Israel. Few original contributions to multilateralism have come from the region, apart from a weak and fractured Arab League, which only the spectre of a Syrian civil war seems to have rescued from irrelevance. Past attempts to generate stronger cooperation or even integration, such as among Maghreb states following the model of the neighboring European Community, failed completely. Random proclamations of unity by two or more countries have not had any serious content. In sum, at first glance the Arab world appears to be a grey area lying between a declining but still decisive North Atlantic space and the rising Asian continent: hardly an important contributor and potentially a disturbance to the scenario of a new East-West duopoly.

The current state of affairs was preceded by developments predominantly influenced by external actors, once the fight for independence, largely the result of endogenous forces, was over. The end of colonization became entangled with the advent of the cold war, an external, tough rivalry that had both direct and indirect consequences in the region, including the establishment of secular states—more or less socialist, more or less capitalistic—that turned into regimes. The petrodollar bonanza did little in terms of modernizing and empowering Arab nation-states, including those hugely endowed with black gold. The end of the oil boom brought about the tutorship of the international financial institutions, the International Monetary Fund and the World Bank in particular, with their well-known criteria. Throughout, the United States has exerted the strongest external influence, dictated, however, by changing national security imperatives (containing the Soviet Union, ensuring oil supplies, and fighting terrorism) and by the increasingly demanding unconditional guarantee extended to Israel.

The European countries and their common institutions were potentially the most important partners, but they have largely failed to fulfill the task, absorbed as they have been by other priorities, such as institutional reform and the geographic extension of the integration process (while maintaining close relations with the United States). The EU's policy of spreading democratic contagion toward the East has frequently been employed as a policy template to be applied in the southern Mediterranean. However, the feasibility of such a scenario is obviously questionable because of the differences between the two theaters. The fact remains that Europe has been seen as seriously underperforming in the case of North Africa, at the risk of being overtaken by some new non-Western external actors, such as distant China or nearby Turkey. The latter in particular has gained huge popularity in the region following the uprisings.

The polities of the Arab states, above all those in North Africa and the eastern Mediterranean, have resented these exogenous factors of influence. Many of the internal power elites have been able to consolidate thanks to their ability to adapt to, entrench with, and exploit these outside influences. The main request from external political and economic actors has been stability—a priority that has contributed to the securitization of public affairs and the consequent enhancement of the internal role of the military, in Egypt in particular. Another typically Western request has been legitimacy. Especially in the eyes of the Americans, however, legitimacy was to be obtained essentially through democracy, and democracy through elections. Other features of a modern state, such as civil rights, the rule of law, separation and balance of powers, an independent judiciary—in sum, a state apparatus not limited to the armed forces—did not receive comparable attention. It was thus sufficient for the regimes to periodically organize more or less fake elections, often plebiscites. Then economic growth, however unstable, unfairly distributed, and plagued with cronyism corruption and clientelism, was used to obtain as much domestic consensus as possible, with the security apparatus taking care of the remainder—a conspicuous remainder.

Speaking of democracy, a survey by the Center for Systemic Peace reveals a gradual increase in the number of democratic states in the world since the final phase of the cold war.[15] The survey distinguishes between democracies, autocracies, and "anocracies," that is, states with incoherent or inconsistent authority patterns—partly liberal, partly authoritarian. The trend in the number of countries seen to belong to each of these three groups, in the 1945–2010 period, is shown in figure 11-1 for the world and figure 11-2 for the Middle East and North Africa (MENA) region. The latter partly shares the global trend, including the decline in autocracies since the mid 1980s, but at least until 2010 remained the only region on earth where democracies came last. It is obviously too soon to assess the impact of the so-called Arab Spring on that finding, which came from data before the uprisings began, but a new light is being cast upon the long-standing debate on whether the impediments to democracy in these countries derive from endogenous cultural, historical, and religious factors or from excessive securitization and premature liberalization enhanced by the aforementioned exogenous pressures.

Figure 11-1. *Global Trends in Governance, 1946–2011*[a]

Number of countries

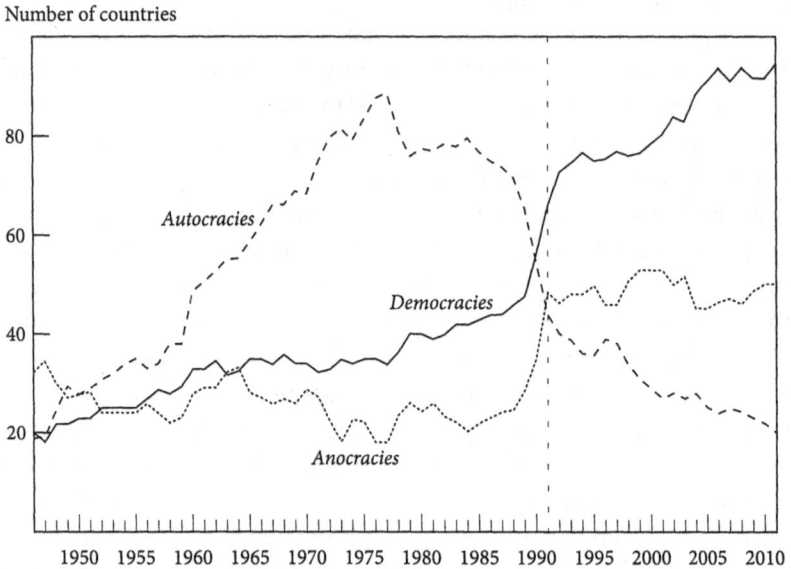

Source: Center for Systemic Peace, "Global Conflict Trends: Measuring Systemic Peace," figure 12 (http://www.systemicpeace.org/CTfig12.htm).
a. Countries with populations exceeding 500,000.

Western democratic states have descended from the Renaissance and the Enlightenment, along a bloody road. The Arabs had their own school of humanist thought, of such richness as to be comparable to the European one, but they did not experience a European-style Enlightenment; rather, the legacy of the latter, including state culture, reached them from the outside via colonization. They have multiple selves, like people in all nations, and the relative importance of each can change according to circumstances. Scores have migrated to other Arab as well as non-Arab countries. National secular institutions are generally weak, the significant differences from country to country notwithstanding. Their current search for an identity, either at home or abroad, is inevitably affected by the perceptions they have of the above problems of belonging, citizenship, and place in a globalized world, in addition of course to those related to subsistence now and well-being in the future.

A survey conducted in October 2011 by the Saban Center of the Brookings Institution in five Arab countries (Egypt and Morocco in North Africa, the United Arab Emirates, Lebanon, and Jordan in the Middle East) shows that the

Figure 11-2. *Middle East Regimes by Type, 1946–2010*

Number

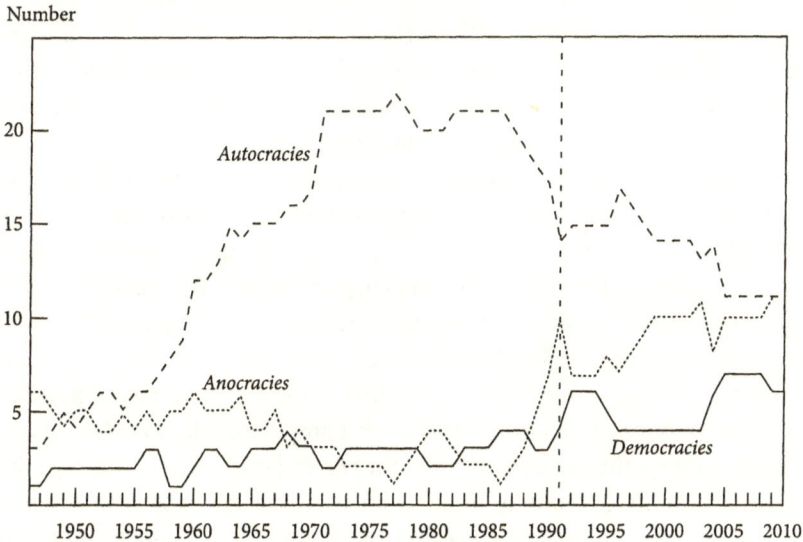

Source: Monty G. Marshall and Keith Jaggers, "Polity IV Country Reports 2010: North Africa and Middle East" (www.systemicpeace.org/polity/polity06.htm).

primary importance given by the sample to their being Muslim—31 per-cent—seems to be closer to the priority given to their national identities—33 percent—than it was two years earlier, with 27 percent and 38 percent, respectively.[16] The Arab identity now ranks third, at 26 percent, while in 2009 it was second, at 33 percent. This may come as a confirmation of the current strength of the religious factor, but this need not be specific to Arab Islam. For example, many Americans see their Christian faith as an identity factor that is as strong as their nationality (46 percent in each case). In contrast, signifi-cant majorities of European Christians identify primarily with their nation-ality rather than with their religion, though with differences from country to country.[17] The Saban Center's survey also anticipated the intention of many Egyptians to vote for an Islamic party in the upcoming parliamentary elec-tions, though it underestimated the degree to which that would happen. On the other hand, it also asked individuals whether they thought their respective governments should base their decisions on what would be best for the coun-try, for Islam, or for the Arab community, and the responses were, respectively, 58 percent (up from 55 percent in 2009), 16 percent (down from 20 percent), and 14 percent (down from 23 percent).

Tunisia seems to be the most promising case in which a transition to democratic governance based upon the national, rather than religious, interest could happen with full participation of Islamist parties. But it is Egypt that will in the end decide the historic relevance of the Arab uprisings, because of its size and history as well as its critical strategic importance in the region. The late Colonel Qaddafi left behind a country that he successfully prevented from becoming either a state or a nation (symbolic may be the fact that this was the only revolt in which the rebels and the regime waved two different flags throughout their fighting). Thus a new, national—though multiethnic—state structure will have to be built from scratch, provided that protracted interethnic or interfaction tensions can be prevented from degrading into a civil war. Morocco is going through a different experiment, with the monarch trying to steer the transition while holding on tightly to the scepter of power, possibly confirming once more author Tomasi di Lampedusa's famous line about changing everything to keep things as they are.[18] Finally, there is Algeria, the forgotten country: according to many analysts, the still fresh memory of a civil war has discouraged the social and political discontent from turning into revolt the way it did in neighboring Tunisia. However, civil society there has been undergoing no less profound a change, so that the question of the future stability of this nation is bound to remain wide open.

Changing Society in North Africa: the Impact of Old and New Western Models

When the project at the origin of this book was in process, the societal change that was occurring on the southern shores of the Mediterranean was subdivided into five categories: demographics, religion, entrepreneurship, gender, and the Internet. For three of these there were precedents in critical passages of history. Religious differences and consequent clashes have been recurrent. In the realm of demographics, there have been issues in the past related to the movement of migrants between North Africa and Europe—and America, too, though on a different scale—since colonial times. The gap between big business, including oil companies, and microbusiness, as in the *suq*, is certainly not a new problem in the region. But the remaining two instances of transformation are unprecedented and deserve more attention than they customarily receive in the West. One is what might be called a metamorphosis in the role of women over the last one or two generations. The other is the dramatic spread of telecommunications, above all the use of the Internet, which in

Figure 11-3. *Fertility Rate, Worldwide and by Region, 1960–2009*

Average total births per woman

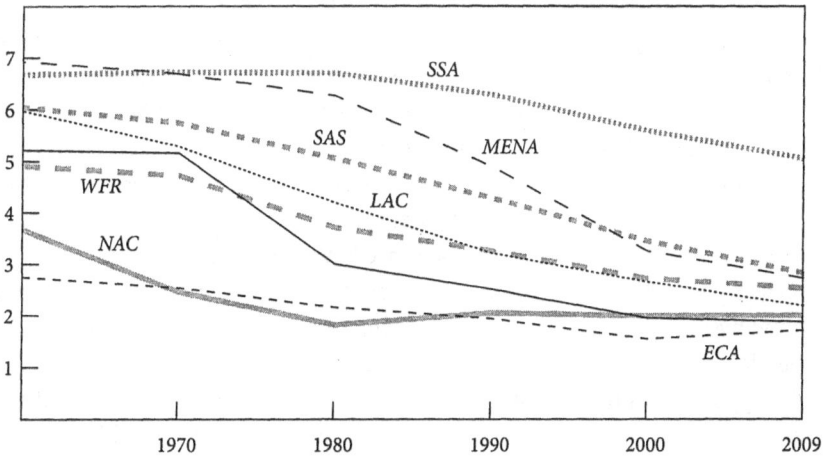

Source: Graph compiled by author based on World Bank data.
SSA = Sub-Saharan Africa; MENA = Middle East and North Africa; SAS = South Asia; LAC = Latin America and the Caribbean; WFR = World Fertility Rate; NAC = North America; ECA = Europe and Central Asia.

most non-Western countries exploded only ten years ago. (Incidentally, these two phenomena happen to be those most shared by American and European societies, as mentioned above.)

The fall in fertility rates is a major symptom of the female revolution. As figure 11-3 shows, over the last fifty years there has been a decline in the total births per woman in all regions of the world. Noteworthy is the fact that the numbers for the MENA, which was still around the same level as sub-Saharan Africa in the 1960s and 1970s, underwent a rapid decrease in the 1980s and 1990s so as to rank just slightly below South Asia in the last decade. As a consequence, the Arab family structure has undergone a profound transformation and in a time interval approximately one-tenth that of European families in the nineteenth and twentieth centuries, that is, throughout the industrial revolution. Although Middle Eastern fertility rates remain higher than the world average, they appear to be converging along with the other regions of the world (with the only—temporary?—exception of sub-Saharan Africa) toward the so-called subsistence rate. How long it will take to reach that goal will have an important impact on how our earth will look in the coming decades. It may be worth noting, by the way, that the convergence of fertility rates in all world regions is occurring without visible distinctions related to civilization, culture, or religion, thus supporting the argument that the role of women in society is dictated prevalently by socioeconomic conditions.

The growing and increasingly open presence of women in public life is another manifestation of the gender revolution, a phenomenon that Maria Cristina Paciello and Renata Pepicelli explore in chapter 3. Public offices, religious (mainly Muslim) circles, and small enterprises in the Arab countries, but also in the diaspora, are witnessing this development. Women took to the streets in past, occasionally violent, demonstrations, as in Egypt against British rule as far back as 1919, but their presence in the recent and current uprisings appears to be different in nature as a consequence of their emancipation in a growing middle class and of the changing family structure. Participation in public life, however, proceeds at a much slower pace than birth control because the opposition of men and institutions is more effective here than in the sphere of personal choice, unless the latter is coerced. Both the drop in fertility and the increase in public presence are products of various factors, the most important of which is probably the spread of education among young women—by the way, often with more significant results than among young men.

The West's influence on the process of empowering Arab women has taken various forms, from the colonial heritage in the homeland to the interaction between migrant women and host societies in the diaspora. Then there have been the diffusion of content from TV and music (with the interesting phenomenon of intercultural mixing) and the more recent influence of the Internet, which provides women with a new instrument of communication and interaction with the outside world from inside the perimeter of the home. Third, there are the substantial number of religious and secular private organizations that explicitly or implicitly deal with gender issues.

The second unprecedented transformation is occurring through the relatively new agent of digital telecommunications and is manifested in the skyrocketing number of ordinary people accessing the web. From 2001 to 2011, Internet users in the MENA region increased more than twentyfold, constituting some 35 percent of the population.[19] That is in fact slightly above the global average but still well below the average in Europe and North America. Moreover, of North African countries, only in Tunisia was Internet use above the regional average on the eve of the uprisings, while prerevolution Libya trailed far behind at a meager 5 percent—another meaningful indicator of the backwardness in which the relatively bloody regime change has been occurring in that country.

The importance of closely interconnected PCs and cell phones in bringing about the successful mobilizations of the "Arab Awakening" was a phenomenon widely reported as well as used by the major media. Equally widely discussed has been the subsequent failure of those communication tools to build up structures because of their "horizontal" nature, and to generate a durable countervailing power to "pyramidal" bodies such as the military and the religious organizations, however fissured or fractured. The resilience of the former, particularly in Egypt, and the show of electoral strength of the latter stand out in comparison with what is left of the role of the mostly secular circles that were protagonists in the uprisings. Nonetheless, it would be a mistake to consider the involvement of Arab individuals in various forms of the web (such as through blogs, Twitter, and cell phones) just a flash in the pan. No less than 35,000 Arab blogs could be counted back in 2009.[20] Something profoundly new and irreversible has happened. The reporting on events enriched by forceful images and the spreading of messages occur instantly for the benefit of small and large audiences alike: in the neighborhood, the city, the country, and all over the world. Despite their greater means of repression, often through the same web-based technologies as popular expression, governments are now more susceptible than in the past to requests for transparency, accountability, and justice coming from people they now realize have new capabilities for mobilization. The Islamist hierarchies also may be confronted with unwanted swerves of the same Internet tiger they have chosen to ride to spread God's word, as Gary Bunt discusses in chapter 4. Thus has emerged the challenge to the traditional top-down model in both the political and religious realms, which Western analysts and policymakers would be well advised to consider with great attention.

The other facets of transformation in southern Mediterranean societies may not be as revolutionary as the two discussed above, but they are certainly not negligible either. All are remarkably interwoven. Religion is probably the one that has received the most acute attention in the West, though with some different assessments on the two sides of the Atlantic, partly reflecting the aforementioned mismatch in the role religious faith plays in each society. As a result of the uprisings, as was predictable, Islamists have gained decisive influence in the political sphere, from which they were excluded by the fallen regimes. But they will now have to deliver a more effective and less corrupt state to their voters, and do so by adjusting *sharia* law. Indeed, religiosity is becoming increasingly personal among those deemed faithful, as Olivier Roy argues in chapter 2 on North African Islam.

If fertility rates are in decline, the current youth bulge in the region is the legacy of the previous, very prolific epoch. The movements that brought about the endogenous regime change in Tunisia, Egypt, and Libya were largely the product of a relatively educated but highly frustrated young generation, whose existential options were often confined to either protest at home or emigration abroad, that is, to other Arab countries or to the north of the Mediterranean. Philippe Fargues, in chapter 1 of this book, underlines that intraregional migrations tend to be underestimated by the Europeans, and Westerners in general, so as to focus attention, and occasionally generate tension, on the issue of those few tens of thousands who have landed, when they made it, in Italy, Spain, or elsewhere across the sea. The lucky ones who remain in these or other European host countries, or even make it to the United States, have joined the so-called Arab diaspora of immigrants, an important factor of cultural exchange with the land of origin, in addition to the economic input from their remittances. The North African youth generation now finds itself in an even worse situation—temporarily, one hopes—squeezed between the negative impact on the local economies of the uprisings and the broader economic downturn affecting Europe in particular, with a consequent further drop in job opportunities, as Carlos Braga and Caroline Freund note in chapter 6.

Southern Mediterranean small and medium-size enterprises (SMEs) have featured least in the transformative process. This is not to underestimate the role they play—and have the potential to play—as drivers of social change in their respective countries, as Gonzalo Escribano and Alejandro Lorca convincingly explain in chapter 5. Rather, it is to stress what these authors say about the inadequate attention the West devotes to this particular business sector versus that reserved for large, well-established companies, at the risk of leaving this engine for change open to the rival influence of third-country actors, such as the Turks and the Chinese. Something similar may be said concerning social entrepreneurship, though in this case religious—Islamic—and local cultural factors have more relevance than in the commercial realm of SMEs. Thus possible cooperative initiatives by European or American public or private bodies active in this arena require careful calibration, as suggested at the end of this chapter.

In sum, these various forms of societal transformation that have been occurring in the Arab Muslim world—North Africa, in this particular case—now appear to be characterized by two features, one endogenous and one exogenous. The former consists of the rediscovery of national, cultural, and religious roots; phenomena such as Islamic feminism, pious commercial or social entrepreneurship, the Muslim blogosphere—discussed in the respective contributions to this volume—are clear examples. The exogenous aspect arises from globalization affecting communication, faith, and gender roles as well as the economy, with the consequent partial fade-out of the Western imprint into a broader, transcultural blend.

Transatlantic Policy Options toward the Changing Mediterranean Microcosm

The Mediterranean has rarely been an area of high priority or harmony in the transatlantic relationship. Most concerns are broadly shared, but the priorities have often been different and shifting. The United States was committed to strategic stability in the region during the cold war, but subsequently it steadily reduced its military presence in what used to be called NATO's southern flank. It's attention instead has been shifted to the Gulf and above all Israel, with the terrorist threat hidden among visitors and immigrants from the area being a critical issue since 9/11. Broadly speaking, the Mediterranean basin has been rather marginal in the American strategic debate, which has traditionally been about an Atlantic focus versus a Pacific focus. As clearly stated in the latest Defense Strategy of the Obama administration, the latter currently receives top priority—as in the 1980s in relation to Japan—at the expense of the former.[21] For quite some time now, U.S. troops in Europe have been gradually reduced, but present budgetary pressures and new requirements concerning the East Asian seas are accelerating the process. Moreover, the United States is likely to reduce its energy dependence on the Middle East, while other external actors, such as China, India, and indeed Europe will probably do the opposite.

The long-standing European stakes in ensuring a safe energy supply from the southern Mediterranean are thus bound to remain high—and so are the vulnerabilities. Lately, crime and religious fundamentalism infiltrating via immigration also have been a source of concern, even while demographic trends keep suggesting that the need for imported labor will continue once the economic recession has been overcome. This explains the importance Europeans give to Mediterranean stability and their consequent frequent alignment with the United States policies, even if sometimes at the expense of interdependence and cooperation with the MENA region, in particular North Africa. Economic development and societal exchange are critical and appear to be of direct interest to the "old continent"—and not necessarily in contradiction with security imperatives. As is quite evident from chapter 9, by Roberto Aliboni, Euro-Mediterranean relations have been punctuated by many initiatives of European states or the EU, whose number and list of good intentions are inversely proportional to their cooperative efficacy and local impact. The crowd of labels and acronyms was eventually joined by NATO, a transatlantic body, with its Mediterranean Dialogue constituting no exception to the said rule, except possibly for the circle of communication it has provided with the military present on the southern shore of the basin—for better or for worse.

Even though they lie on the eastern border of the North African geopolitical area of concern here, three other problem countries or areas deserve brief mention in this context because of their relevance to Western policy options and their relationship to societal change. The reference is to Turkey, Palestine, and the Gulf. In all three cases, the role of the United States is dominant, but that does not make a European contribution any less necessary, occasionally indispensable. Actually, the main thrust of U.S. policy vis-à-vis Ankara has been to push for its entry into the EU, thus transferring the onus of determining Turkey's regional role onto the shoulders of the Europeans, already struggling with the consequences of the previous ambitious enlargements. While the issue has accentuated transatlantic divisions and mutual dissatisfaction, Turkey has been undergoing significant changes in both its international role and its society, so as to become a paradigm of Islamic governance in the region, with pros and cons varyingly appreciated on each side of the Atlantic.

Possibly an even more divisive issue in the transatlantic relationship is the perhaps undoable Israeli-Palestinian knot. The respective special envoys to the area have oscillated between inefficacy and irrelevance, despite the conspicuous political investment by Washington and the nonnegligible economic investment by Brussels. The Quartet formula has failed as a useful, broader multilateral actor. The governments of Israel, with the help of the powerful Jewish lobby in the United States and a bit of bad conscience in Europe, have long operated on the assumption that time is on their side, though the upheavals in the Arab neighborhood may now challenge its validity. Meanwhile, the polity and society of the country have evolved significantly, with the former moving to the right of the political spectrum and the latter experiencing an increasing fundamentalist religious influence. The definition of Israel as a Jewish state, notwithstanding the one-fifth of its citizens who are Muslim, now raises obvious questions in a West feeling uneasy every time a formal Islamic connotation is attributed to a state with a prevalently Muslim population.

On the shores of the Persian Gulf where its allies are located, the United States, and the West more broadly, has abundantly applied double standards in relation to democracy and secular human rights, accommodating authoritarian regimes even more than it has in North Africa. On the opposite shore of the Gulf, a theocratic regime has been oppressing a society that happens to be closer to Western-style secularism than its Arab counterparts. Tehran's pursuit of a military nuclear capability, in violation of its commitments to the Nuclear Non-Proliferation Treaty, raises strategic dilemmas between cold war–style containment and military rollback. Until France displayed some activism on the issue last year, the Europeans largely have been towed along by the Americans, as in all Gulf matters, occasionally dragging their feet for individual national interests.

Most analysts agree that while Turkey appears to have gained in standing from the Middle Eastern events, antithetic Israel and Iran have both turned out to be losers. But the West has not fared well either. The fact that the uprisings that began in Tunisia at the end of 2010 and took both the Americans and the Europeans by surprise, even though they were aware that the regimes were unsustainable, has been repeated ad nauseam. The truth of the matter is that after a long period of nearly totally dominant external influence—essentially Western—the rapid buildup of antiauthoritarian movements has been largely endogenous, like the anticolonial movement decades before. Even though due appreciation must be given to the Western cultural influences that permeated the background of several of the groups that initiated the demonstrations, the events largely have been the result of a new civil society trying to take matters into its own hands. As a consequence, the West has found itself far less relevant in the region than it was in the past and has had to embrace quickly, though with nuances and different reaction times, what at the beginning of the uprising was optimistically called the Arab Spring. But it has tended to frame it in its own image and paradigms rather than in the context of changing local realities, using the post–cold war Eastern European transformation as a misleading precedent.

Before going into the policy implications of all this, reference should be made to Libya as a partly separate case. The uprising was endogenous there, too, but differed from the neighboring countries in that it probably could not have succeeded without external, especially Western, support. The outcome of the operation is open to almost opposite readings. On the positive side, unlike what happened in the Balkans, the Europeans took the initiative in this case while the United States adopted a low-key role, famously described as "leading from behind." NATO military operations from the sky were on the whole a success, without losses and with reduced collateral killings thanks to the use of precision guided munitions. The mission mandated by the UN was the first opportunity to apply the R2P (Responsibility to Protect) provision and was implemented and extended to regime change with decently managed ambiguity. Incidentally the Arab League was also involved, although it responded in rather ambiguous and vacillating terms (not to mention the African Union, which acted mostly as an obstacle). And an important diplomatic success was the participation of a number of Arab states. In sum, the operation in Libya turned out much better in comparison with, say, Afghanistan.

However, there were negative outcomes as well. Serious discrepancies surfaced in the Atlantic alliance, with a reluctant United States pointing out the insufficient European capabilities to act militarily in an area of their prime interest. Even deeper were the divisions among the Europeans, with Poland joining Germany in preferring the company of Russia and China over that of their allies when voting in the UN Security Council; protagonists Sarkozy (France) and Cameron (Britain) overshadowed participation by other states, including Italy, and totally eclipsed the EU's High Representative and the newborn European External Action Service. In Washington the Libya operation, until its successful accomplishment became imminent, was frequently mentioned as the number one example of what U.S. foreign policy should no longer contemplate.

In keeping with the two opposite readings, there are those who considered the procedure adopted by the alliance on this occasion as a potential paradigm for future action, while others suggest that this should be the last joint NATO operation ever.

The Imperative of Doing Better with Less

While the fate of the Libyan tyrant has followed a rather traditional script, two different kinds of developments are taking place in the surrounding area. One is the reform process occurring in a number of North African countries; the other is the tangle of critical situations arising on the Middle Eastern flank, such as in Syria, with a civil war ignited by the spirit of the Arab Spring, the growing tensions in the Gulf, and the Palestinians seeking international recognition. The main difference between these two developments is that the latter has far more geopolitical implications than the former. In other words, the original pre–Arab Spring assumption of this project—that North Africa was a comparatively isolated case study of social transformations leading to political innovation—has been confirmed now by the way the polity and the institutions of these countries—post-upheaval—are evolving. Of course, the outcomes of this process will continue to influence the hopes of other Arab movements to a significant extent. Moreover, the situations and roles of practically all Middle Eastern actors—not just Turkey, Israel, or Iran—have been affected by the events. But the process under way in North Africa, whatever its future successes or failures, will remain essentially local, with the only and partial exception of historically cosmopolitan Egypt, which inevitably has a stake in what happens east of the Sinai.

Thus the national security of Western countries is unlikely to be greatly affected by the outcome of such process. Even the European vulnerabilities related to energy supplies and migratory inflows may find ways to be addressed separately from the broader geostrategic outlook—hopefully cooperatively in view of the mutual interests that occasional misgivings and tensions should not hide. Add to that the U.S. focus on the crisis-prone Middle East and the severe financial constraints on U.S. and European foreign policies (no room, in other words, for indulging in the rhetoric of Marshall Plans), and the conclusion one draws is that the significance of the southern rim of the Mediterranean will remain de facto secondary and deserve, as such, only marginal attention from the West, except for the specific interests of this or that country.

Two considerations may help clarify why this would be an erroneous conclusion. The first one is about building a new relationship with that complex, but relatively separate, geographical strip in a way that can provide a useful test case and a vehicle for a comprehensive approach to the broader Arab Muslim world—which is an imperative rather than a wish. As Jonathan Laurence (chapter 7) and Roberto Aliboni (chapter 9) point out, the opportunity to transcend American and European stereotypes has to be grasped, as does the potential for transformation of an Islam that is now part of a new power structure and a more or less democratic process. That includes consistency in addressing the issue of Islamic immigrants and in choosing policies toward the countries of origin. The stereotypes hindering more open approaches are largely different on the two sides of the Atlantic. In Europe the new problem of multicultural community life, discussed by Olivier Roy in chapter 10, combines with hypersensitivities about crime and, now, job competition. In the United States, the anti-Muslim rhetoric of the Christian right is particularly audible during electoral campaigns and exploits the need for Americans to choose an adversary—Islam in this case—and to define it as evil, as Alan Wolfe explains in chapter 8.

That leads to the second consideration: given that security implications and related priority differences between the United States and European countries are less important in this part of the MENA region, can the transatlantic community, to the extent that there still is one, act jointly rather than separately here? Or can they at least adopt a sufficiently consensual, preferably coordinated division of labor, given the current imperative to do better with less? As usual, the preferable scenario of synergy in whatever form encapsulates the need for the Europeans to get their acts together, particularly in the areas of immigration and energy policies, and to sort out whether they want to continue toward an intergovernmental approach in their Mediterranean policies, despite its manifest inefficacy, or make better use of the instruments offered by the Lisbon Treaty in order to "speak with one voice"—a famous, possibly mythical objective by now.

To further limit optimism that the two considerations will be taken into due account, one has to add the extreme differentiation of the single national cases in the region and the uncertainty of their respective futures. While Tunisia contaminated Egypt with its uprising in the name of democracy and justice, the ensuing change has not been the same, including the way political Islamism has taken shape. The specificity of the Libyan revolution has been confirmed by the developments there, consequent to the aforementioned absence of a true nation. In Morocco the monarch has tried to steer the transition from the throne. Algeria, whose regime has so far survived while the civil society undergoes transformations similar to those of its neighbors, may end up being a test case for the West to show that it has learned from the recent past. Thus the said options for transatlantic action in the area risk having to be mostly aimed at, and tailored to, each individual country.

The purpose of this exercise, however, is to transcend the traditional foreign policy sphere and to try to advance a broader and longer-term strategy for Europeans and Americans to regain a satisfactory degree of cooperative leverage in the area as part of a more balanced relationship, one that takes account of the rapidly changing societies but also the painfully slow-to-change polities. The various societal dynamics discussed earlier in this book suggest that both the extent and nature of the change may make understanding between peoples more important but possibly less difficult today than under the ambiguous conditions that existed under the regimes.

Two directions are suggested as deserving priority. One concerns an innovative institutional approach, at both the local and the international level, and the other concerns the role of the private sector and civil society. They will be explained by means of examples rather than through a comprehensive analysis.

Isolationism and sovereignism both assume that multilateralism is obsolete, if not wrong altogether. One wonders, however, whether going down that road is the best way to stem the West's loss of influence in the area. The United States has a long-standing tradition in institution building, possibly a little rusty of late. The European Union is itself the most advanced experiment of a partly shared sovereignty within a regional institution providing peace and growth among its members. It remains also a paradigm for other regions, the current tendencies toward renationalization notwithstanding. A return to liberal internationalism in the United States and a solution to the euro crisis via deeper integration within the EU could help revive multilateral approaches in the West's international action.

At the global level, the United Nations framework cannot be brought in only when it is convenient, as with the role played by the Security Council in "protecting" Libyan civilians or trying to stop the bloodshed in Syria. Other UN bodies, such as UNDP and UNESCO, can also be of value. (By the way, in light of the huge cultural legacy located in North Africa, the latter should not be held hostage to unrelated issues like Israeli-Palestinian differences.) At the regional level, one interesting project concerns the establishment of a Middle Eastern nuclear-weapon-free zone, to join the other five existing ones, as an intermediate step toward the eventual so-called zero option at the world level. Since the main objective is de facto to defuse Iran's ticking bomb, North Africans have less direct stakes in the matter, but this could help to give them, Egypt in particular, some room for initiative. The chances of success may not be as remote as some say if it is true that the idea is popular in the region, including in its only nuclear armed country, Israel, 64 percent of whose citizens say they are in favor.[22]

Western countries have little leverage with the Arab League, but even that little bit should not be wasted. It was wise to involve the organization in the Libyan operation, after which, under the leadership of the Gulf countries—Qatar above all—it became involved to an unprecedented degree in a crisis in which the West had to stay at a distance: the uprisings and near civil war in Syria. But, to return to North Africa, the medium-term development of the regional economic fabric is of primary importance, as stressed in chapter 6. Western, above all European, action should be aimed at enhancing an institutionally framed open trade among locals, which at the moment contributes as little as 4 percent to the regional GDP (by comparison, it contributes 60 percent in Europe). A second objective would be to devise multilateral ways to enhance small and medium-size commercial or social entrepreneurship, as mentioned earlier.

Addressing the question of what multilateralism has to do with changing societies may be in order here. The answer is rooted partly in the clauses of conditionality that are applied to multilateral as well as bilateral cooperation and aid, in that they most frequently concern human rights, protection of minorities and women, access to information, and the like, which interact with societal features. Conditionality, of course, becomes less effective if the Western actor has less economic (or strategic) leverage. Yet Western countries should learn how to better apply standards that are shared rather than imposed, in the assumption permeating this book that societal change helps convergence between their societies and those on southern shores of the Mediterranean in identifying common paradigms in due time. But conditionality is only part of the answer. Multilateralism can have a broader, environmental effect on intersocietal relations insofar as it provides the institutional framework in which they can develop, not only in terms of reaching shared standards but also in helping to form a civil society made of managers, social operators, and government employees, both civil and military. The post–World War II European experience is illuminating in that respect—and the current oppositional populist tendency in many Western countries to disparagingly downgrade civil servants (or *commis de l'état*, as the French call them) to bureaucrats and technocrats should not distract us from such an important goal.

The need to contribute to the buildup of the human fabric of a modern state and the broader public sphere leads to the issue of how to help reinforce domestic institutions. This purpose should be pursued to allow the local culture—including Islamism—to come to terms with civil and social forms, now increasingly recognized by a spectrum of countries stretching beyond what we have called here the West. As already said above, the imperative is to look beyond the requirement of electoral democracy to address the broader and complex transformations Europe and North America have been going through over the last two or three centuries, including the achievements of the rule of law, the balance of powers, economic fairness, and the supply of common goods. Acceptably free and fair elections, as apparently occurred recently in some North African countries, are certainly a step forward, but they also carry the risk of disenchantment vis-à-vis politics, and public affairs in general, to the advantage of religious or sectarian allegiances once the democratically legitimized bodies are not allowed, or able, to perform and deliver according to citizens' expectations.

The Role of the Private Sector

The ensuing job for Western countries requires time, some division of labor, and a partly new array of instruments, the detailed discussion of which would go beyond the scope of this final chapter. It can only be suggested here that we should not get unduly discouraged by the possibly inevitable setbacks the process has been going through in the immediate aftermath of the uprisings. The advantages are likely to become evident only in the medium run, but action should be taken now at costs that appear containable and affordable— and by sharing the burden beyond the public sector. This leads to the second priority: devising a more effective role for the vast array of instruments the Western private sector has at its disposal, ranging from business circles to think tanks and secular or religious nongovernmental organizations (NGOs).

This sector in the United States and Europe has had a remarkable, though variable, record in their dealings with counterparts in Japan, South Korea, Latin America, Eastern Europe, and Turkey, that is, with those regions or countries that were listed earlier as being on the periphery of the West or potential bridges between the West and other cultures. Sometimes the initiatives are shared by both sides of the Atlantic, sometimes they reflect different national interests and degrees of communication with the concerned partners. Sometimes they are strictly private; sometimes they involve governments and other public bodies. The Americans have played a leading role in this field, thanks above all to their richly endowed foundations and their special tradition of personal and corporate giving. The results have not always been useful in helping transcultural dialogue and people-to-people exchanges, but in several instances they have.

The shared rapid transformation of North Africa's civil society and private sector and the different political processes that the various countries have painfully been undergoing as a consequence could offer an opportunity for all interested circles to explore the interlocking option with more determination and with all due consideration for cultural differences, including the religious factor.

A widespread perception, however, is that the initiatives taken by the few components of the Western private sector that have already been operating in the region—whether social, political, or business oriented—often tend to frame the dialogue within Western images and standards, including political paradigms, economic schools of thought, or religious denominations. A case in point is the controversy that broke out in Egypt early in 2012 over foreign, primarily American funding to NGOs active in the fields of freedom and human rights. Of course, the related local criticisms are mostly self-serving for domestic purposes and can be used to justify repressive actions by regime-prone governmental bodies or intolerant Islamist factions. Nonetheless, not all such criticisms are gratuitous. It thus may be appropriate to first assess the adequacy and efficacy of the said initiatives, whether coming from Europe or the United States. Then a greater effort may be in order in the fields of culture and religion, polity and society to explore ways in which the dynamics affecting all four of these areas can make understanding and eventual convergence easier.

The West is not alone in the endeavor. The remarkable activism of wealthy Gulf countries in the region is a new development. Intrinsic to these countries is the lack of separation between a public and a private sphere, including their huge sovereign funds, as well as the peculiar hybridization between Arab conservatism, often in overt contradiction with the societal dynamics discussed here, and cultural importation from the West, of which the Louvre Abu Dhabi or the Brookings Doha Center are just two examples. The European and the American governmental and nongovernmental actors have been increasingly dealing with these players who project an alternative influence—occasionally an ambiguous one, as in the religious realm—into the North African region, in particular after the events of last year. The assessment suggested here should include an analysis of the related convergences or contradictions arising from this reality.

The short-term scope for transatlantic cooperation in dealing with the transformation occurring in the North African countries is limited and unlikely to have a significant amplifying effect on the separate policies the United States and the European countries are capable of implementing—the latter either at the national or the integrated level. Moreover, such policies are currently affected by several constraints, above all economic, with the consequence of further reducing Western influence in a process that is essentially endogenous. The limitations arising from this reality can be compensated for by addressing the roots of the discontent expressed in the Tunisian and Egyptian squares, which are to be found in societies undergoing a rapid and profound change. Thus the scope of action and cooperation should be broadened and projected over the medium term, to devise a strategy that takes advantage of, rather than suffers from, the complementarity between American and European priorities or capabilities, and makes use of those policy instruments that have made the West strong, rather than consider them obsolete. Multilateralism, institution building, and the development of relations with the local—mostly Arab and Muslim—civil society and private sector are suggested here as exemplary arenas for this strategy.

Notes

1. See, for instance, Fareed Zakaria, *The Post-American World* (New York: Penguin Books, 2009); Andrew J. Bacevich, *The Limits of Power: The End of American Exceptionalism* (New York: Henry Holt, 2009); Niall Ferguson, *Colossus: The Rise and Fall of the American Empire* (New York: Penguin Books, 2005).

2. Oswald Spengler's famous two-volume study, *The Decline of the West,* was first published in 1918. The second volume appeared in print in 1923.

3. Thomas L. Friedman and Michael Mandelbaum, *That Used to Be Us: How America Fell Behind in the World It Invented and How We Can Come Back* (New York: Farrar Straus and Giroux, 2011). For a recent and somewhat opposing take on this issue, see Robert Kagan, *The World America Made* (New York: Alfred A. Knopf, 2012).

4. Cesare Merlini, "The Lessons of Ancient History and the Future of Transatlantic Relations," *International Spectator* 44, no. 1 (March 2009): 23–31; Cesare Merlini, "U.S. Hegemony and the Roman Analogy: A European View," *International Spectator* 37, no. 3 (2002): 19–30.

5. Richard N. Haass, *The Reluctant Sheriff: The United States after the Cold War* (Brookings, 1997). Former U.S. secretary of state Madeleine Albright described America as the "indispensable nation" during a speech delivered in December 1996.

6. See, for instance, Michael Mandelbaum, *The Frugal Superpower: America's Global Leadership in a Cash-Strapped Era* (New York: Public Affairs, 2010); John Ikenberry, "The Future of the Liberal World Order. Internationalism after America," *Foreign Affairs* 90, no. 3 (2011): 56–68.

7. Anti-European, antisocialist rhetoric has flooded the Republican debates. Speaking at a Republican fundraising dinner ahead of the Iowa caucus in December 2011, Republican candidate Newt Gingrich described Europeans as "subjects" in comparison to Americans, who are "citizens."

8. Joseph S. Nye Jr., *The Future of Power* (New York: PublicAffairs, 2011); Daniel Hamilton and Kurt Volker, eds., *Transatlantic 2020: A Tale of Four Futures* (Center for Transatlantic Relations, Johns Hopkins University, 2011); Hillary Rodham Clinton, "Leading through Civilian Power. Redefining American Diplomacy and Development," *Foreign Affairs* 89, no. 6 (2010): 13–24.

9. Gideon Rachman, *Zero-Sum World: Politics, Power and Prosperity after the Crash* (London: Atlantic Books, 2010).

10. Internet World Stats, "World Internet Users and Population, December 2000–December 2011" (www.internetworldstats.com/stats.htm [March 2012]).

11. Pew Research Center, *Millennials: A Portrait of Generation Next* (Washington, February 2010) (http://pewsocialtrends.org/files/2010/10/millennials-confident-connected-open-to-change.pdf [March 2012]).

12. Pew Global Attitudes Project, "The American-Western European Values Gap: American Exceptionalism Subsides," November 17, 2011 (www.pewglobal.org/files/2011/11/Pew-Global-Attitudes-Values-Report-FINAL-November-17-2011-10AM-EST.pdf [March 2012]).

13. Pew Forum, "The Future of the Global Muslim Population: Projections for 2010–2030," January 27, 2011 (www.pewforum.org/The-Future-of-the-Global-Muslim-Population.aspx [March 2012]).

14. In late 2005 Goldman Sachs coined the term "Next-11" (N-11), a list of eleven countries that have a high potential, together with the BRICS (Brazil, Russia, India, China, and South Africa), of becoming the world's largest economies in the twenty-first century. The list includes Bangladesh, Turkey, Egypt, Vietnam, Iran, Indonesia, Korea, Mexico, Nigeria, Pakistan, and the Philippines.

15. Monty G. Marshall and Benjamin R. Cole, *Global Report 2011: Conflict, Governance, and State Fragility* (Vienna, Va.: Center for Systemic Peace, 2011), p. 10 (www.systemicpeace.org/GlobalReport2011.pdf [March 2012]).

16. Shibley Telhami, "The 2011 Arab Public Opinion Poll," November 21, 2011 (www. brookings.edu/reports/2011/1121_arab_public_opinion_telhami.aspx [March 2012]).

17. Pew Global Attitudes Project, "The American-Western European Values Gap."

18. Giuseppe Tomasi di Lampedusa, *The Leopard*, English trans. (New York: Signet, January 1961).

19. Internet World Stats, "World Internet Users and Population." See reference in note 10.

20. Bruce Etling and others, "Mapping the Arabic Blogosphere: Politics, Culture, and Dissent," Research Publication 2009-06 (Berkman Center, Harvard University, June 2009) (http://cyber.law.harvard.edu/sites/cyber.law.harvard.edu/files/Mapping_the_Arabic _Blogosphere_0.pdf [March 2012]).

21. U.S. Department of Defense, "Sustaining US Global Leadership: Priorities for 21st Century Defense," January 2012 (www.defense.gov/news/Defense_Strategic_Guidance.pdf [March 2012]).

22. Shibley Telhami, "The 2011 Public Opinion Poll of Jewish and Arab Citizens of Israel," December 2011 (www.brookings.edu/reports/2011/1201_israel_poll_telhami.aspx [March 2012]).

Contributors

ROBERTO ALIBONI is senior research adviser for the European Institute of the Mediterranean, Barcelona, and a scientific counselor for the Italian Institute of International Affairs (IAI), Rome. He served as both director and vice president at the IAI, has held research positions with various Italian think tanks, and has taught at the universities of Naples and Perugia. In 1993–94 he conceived of and successfully established the Mediterranean Study Commission, a network of Mediterranean institutes dealing with security and international affairs, which became the Euro-Mediterranean Study Commission in 1996. He has published numerous articles and books on Mediterranean and Middle Eastern security and international relations.

CARLOS A. PRIMO BRAGA has been the special representative and director for Europe, External Affairs Vice-Presidency, at the World Bank since January 2011. In 2008–10 he was director of the Economic Policy and Debt Department at the World Bank. He has also served as the acting vice president and corporate secretary of the World Bank Group and as acting executive secretary of the Development Committee. Braga has a degree in mechanical engineering and masters and doctoral degrees in economics. He has contributed to the economics literature on sovereign debt, growth and innovation, and international trade.

GARY R. BUNT is a reader in Islamic studies and the director of the masters Islamic studies program at University of Wales Trinity Saint David. His primary research focuses on Islam, Muslims, and the Internet. His most recent book is *iMuslims: Rewiring the House of Islam*, which discusses how, in some contexts, the Internet has had an overarching transformational effect on how Muslims practice Islam, how forms of Islam are represented to the wider world, and how Muslim societies perceive themselves and their peers. Bunt is preparing a work on Muslims in Britain and on social networking–web 2.0 issues. His research website can be found at www.virtuallyislamic.com.

GONZALO ESCRIBANO is director of the Energy program at the Real Instituto Elcano de Relaciones Internacionales and professor at the Department of Applied Economics, Spanish Open University (UNED), Madrid. He is a member of several Euro-Mediterranean networks and a researcher with the Research Group on International Political Economy (UNED). Escribano has lectured at several universities and masters programs in Spain and abroad and has published more than 100 articles, book chapters, and other pieces of research on the political economy, geoeconomics, and geopolitics of the Mediterranean and the Arab world and Euro-Mediterranean economic relations. He holds a Ph.D. in economics from the Universidad Complutense de Madrid.

PHILIPPE FARGUES, a sociologist and demographer, is currently the director of the Migration Policy Centre, which he founded at the European University Institute in Florence. He has been director of the Center for Migration and Refugee Studies at the American University in Cairo, senior researcher at the French National Institute for Demographic Studies in Paris, visiting professor at Harvard, and director of the Centre for Economic Legal and Social Studies in Cairo. His research interests include migration and refugee movements, population and politics in Muslim countries, family building, and demography and development. He has published more than 150 scientific articles and books on these topics and lectured at a number of universities in Europe, America, Africa, and the Middle East.

CAROLINE FREUND is chief economist for the Middle East and North Africa Region, World Bank. She has also worked at the International Monetary Fund and the Federal Reserve Board. Freund is an expert on economic growth, international trade, and international finance; her work covers the developing world and transition countries. She has authored numerous academic and policy papers on international trade, development, and current account adjustment. Freund holds a Ph.D. in economics from Columbia University.

JONATHAN LAURENCE is associate professor of political science at Boston College and nonresident senior fellow at the Brookings Institution. He recently served as a senior fellow at the Transatlantic Academy and as a visiting researcher at the Wissenschaftszentrum Berlin, and is a term member of the Council on Foreign Relations. Laurence's most recent book is *The Emancipation of Europe's Muslims*, and he has published numerous essays in such journals as *European Political Science* and *Foreign Policy*. He has a Ph.D. in political science from Harvard University.

ALEJANDRO LORCA is program director for the Master of International Relations and Security: Geo-economics and Geopolitics at the Lauren Klein Institute of the Autonomous University of Madrid, where he holds the Jean Monnet Chair. The objective of his work is the introduction of mathematical tools of analysis into the field of international relations. His geographic focus is the four seas zones (Mediterranean, Black, Caspian, and Gulf seas). Lorca has taught at more than ten universities in eight countries and has consulted for steering committee members of the Forum Euroméditerranéen des Instituts de Sciences Économiques. He holds a degree in law and a Ph.D. in economics. He has published seven books and nearly 250 articles in the field of economics.

CESARE MERLINI is chairman of the board of trustees of the Italian Institute for International Affairs in Rome, of which he had been the president for many years. He is also a nonresident senior fellow with the Brookings Institution in Washington. Until the end of 2009 he was executive vice chairman of the Council for the United States and Italy, an organization he cofounded in 1983. His areas of expertise include transatlantic relations, European integration, nuclear nonproliferation, and, more recently, the impact of societal change on international relations. He has written numerous publications, including the conference paper "Religious Revival and Megatrends in Global Security, Economy and Governance" (University of Sussex, UK, October 27–29, 2011) and "Europe in the International Scene: A Union of Necessity after a Union of Choice?" a chapter in *The European Union in the 21st Century*, CEPS, Brussels, 2009.

MARIA CRISTINA PACIELLO is a socioeconomist with extensive research and field experience in the North African region. Since 2006 she has been a lecturer at La Sapienza University of Rome. Paciello also works as a research consultant for Istituto Affari Internazionali, Rome, on projects concerning the southern Mediterranean area. She has conducted research on gender and development studies for a number of major international organizations. Her most recent publications have focused on Tunisia, Egypt, and Morocco. Paciello has a Ph.D. from the University of Florence in the politics and economics of developing countries.

RENATA PEPICELLI holds a Ph.D in geopolitics and cultures of the Mediterranean" (Sum–Italian Institute of Human Sciences, University of Naples). She has a postdoctoral fellowship at the Department of Politics, Institutions, and History of the University of Bologna. Her main topics of research are contemporary Islam, Euro-Mediterrenean relations and migrations focusing mostly on the gender perspective. She is author of several national and international publications, including the books *Il velo nell'Islam. Storia, politica, estetica* [The veil and Islam. History, politics, and esthetics] (Carocci, 2012); *Femminsmo islamico. Corano, diritti, riforme* [Islamic feminism. Quran, rights, reforms] (Carocci, 2010); *2010, un nuovo ordine mediterraneo?* [2010, a new mediterranean order?] (Mesogea, 2004).

OLIVIER ROY is a professor at the European University Institute, Florence, where he also heads the Mediterranean progam at the Robert Schuman Center for Advanced Studies. He has been a senior researcher at the French National Center for Scientific Research, professor at the Ecole des Hautes Etudes en Sciences Sociales, and visiting professor at the University of California, Berkeley. He headed the Mission for Tajikistan (Organization for Security and Cooperation in Europe, 1993–94) and consulted for the UN Office of the Coordinator for Afghanistan (1988). His field work has covered political Islam, the Middle East, Islam in the West, and comparative religions, and he has written a number of books on Islam in modern contexts, including the recent *Holy Ignorance* (Columbia University Press, 2010). His current focus is on religious norms in the public sphere, conversions, apostasy, and comparative religions. Roy received an "Agrégation de Philosophie" and holds a Ph.D. in political science.

ALAN WOLFE is professor of political science and director of the Boisi Center for Religion and American Public Life at Boston College. Wolfe is also a senior fellow with the World Policy Institute at the New School University in New York. He served as an adviser to President Clinton in preparation for his 1995 State of the Union address and has lectured widely at American and European universities. In fall 2004 Wolfe was the George H. W. Bush Fellow at the American Academy in Berlin. The author and editor of more than twenty books, Wolfe is also a contributing editor and author for numerous major magazines and newspapers.

Index

Page numbers followed by *f* or *t* refer to figures or tables, respectively.

digital media in uprising in, 86, 90; parliamentary elections, 8, 69–70, 148; private sector characteristics, 99; private sector involvement in revolution, 104–05; prospects for gender equality in, 69–70; public sector employment, 128; religion in politics in, 49, 50–51, 236; social associations, 106; start of revolution in, 86, 128; unemployment patterns in, 30, 57; Western policies and perceptions, 157, 159, 203, 204, 243; women in politics in, 60, 62, 68–69; women in protest movement in, 65

Turkey, 227, 243; geostrategic implications of Arab uprisings, 10; Islamic politics in, 196–97; migration patterns, 33–34; as model for Arab reform, 51–52, 150; public sector employment, 124; U.S. relations, 155, 242

Ullstein, Leopold, 174
Union for the Mediterranean, 115, 139, 186, 205
United Arab Emirates, 156
United Nations, 2, 11, 244
United States: democracy-promotion before uprisings, 147–49, 151–53; economic relations with North Africa, social change and, 113–17, 149; foreign assistance to MENA countries, 151–55; in future of Arab sociopolitical evolution, 11–13; geostrategic implications of Arab uprisings, 10–11, 245–46; global status, 3, 228–31; Israel and, 150; Middle East Transitions Office, 162; misperception of events in MENA, 181, 182; Muslim public opinion of, 155–57, 156*t*, 162; Obama administration response to uprisings, 149–50, 153–55; relationship with Persian Gulf countries, 243; religious identity, 214, 230, 235; September 11,

2001, terrorist attacks, 169; sociocultural transformation in, 7–8; strategic interests in Mediterranean, 241; support for corrupt and nondemocratic regimes, 147, 151, 162. *See also* Bush (George W.) administration; Obama administration; Western countries
Urban-rural populations: fertility patterns and trends, 22; recent electoral outcomes, 8
U.S.-Maghreb Entrepreneurship Conference, 155

Western countries: ability to influence events in Arab Middle East, 10–12; boundaries and membership, 227–28; distribution of global power and influence, 228–31; in empowerment of Arab women, 238; fears of Islamism, 180, 199; neglect of small- and medium-size enterprises in MENA, 240; perceptions of Arab uprisings, 3–4, 8, 180, 195–98, 204, 243–44; perceptions of Muslim Middle East, 13, 47; recommendations for MENA relationships and policies, 247–51; religious identity, 214–16; trends in international power relations, 3. *See also* Europe; United States
Wheat, 125–26
WikiLeaks, 85
Wittes, Tamara, 151, 158; 152
Women, 12; in Arab uprisings, 53–54, 65, 66–67, 238; domestic work burden, 58–59; educational access and attainment, 24–28, 54; in Egyptian uprising and transition, 66–68; entrepreneurship, 111, 117; European programs in Mediterranean, 208; feminist and women's organizations, 63–65; fertility patterns and trends, 21–24, 42–43, 237–38, 237*f*; future

www.ingramcontent.com/pod-product-compliance
Lightning Source LLC
Chambersburg PA
CBHW030644270326
41929CB00007B/202